Shakespeare and Judgment

Shakespeare and Judgment

Edited by Kevin Curran

EDINBURGH
University Press

Edinburgh University Press is one of the leading university presses in the UK. We publish academic books and journals in our selected subject areas across the humanities and social sciences, combining cutting-edge scholarship with high editorial and production values to produce academic works of lasting importance. For more information visit our website: www.edinburghuniversitypress.com

Edinburgh University Press Ltd
The Tun – Holyrood Road, 12(2f) Jackson's Entry, Edinburgh EH8 8PJ

First published in hardback by Edinburgh University Press 2017

Typeset in 11/13 Adobe Sabon by
IDSUK (DataConnection) Ltd, and
printed and bound in Great Britain by
CPI Group (UK) Ltd, Croydon CR0 4YY

A CIP record for this book is available from the British Library

ISBN 978 1 4744 1315 2 (hardback)
ISBN 978 1 4744 3161 3 (paperback)
ISBN 978 1 4744 1316 9 (webready PDF)
ISBN 978 1 4744 1317 6 (epub)

Contents

Acknowledgments   vii
List of Contributors   viii

Introduction   1
Kevin Curran

Part I: Staging Judgment: Deliberation in the Plays

1. Preventive Justice in *Measure for Measure*   21
   Virginia Lee Strain

2. Believing in Ghosts, in Part: Judgment and
   Indecision in *Hamlet*   45
   Vivasvan Soni

3. Shakespeare's Law and Plowden's Authority   71
   Constance Jordan

Part II: Audience Judgment: Deliberation in the Theater

4. "Gently to hear, kindly to judge": Minds at
   Work in *Henry V*   93
   Katherine B. Attié

5. "Practis[ing] judgment with the disposition of natures":
   Measure for Measure, the "Discoursive" Common Law,
   and the "Open Court" of the Theater   115
   Carolyn Sale

6. The Laws of *Measure for Measure*   139
   Paul Yachnin

7. Prospero's Plea: Judgment, Invention, and Political Form
   in *The Tempest*   157
   Kevin Curran

Part III: The Ethics of Judgment

8. Antinomian Shakespeare: English Drama and Confession
    Across the Reformation Divide   175
    John Parker

9. Bracketed Judgment, "Un-humanizing," and Conversion
    in *The Merchant of Venice*   195
    Sanford Budick

10. The Judgment of the Critics that Makes us Tremble:
    "Distributing Complicities" in Recent Criticism of
    King Lear   215
    Richard Strier

Index   235

Acknowledgments

I wish to thank the contributors to *Shakespeare and Judgment* for their generosity, reliability, and rigor. I've always loved collaboration, but this has been an exceptionally rewarding team to work with. It should also be said, though, that this volume is actually the product of an even earlier collaboration, one that took place before I decided to put together an edited collection. In 2014, I directed a seminar on "Theater and Judgment in Early Modern England" at the meeting of the Shakespeare Association of America in St. Louis, MO. I owe a great deal to the participants in that event, each of whom in some way or other influenced my thinking. For illuminating and sustained conversations about Renaissance judgment over the last several years, I thank Heather Hirschfeld, Julia Reinhard Lupton, Richard Strier, Garrett Sullivan, and Paul Yachnin. Other shrewd interlocutors have included Heidi Cephus, Stephanie Elsky, Virginia Lee Strain, and Jennifer Waldron. Finally, I must insist on what a pleasure it is to work with Edinburgh University Press. This volume has benefitted immeasurably from the expert advice of the two anonymous readers they secured. At EUP headquarters, Jackie Jones, Michelle Houston, Adela Rauchova, Rebecca MacKenzie, and Carla Hepburn have been models of that rare and wonderful triumvirate: professionalism, promptness, and pleasantness.

Kevin Curran
Lausanne, Switzerland

Contributors

Katherine B. Attié is Assistant Professor of English at Towson University. Her work has appeared in *English Literary Renaissance*, *Modern Philology*, *Shakespeare Quarterly*, *SEL*, and *ELH*. Her book project, *Patterns of Power: Shakespeare's Everyday Aesthetic*, explores how representations of habitual activity are politicized in the Henriad and other plays.

Sanford Budick served as Professor of English at Cornell University and was subsequently appointed Professor of English at The Hebrew University of Jerusalem, where he was founding-director of the Center for Literary Studies. He has written on Shakespeare, Milton, eighteenth-century poetry, Wordsworth, Kant's relation to Milton, and the theory of tradition.

Kevin Curran is Professor of Early Modern Literature at the University of Lausanne in Switzerland and editor of the book series "Edinburgh Critical Studies in Shakespeare and Philosophy." He is the author of *Shakespeare's Legal Ecologies: Law and Distributed Selfhood* (Northwestern, 2017) and *Marriage, Performance, and Politics at the Jacobean Court* (Ashgate, 2009).

Constance Jordan is Professor or English, Emerita, at Claremont Graduate University. She is the author of many books and editions, including *Renaissance Feminism: Literary Texts and Political Models* (Cornell University Press, 1990), *Shakespeare's Monarchies: Ruler and Subject in Shakespeare's Romances* (Cornell University Press, 1997), and *Reason and Imagination: Selected Correspondence of Learned Hand* (Oxford University Press, 2013).

John Parker is Associate Professor of English at the University of Virginia. He is the author of *The Aesthetics of Antichrist: From Christian Drama to Christopher Marlowe* (Cornell University Press, 2007), along with several book chapters, articles, and reviews.

Carolyn Sale is an Associate Professor in the Department of English & Film Studies at the University of Alberta (Canada), where she teaches courses in Shakespeare, especially Shakespeare and the law and Shakespeare and political theory. She is completing a book manuscript, "The Literary Commons: The Law and the Early Modern Writer, 1528–1628."

Vivasvan Soni is Associate Professor of English at Northwestern University. He is the author of *Mourning Happiness: Narrative and the Politics of Modernity* (Cornell University Press, 2010) and a special issue of the journal *ECTI* on "The Crisis of Judgment." He has held fellowships from The American Philosophical Society and the NEH/ Andrew W. Mellon Foundation.

Virginia Lee Strain is an Assistant Professor of English at Loyola University Chicago. She has held fellowships at Vanderbilt University, Washington University in St. Louis, and The Huntington Library. Her publications include articles in *The Oxford Handbook of Law and Literature, 1500–1700* and *ELH*. Her dissertation won the J. Leeds Barroll Dissertation Prize from the Shakespeare Association of America (2011).

Richard Strier is the Frank L. Sulzberger Distinguished Service Professor Emeritus in the English Department at the University of Chicago. His books include *The Unrepentant Renaissance from Petrarch to Shakespeare to Milton*; *Resistant Structures: Particularity, Radicalism, and Renaissance Texts*; and *Love Known: Theology and Experience in George Herbert's Poetry*.

Paul Yachnin is Tomlinson Professor of Shakespeare Studies at McGill University. Among his publications are the books, *Stage-Wrights* and *The Culture of Playgoing* (with Anthony Dawson); editions of *Richard II* (with Dawson) and *The Tempest*; and six edited books, including *Shakespeare's World of Words* and *Forms of Association* (with Marlene Eberhart). His book-in-progress, *Making Publics in Shakespeare's Playhouse*, is under contract with Edinburgh University Press.

Introduction

Kevin Curran

Shakespeare and Judgment. It's a simple enough proposition. "Shakespeare" and "judgment": two keywords, both fairly recognizable, each offering a context for the other. And yet the title of this book immediately raises some questions. First of all, what exactly *is* "judgment"? Is it an act or a process? A concept or an experience? To which cultural or theoretical field does it belong, and to what set of social practices? Also – and perhaps most importantly – what does it have to do with Shakespeare? Given how many items have appeared on the other side of the "Shakespeare and" formulation – from religion, law, appropriation, the book trade, and national culture to masculinity, republicanism, Ovid, music, and language – what justifies adding yet another? What, that is, does judgment offer Shakespeare studies as a category of critical inquiry? This introduction will begin to provide some answers to these questions, setting the scene for the more specific projects that follow. Grounding the volume are two core contentions: (1) that attending to Shakespeare's treatment of judgment leads to fresh insights about the imaginative relationship between theater, law, religion, and aesthetics in early modern England; and (2) that judgment offers new ways of putting the historical and philosophical contexts of Shakespeare's plays into conversation.

This is a new undertaking, the first attempt to articulate the central place of Shakespearean drama in the cultural and intellectual history of judgment. That said, the volume builds on a number of earlier studies. Richard Strier, for instance, discusses what he views as Shakespeare's skepticism about moral judgment in chapter three of *The Unrepentant Renaissance: From Petrarch to Shakespeare to Milton*, and returns to the idea in an essay called "Shakespeare and Legal Systems: The Better the Worse (but Not Vice Versa)."[1] Julia Reinhard Lupton explores the idea of judgment at a number of points in *Thinking with Shakespeare: Essays on Politics and Life*, especially in a chapter devoted to *The*

Winter's Tale which draws compelling parallels between Shakespeare's and Hannah Arendt's conceptions of judgment. Lupton extends this line of thought in a more recent essay dealing with the relationship between judgment and forgiveness in *The Winter's Tale*.[2] Judgment is also discussed at various points in Lorna Hutson's seminal study of theater and law in early modern England, *The Invention of Suspicion: Law and Mimesis in Shakespeare and Renaissance Drama*.[3] Hutson is primarily interested in the perception and practice of judgment within English common law, but she also examines the way ideas about legal judgment are connected to discourses of religion and civility in early modern England. The place of judgment within rhetorical theory has been addressed by Kathy Eden in *Poetic and Legal Fiction in the Aristotelian Tradition*, Joel Altman in *The Improbability of Othello: Rhetorical Anthropology and Shakespearean Selfhood*, and Quentin Skinner in *Forensic Shakespeare*.[4] Paul Yachnin's chapter on "The Theater of Judgment" in his forthcoming book, *Making Publics in Shakespeare's Playhouse*, will constitute yet another significant contribution to this growing body of scholarship.[5] Related work that deals with judgment beyond the historical parameters of early modernity includes, most importantly, Vivasvan Soni's special issue of *The Eighteenth Century* on "The Crisis of Judgment" and Thomas Pfau's wide-ranging inquiry into the roots of modernity, *Minding the Modern: Human Agency, Intellectual Traditions, and Responsible Knowledge*, which takes up judgment – along with will, personhood, and action – as one of the foundational concepts in Western intellectual history.[6]

As the notes to the chapters that follow indicate, *Shakespeare and Judgment* is in close conversation with these studies. Taken as a whole, though, the volume also offers something quite distinct: the first sustained consideration of the way judgment, in its various cultural and conceptual formations, shapes and is shaped by Shakespeare's language and dramaturgy. Such a project stands to reinvigorate our understanding of the imaginative and cultural geography of Shakespeare's plays, since judgment was, and remains, a point of intersection for a wide variety of social practices and intellectual traditions. Conversely, the plays themselves help us map out judgment's assemblage-like structure across the sprawled thought-worlds of law, religion, aesthetics, rhetoric, and philosophy. Shakespeare, of course, was not the only early modern dramatist to engage with judgment. Ben Jonson, for example, deals with it quite regularly. But Shakespeare's plays offer a richer, more wide-ranging account of what judgment is and what judgment can make possible (politically, ethically, and socially) than any of his contemporaries.

What is Judgment?

Judgment is something *out there* – in the law courts, in the universities, on the tip of God's tongue, and in the codes of socialization. But it's also something *in here*. Judgment is a psychological faculty possessed by each person, even if its effectiveness may vary depending on circumstance and other factors. Early modern scholars such as Pierre de la Primaudaye, Thomas Wright, Philippe de Mornay, and others describe the capacity to judge as part of a complex ecology of cognitive and sensory aptitudes. Memory, for example, as Garrett Sullivan has shown, was thought of as crucial to judgment, providing a storehouse of experience-based data on which future decisions could be based.[7] Emotion, on the other hand, conceived of in physiological terms and referred to as "passions," impeded judgment. In *Passions of the Minde* (1601), Thomas Wright explains,

> Those actions then which are common with us, and the beasts, we cal Passions, and Affections, or perturbances of the mind . . . They are called Passions (although indeed they be acts the sensitive power, or faculties of our soul . . .) because when these affections are stirring in our minds, they alter the humours of our bodies, causing some passion or alteration in them. They are called perturbations, for that . . . they trouble wonderfully the soule, corrupting the judgment, & seducing the will . . .[8]

Similarly, Philippe de Mornay in *The True Knowledge of a Man's Owne Selfe* (1602) instructs that "The knowledge of a mans owne selfe, availeth, not onely for preservations of the bodies health, but likewise to moderate the vehemcie of inordinate affections, which hinder and impeach the health of judgment."[9]

According to these writers, judgment is rational and practical, and in this sense quite opposed to the operations of the body. But this was not the only version of judgment made available by early modern faculty psychology. As David Summers has demonstrated, there is also "a long tradition of speculation concerning prerational sensate judgment upon which Renaissance writers drew."[10] Aristotle, for example, argued that the capacity to judge was common to both thought and perception. "Each sense," he writes, "judges the specific differences of its own sensible object . . . Sight produces upon white and black, taste upon sweet and bitter, and so with the rest."[11] Later, we find the English scholar Abraham Fraunce advancing a similar line about the relationship between judgment and sensation in *The Lawyers Logike* (1588):

For as Aristotle teacheth in the second of his demonstrations, every
sensible creature hath a naturall power and facultie of judging, which
is called sence; & this sence (2. Topic) is of him sayde to bee a certayne
kinde of judgement: and without doubt, the sence is a most upright
judge of suche thinges as are properly under his jurisdiction, as
the sight of colours, the hearing of soundes, the smelling of smelles
(4. Metap).[12]

For Thomas Wright and Phillipe de Mornay, judgment is something that distinguishes humans from animals because it is a property of reason rather than sensation. For Fraunce, following Aristotle, however, judgment is common to "every sensible creature" because sensation constitutes a "certayne kinde of judgment."

It is the latter tradition that Shakespeare has in mind when Hamlet confronts his mother with portraits of her old husband, Hamlet Sr., and her new husband, Claudius:

This was your husband. Look you now what follows:
Here is your husband, like a mildewed ear,
Blasting his wholesome brother. Have you eyes?
Could you on this fair mountain leave to feed,
And batten on this moor? ha, have you eyes?
You cannot call it love, for at your age
The heyday in the blood is tame, it's humble,
And waits upon the judgment, and what judgment
Would step from this to this?
. . .
Eyes without feeling, feeling without sight,
Ears without hands or eyes, smelling sans all,
Or but a sickly part of one true sense
Could not so mope. (3.4.63–71, 78–81)[13]

In the course of Hamlet's withering rebuke, judgment emerges as a species of spectatorship ("have you eyes?"). Good judgment, it seems, involves a clear alignment of perception and emotion while bad judgment (Gertrude's judgment) results from a misalignment of perception and emotion: "Eyes without feeling, feeling without sight."[14]

Faculty psychology underpinned much of the discourse on self-hood in early modern England, but the context in which most of Shakespeare's contemporaries would have encountered judgment was, in fact, the study of rhetoric. Roman rhetorical theory was central to the humanist curriculum in Tudor grammar schools. The *Rhetorica ad Herennium*, Cicero's *De inventione*, and Quintilian's

Institutio oratoria were used as textbooks, offering students training in the kind of analytical and pragmatic method of argumentation central to what Aristotle called the *genus iudiciale*, or legal speech.[15] This involved the carefully synchronized deployment of two skills: invention and judgment. Invention is the process of choosing the ideas and subjects most likely to persuade your audience while judgment is the process of ordering and deploying those ideas in a way designed to achieve maximum effect. In this context, judgment is best understood as "a faculty of form and structure, arranging the matter of invention by deciding which type of argument to use and how to compose a total sequence."[16] This formal dimension of judgment is noteworthy as it lies behind much of the vernacular literary criticism that emerged in the sixteenth and seventeenth centuries. Programmatic descriptions of good writing and right reading by figures such as Philip Sidney, George Puttenham, Samuel Daniel, and Henry Peacham cite judgment as both the faculty responsible for proper discernment and the attribute that stands to benefit from superior writing and oratory. The easiest way to identify first-rate poetry, so the argument runs, is to assess its level of *decorum*, the quality of adhering to formal rules of concurrence among genre, plot, character, and language. *Decorum* was the gold standard of aesthetic quality for early modern literary critics and it was understood primarily as an expression of sound judgment.

If the *genus iudiciale* relied on a practical and evaluative version of judgment native to both humanist pedagogy and literary criticism, the term itself also reminds us that judgment found its primary institutional home in the law courts. In the case of legal pleas it took a form consistent with the requirements of humanist oratory. A plea, that is, involved both choosing and effectively arranging arguments. At the same time, judges, juries, and Justices of the Peace practiced judgment not just in the sense of handing down decisions, but also in the sense of using specific criteria to measure the quality and persuasiveness of legal arguments. In this respect, judges engage in a practice very similar to literary critics, a correspondence that Kathy Eden traces back to Aristotle:

> The rapport between poetry and law, so fundamental to the Aristotelian literary tradition, is not only preserved but enriched. For, in an attempt to chart, for the first time, the invisible workings of psychological judgment, Aristotle turns . . . to the familiar procedures of legal judgment. And this capacity for judging, in turn, is intimately linked in the human soul to the act of imagining, so crucial to both rhetoric and poetry.[17]

For the judge as for the poet or dramatist, judgment is a *method*. It is a procedure designed for measurement and assessment, for breaking things down into their component parts so as to evaluate them more effectively and understand them more accurately.

The Renaissance represents a particularly important passage in the professional and institutional history of legal judgment. The period saw a gradual shift in emphasis from legal doctrine to judge-made law, or *jurisprudence*, which meant that the role of judgment – of judicial decision-making – in creating the law expanded significantly.[18] Whereas in the fifteenth century, Thomas Littleton's landmark *Tenures* (1481) relied almost exclusively on doctrine, or common learning, Sir William Staunford, holding the same judicial office as Littleton less than a century later, wrote, in J. H. Baker's words, "books so crammed with references and quotations that he seemed incapable of venturing an opinion unless it could be derived from someone else."[19] Staunford, in other words, in books like *Les plees del coron* (1557) and *An exposicion of the kinges prerogative* (1561), drew heavily on past judicial decisions to lend his own claims authority. Edmund Plowden's later sixteenth-century law reports exhibit the same tendency, but with more methodological rigor and decisiveness. Plowden was very selective when it came to choosing which cases to report. Unlike more typical yearbooks of the period, he would leave out any courtroom debate that was inconclusive, publishing only those cases in which a specific point of law had been settled by a final judgment of record.[20] These shifts are indicative of a mounting desire among legal professionals and their clientele for law to rest upon clearly recorded facts. It resulted, gradually, in a more authoritative judiciary and judgment came to loom larger in the conceptual landscape of English common law.[21]

Despite the steadily growing importance of judgment – or perhaps because of it – there was also anxiety about the methods and effects of meting it out. Some of these anxieties were religious. Writings on the sacrament of penance, for example, frequently presented secular judgment as demonic, both severely formal and dangerously fallible in comparison with the equitable and restorative principles of the Church.[22] One such text is *Jacob's Well* (c.1450), a sequence of penitential sermons composed for oral delivery between Ash Wednesday and the Vigil of Pentecost, now widely recognized as an early source for the morality play *Mankind* (c.1465).[23] Each sermon fits into a larger allegorical scheme in which the soul struggles out of a pit of corrupt waters into the pure well of Jacob, assisted by various tools that represent contrition, confession, and satisfaction. The aim of these sermons was to urge parishioners to make confession and embrace the Church's penitential system for managing and purging sin. The diabolical alternative is the secular common law courts in which "thou schuldst be convict in thi cause, for thou art gylty in wrong . . . and the sentens of dampnacyoun shulde be gouyn agens the." Better to go "to the juge of god, that is, to the preest."[24] Whereas God's justice offers a shot at redemption, the inflexible justice of the common law courts leads directly to death and damnation. Hutson explains that in *Jacob's Well*, "jury trial emerges as no kind of trial at all, and salvation is imagined as a repeated escape from the rigors of Common Law Hell, first by the priestly judge's absolution, and then by Purgatorial pains, figured as our escape, by pleading clergy, to the canonical purgation of the spiritual courts."[25]

The attitude toward secular judgment in *Jacob's Well* is indicative of a deeply entrenched habit of thought, a core distrust of secular law that persisted even despite the momentous shift in jurisdictional authority from spiritual to temporal institutions over the course of the sixteenth century. As late as 1578, Thomas Garter's dramatic interlude, *The Commody of the most virtuous and Godlye Susanna*, portrays a miscarriage of justice in a secular court set right at the last moment by divine intervention. Here, the concern is less with the diabolically stringent, either/or conditions of common law courts than it is with the basic competence of human judges, fallen and imperfect as they are, to identify truth and arbitrate accordingly. The Judge in Garter's interlude, persuaded by the false testimony of the elders, sentences Susanna to death. However, as "*she is led to execution . . . God rayseth the spiritte of Danyell,*" who insists that "*they return all backe to judgment.*"[26] In due course, Susanna is proclaimed innocent and the other participants in the trial roundly condemned. Garter's interlude is comforting to the extent that it portrays a caring God who intercedes on behalf of the downtrodden, but it certainly would not have left readers with much confidence in temporal judgment. Daniel refers to the members of the legal community in the interlude as "foolish folke . . . that know not ill from good"[27] – hardly an endorsement of the efficacies of English common law.

Anxieties about the role of judges and the effects of their decisions can be found issuing from within the legal community, too. Edward Coke, for example, though confident enough that a judge would not completely misinterpret evidence and testimony, nevertheless urged those charged with the task of adjudication not to overstep their bounds. The role of the judge, Coke insisted, is to declare law, not to make it, "for that which hath been refined and perfected by the wisest men in former succession of ages, and proved and approved by continual experience to be good and profitable for the commonwealth, cannot without great hazard or danger be altered or changed."[28] He returned to the issue in his *First Institutes*, noting that "commonly a new invention doth offend against many rules and reasons of the common law, and the ancient judges and sages of the law have ever ... suppressed innovation and novelties in the beginning."[29] Coke was not the only one to weigh in on the "hazard" of judicial innovation. John Davies makes a similar point in the preface to *Le Primer Report des Cases en Ireland* (1615) and Francis Bacon opens his essay "Of Judicature" with an extended statement on the matter:

> Judges ought to remember that their office is *jus dicere*, and not *jus dare*; to interpret law, and not to make law, or give law. Else it will be like the authority claimed by the church of Rome, which under pretext of exposition of Scripture doth not stick to add and alter; and to pronounce that which they do not find; and by show of antiquity to introduce novelty. Judges ought to be more learned than witty, more reverend than plausible, and more advised than confident. Above all things, integrity is their portion and proper virtue.[30]

Judgment, Bacon asserts, is a strain of applied scholarship, not a maverick performance. He urges a kind of learned modesty and deference to legal doctrine. As long as the laws themselves speak through the judge, rather than vice versa, there is minimal risk of corruption and error.

The anxieties of jurists and clergymen notwithstanding, legal judgment was, with few exceptions, a thoroughly collaborative affair. It was a *process* involving multiple parties. We get a sense of how this worked in the manuals produced for Justices of the Peace in the period. Essentially printed how-to guides, these manuals were aimed at the gentlemen charged with presiding over the Quarter Sessions – county courts that met four times per year (Epiphany, Easter, Trinity, and Michaelmas) – though they were no doubt consulted by other legal amateurs, too. Justices of the Peace were appointed annually and the primary qualification for the job was local standing, not legal expertise. They would hear cases having to do with comparatively minor offenses, such as trespass, assault, licenses for alehouses, and theft.[31] Cases involving the most serious felonies, such as murder, were typically heard at the Assizes, which met twice per year and were presided over by professional barristers from the central courts. Responding to a clear need among England's many legal amateurs for procedural guidance, Justice of the Peace manuals began being printed in the late sixteenth century and increased steadily in popularity over the course of the seventeenth century. Almost all Justice of the Peace manuals went through multiple print runs and successive editions, so we can assume that they were in demand. Small books ranging in size from sixteenmo to octavo, they were meant to be carried around and referred to while on the job or shortly beforehand. Accordingly, the tone and style of the Justice of the Peace manuals tend to be practical and concise. From the mid-seventeenth century, in particular, a premium seems to have been placed on usability. The anonymously authored *The Complete Justice* (1637), for example, simply lists alphabetically a series of key technical terms and procedures followed by brief descriptions. This is a manual designed for quick and easy reference. The same format is adopted in *The justice of peace, his clarks cabinet* (1654), written by the prolific William Shepherd who also produced law lexicons and manuals for parsons, constables, and other minor legal professionals.

All of these texts show legal judgment to be a process involving various individuals working in close partnership. Take William Lambarde's *Eirenarcha: or the office of the justices of the peace* (1581). As an early example of the genre, *Eirenarcha* is more discursive and descriptive than its later seventeenth-century counterparts. Lambarde overviews the duties of Justices to their community, the central courts, the king, and God, and tries to differentiate between those situations in which strict conformity to certain recorded statutes is appropriate and when more discretionary judgment is called for.[32] Significantly, during the lengthy discussion of the protocols of trial and sentencing, Lambarde describes this "Session of the Peace" as "An assemblie," and he stresses the fact that not one, but "two (or moe) Justices" must be present "to heare and determine" a case.[33] This plurality of adjudicators is essential, and "if any of them be absent," Lambarde explains, "their fellow justices cannot amerce them . . . for . . . the auctoritie of all the Justices of the Peace at the Sessions is equall."[34] Lambarde goes on to describe in some detail each of the other figures who must be present for a trial to go forward and judgment to be passed: the "Shirife," the "Baylifes," and the "Juries," which "ought to containe 12. in number at the leaste."[35] *Eirenarcha* presents judgment as a participatory "assemblie," one in which complex bureaucratic procedures knit together a diverse network of both amateur and professional legal agents. Michael Dalton, a member of Lincoln's Inn, stresses this point too, opening his manual, *The Countrey Justice* (1618), with a narrative sketch of where the Justice of the Peace stands within the larger legal hierarchy and what that position affords in terms of specific duties, obligations, and dependencies.[36]

At the heart of these Justice of the Peace manuals is a fascination with breaking the legal process, especially adjudication, down into its most essential components. This concern with itemization and procedural detail can be found in other kinds of writing, too. Richard Bernard's stunningly dense allegory, *The Isle of Man, or, The legall proceedings in Man-shire against sinne* (1627), is a good example. In this narrative, self-examination, self-management, and self-regulation are figured through the collaborative procedures of common law. Conscience is represented by the Judge, but this judge operates within a diverse cluster of Justices and other officials:

> The Justices of Peace in the Countrie are there, and doe sit with the Judge and are in Commission with him. Of these some are of the Quorum, and of the better ranke, some are meaner Justices and take their place lower.
>
> The Justices of Peace in the Soule of better ranke are Science, Prudence, Providence, Sapience: the inferiors are Weake Wit, common Aprehension, and some such like.
>
> These Justices have their Clerkes, there ready with their examinations and recognizances. Justice Science, his Clerke is Discourse: Justice Prudence, his Clerke is Circumspection, Justice Providence, his Clerke is Diligence; Justice Sapience, his Clerke is Experience: Justice Weake-wit, his Clerke is Conceit: and Justice Common-Apprehension, his Clerke is onely Sense.[37]

Bernard turns common law into a precise language of cognitive process and spiritual struggle, signaling what Hutson describes as "a new moral confidence . . . in the procedural detail of the Common Law."[38] The allegory demonstrates the power of common law adjudication as an emblem of collaborative decision-making and as a figure for the concatenation of forces involved in moral choice.[39]

One thing that all the types of judgment considered here have in common is a fundamentally social, or at least relational, structure. In faculty psychology, judgment forms an evaluative interface with the outer world of people and things. In the rhetorical tradition, judgment aims at address and response; it presupposes the presence of an other. Legal judgment is a distributed, participatory event. Even when judgment is invoked in the context of self-knowledge, as it is by Stephen Guazzo in his conduct book, *The Civile Conversation* (1581), it is presented as a capacity that links the individual to a larger scene of sociality: "The judgment which we have to know ourselves is not ours, but we borrow it of others . . . the knowledge of ourselves, dependeth of the judgment and conversation of many."[40] To this extent, early modern judgment, in all its various intellectual and institutional iterations, participates in a long philosophical tradition that views judging as a means of connecting the individual to larger collectives. This line of thought begins with Aristotle and the Stoics and is taken up with particular rigor in the eighteenth century when writers like the Third Earl of Shaftesbury, Jean-Jacques Rousseau, and Immanuel Kant formulated new ideas about the role of judgment in social and political life.

Particularly influential was Kant's famous argument that judging requires an "enlarged mentality," a form of decision-making based on a combination of one's own intuitions and the range of other possible intuitions held by those with whom you share a particular space or community. He describes it as "a power to judge that . . . takes account (a priori), in our thought, of everyone else's way of presenting [something], in order as it were to compare our own judgment with human reason in general."[41] Hannah Arendt, Kant's most astute modern interpreter, makes a similar argument: "As logic, to be sound, depends on the presence of the self, so judgment, to be valid, depends on the presence of others"; "Judging," she continues, "is one, if not the most, important activity in which this sharing-the-world-with-others comes to pass."[42] In a series of essays and lectures produced between 1961 and 1975, Arendt explored this link between judgment and collective perception at a level of nuance that surpassed any other twentieth-century philosopher. In this body of work, Arendt is particularly adept at drawing out the political and ethical implications of Kant's theories. In her essay "The Crisis in Culture," for example, she explains,

> That capacity to judge is a specifically political ability in exactly the sense denoted by Kant, namely, the ability to see things not only from one's own point of view but in the perspective of all those who happen to be present; even that judgment may be one of the fundamental abilities of man as a political being insofar as it enables him to orient himself in that public realm, in the common world.[43]

Pushing this assertion further, Arendt maintains that aesthetic judgment, or "taste," should be understood in the same terms:

> Taste, insofar as it, like any other judgment, appeals to common sense, is the very opposite of private feelings. In aesthetic no less than political judgments, a decision is made, and although this decision is always

determined by a certain subjectivity, by the simple fact that each person occupies a place of his own from which he looks upon and judges the world, it also derives from the fact that the world itself is an objective datum, something common to all its inhabitants.

"For judgments of taste," Arendt concludes, "the world is the primary thing, not man, neither man's life nor his self."[44] Arendt didn't look to early modern England to develop these arguments, but she could have. The central idea she advances – that judgment, broadly conceived, is interactive and participatory – is central to the period's understanding of adjudication. Shakespeare bears this out better than anyone.

Shakespeare and Judgment

As even this brief overview indicates, judgment is a more protean phenomenon than may at first appear to be the case. At once a faculty, a practice, a method, and a skill, judgment transforms as it migrates across the realms of psychology, rhetoric, aesthetics, law, religion, and philosophy. One implication of this multidimensionality is that judgment is difficult to contain within a single analytical framework. Accordingly, the chapters in this volume speak from a range of methodological platforms and engage a variety of different aspects of early modern culture, the history of ideas, and critical theory. The result, I hope, is a book that advances an intellectually diverse but still coherent account of the way judgment brings various discourses about justice, religion, beauty, selfhood, time, and performance into contact in Shakespeare's plays.

The chapters in *Shakespeare and Judgment* have been grouped in such a way so as to let the complexities of these crossings emerge. Themed subsections denote fields of action and experience that comprise different forms of judgment (legal, aesthetic, moral, etc.), rather than building artificial walls between them. Part I, "Staging Judgment: Deliberation in the Plays," presents three chapters on the performance of judgment in the playworld itself. Virginia Lee Strain's chapter, "Preventive Justice in *Measure for Measure*," considers the Duke's treatment of Barnardine's case at the end of the play. Frequently grouped among *Measure for Measure*'s several concluding anomalies, Strain shows that there is, in fact, a compelling ethical logic to the Duke's decision. This emerges into view when we read the scene in the context of "preventive justice," a frequently overlooked aspect of legal theory and practice, both in early modern studies and legal studies. Moving from legal history to intellectual history, Vivas-van Soni's "Believing in Ghosts, in Part: Judgment and Indecision in *Hamlet*" discusses the failure of modern philosophers to differentiate sufficiently between decision and judgment in *Hamlet*, arguing for the centrality of the former to the play's treatment of both time and subjectivity. Constance Jordan closes the section with a turn to material and professional contexts. Her chapter, "Shakespeare's Law and Plowden's Authority," considers how judgment in *The Taming of the Shrew* is shaped by developments in the practice of law reporting in the sixteenth century.

Part II, "Audience Judgment: Deliberation in the Theater," features four chapters that expand the frame of reference to include not just the fictional playworld, but also the cognitive, interpretive, and participatory dynamics of theatrical spectatorship. Katherine B. Attié opens the section with a chapter called "'Gently to hear, kindly to judge': Minds at Work in *Henry V*." In it, she demonstrates that in the case of *Henry V*, audience judgment is linked not to law, but rather to a specifically early modern understanding of the intellectual and ethical labor of playgoing itself, one that runs counter to the famous antitheatrical equivalence between theatrical spectatorship and idleness. Carolyn Sale's chapter, "'Practis[ing] judgment with the disposition of natures': *Measure for Measure*, the 'Discursive' Common Law, and the 'Open Court' of the Theater," shifts the discussion from labor back to law. Focusing on *Measure for Measure*, she argues that the play in performance offers audiences the opportunity to experience their own authority in relation to the common law's "discursive" practices of judgment. Paul Yachnin takes us deeper into this play in his chapter, "The Laws of *Measure for Measure*." Like Strain in the previous section, Yachnin is interested in the apparent strangeness of the Duke's judgments in Act 5. But whereas Strain explains it by reference to the history and theory of preventive justice in early modern England, Yachnin views it as an example of the law-making capacity of Shakespeare's theatrical art. By defamiliarizing legal judgment in institutional and historical terms, *Measure for Measure* creates its own legal system. That is to say, it opens a participatory space within the theater where playgoers can engage in the sort of collective evaluation and moral decision that gives meaning and value to the world. Kevin Curran concludes the section with a chapter called "Prospero's Plea: Judgment, Invention, and Political Form in *The Tempest*." Curran shows, first, that the connection Prospero establishes between judgment and invention in the epilogue grows out of early modern rhetorical theory. He then goes on to argue that in translating this tradition into the language of performance, the epilogue makes a uniquely theatrical contribution to a modern body of thought on the relationship between judgment, politics, and form.

The final section of the volume, "The Ethics of Judgment," opens out to a broader set of historical and conceptual questions. Featuring three very different kinds of inquiries, the section offers a wide-ranging meditation on how judgment indexes the larger religious, philosophical, and critical contexts for the way social and moral value is determined. John Parker's "Antinomian Shakespeare: English Drama and Confession across the Reformation Divide" explores how Shakespeare tends to figure forgiveness as an escape from legal and moral judgment. Shakespeare's skepticism about judgment, Parker argues, follows from Christianity's ongoing and sometimes quite radical critique of the law. Sanford Budick's rigorously philosophical chapter, "Bracketed Judgment, 'Un-humanizing', and Conversion in *The Merchant of Venice*," reflects on the way Shakespeare uses judgment in the trial scene to create an impossible moral dilemma, one that actually suspends the audience's own ability to judge. Though at first glance paradoxical, Budick shows through careful philosophical contextualization that this suspension of judgment is in fact one of the play's most powerful and systemic ways of creating human community. Concluding the section, and the volume, is Richard Strier's chapter, "The Judgment of the Critics that Makes us Tremble: 'Distributing Complicities' in Recent Criticism of *King Lear*." In a move that will leave many readers reflecting not just on Shakespeare's plays, but also on their own professional practice, Strier steps outside of staged fictions, outside of the theater, and outside of early modern culture to consider instead the kind of judgment exercised in the world of Shakespeare criticism. Focusing on Stanley Cavell's and Harry Berger Jr.'s influential work on *King Lear*, Strier argues for a mode of literary-critical judgment based on surface rather than depth and on common sense rather than convolution. Judgment, he reminds us, is not just an instinctive response, but a deliberate craft involving stylistic and hermeneutic choice. If we want literary criticism to have real intellectual and ethical purchase, we need to think carefully about how that craft is practiced.

My hope for this volume is that it will offer readers new ways to frame the historical and intellectual contexts of Shakespeare's plays, such that neglected areas of conceptual overlap begin to emerge.

Rooted as it is in so many different aspects of cultural practice and philosophical speculation, judgment stands to make a uniquely generative contribution to Shakespeare studies by opening new spaces of encounter among early modernists working with law, religion, rhetoric, theater history, and critical theory.

Notes

1. Richard Strier, *The Unrepentant Renaissance: From Petrarch to Shakespeare to Milton* (Chicago: University of Chicago Press, 2011) and "Shakespeare and Legal Systems: The Better the Worse (but Not Vice Versa)," in *Shakespeare and the Law: A Conversation Among Disciplines and Professions*, ed. Bradin Cormack, Martha C. Nussbaum, and Richard Strier (Chicago: University of Chicago Press, 2013), 174–200.
2. Julia Reinhard Lupton, *Thinking with Shakespeare: Essays on Politics and Life* (Chicago: University of Chicago Press, 2011) and "Judging Forgiveness: Hannah Arendt, W. H. Auden, and *The Winter's Tale*," *New Literary History* 45 (2014): 641–63.
3. Lorna Hutson, *The Invention of Suspicion: Law and Mimesis in Shakespeare and Renaissance Drama* (Oxford: Oxford University Press, 2007).
4. Kathy Eden, *Poetic and Legal Fiction in the Aristotelian Tradition* (Princeton: Princeton University Press, 1986); Joel B. Altman, *The Improbability of Othello: Rhetorical Anthropology and Shakespearean Selfhood* (Chicago: University of Chicago Press, 2010); and Quentin Skinner, *Forensic Shakespeare* (Oxford: Oxford University Press, 2014).
5. Paul Yachnin, *Making Publics in Shakespeare's Playhouse* (Edinburgh: Edinburgh University Press, forthcoming 2017).
6. Vivasvan Soni, ed., *The Eighteenth Century: Theory and Interpretation* 51 (2010), Special Issue on "The Crisis of Judgment"; Thomas Pfau, *Minding the Modern: Human Agency, Intellectual Traditions, and Responsible Knowledge* (Notre Dame: Notre Dame University Press, 2013).
7. Garrett A. Sullivan, Jr., "'Be this sweet Helen's knell, and now forget her': Forgetting, Memory, and Identity in *All's Well that Ends Well*," *Shakespeare Quarterly* 50 (1999): 51–69. In this section I have relied heavily on Sullivan, whose work on memory and forgetting returns regularly to the notion of judgment in early modern faculty psychology. See also his book *Memory and Forgetting in English Renaissance Drama: Shakespeare, Marlowe, Webster* (Cambridge: Cambridge University Press, 2005).

8. Thomas Wright, *The Passions of the Minde in Generall* (London, 1601), 12–14; quoted in Sullivan, "'Be this sweet Helen's knell'," 57.

9. Philippe de Mornay, *The True Knowledge of a Man's Owne Selfe* (London, 1602), 2.

10. David Summers, *The Judgment of Sense: Renaissance Naturalism and the Rise of Aesthetics* (Cambridge: Cambridge University Press, 1987), 22. Also relevant here is Heidi Cephus, "Corporeal Judgment in Shakespeare's Plays" (PhD diss., University of North Texas, 2016), which makes an important contribution to this line of inquiry.

11. Aristotle, *De Anima (On the Soul)* (London: Penguin, 1986), 426b–c.

12. Abraham Fraunce, *The Lawyers Logike* (London, 1588), 91.

13. G. Blakemore Evans, gen. ed., *The Riverside Shakespeare*, 2d ed. (Boston: Houghton Mifflin, 1997). The version of this speech in Evans's edition includes the lines from the First Quarto (1603) that are not present in the First Folio (1623).

14. I develop this idea further in a forthcoming essay called "Judgment and Emotion in *Hamlet*."

15. See Peter Mack, *Elizabethan Rhetoric: Theory and Practice* (Cambridge: Cambridge University Press, 2002); and Skinner, *Forensic Shakespeare*, 11–47.

16. Henry S. Turner, *The English Renaissance Stage: Geometry, Poetics, and the Practical Spatial Arts, 1580–1630* (Oxford: Oxford University Press, 2006), 50.

17. Kathy Eden, *Poetic and Legal Fiction in the Aristotelian Tradition* (Princeton: Princeton University Press, 1986), 63.

18. John Langbein, *Prosecuting Crime in the Renaissance: England, Germany, France* (Cambridge, MA: Harvard University Press, 1974), 104–28; "The Criminal Trial Before the Lawyers," *University of Chicago Law Review* 45 (1978): 263–316; J. S. Cockburn, *Calendar of Assize Records: Introduction* (London: Her Majesty's Stationery Office, 1985), chs. 6, 8, and Conclusion; J. H. Baker, *The Legal Profession and The Common Law: Historical Essays* (London: The Hambledon Press, 1986), 474–6.

19. Baker, *Legal Profession*, 474.

20. See, for example, Edmund Plowden, *Les commentaries, ou les reportes de Edmunde Plowden* (London, 1571) and *Cy ensuont certeyne cases reportes per Edmunde Plowden* (London, 1579).

21. Baker, *Legal Profession*, 461–76; J. H. Baker, *An Introduction to English Legal History* (Oxford: Oxford University Press, 2002), 195–9; Cynthia Herrup, *The Common Peace: Participation and the Criminal Law in Seventeenth-Century England* (Cambridge: Cambridge University Press, 1987), 158–9.

22. Hutson, *The Invention of Suspicion*, 30–7.

23. Sister Mary Coogan, *An Interpretation of the Moral Play* (Washington, DC: Catholic University of America Press, 1947); Leo Caruthers, "The Liturgical Setting of *Jacob's Well*," *English Language Notes* 24 (1987): 11–24.
24. Arthur Brandeis, ed., *Jacob's Well, an English treatise on the cleansing of man's conscience*, Early English Text Society 115 (Oxford: Oxford University Press, 1900), 256–7.
25. Hutson, *The Invention of Suspicion*, 37–8.
26. Thomas Garter, *The Commody of the most virtuous and Godlye Susanna* (London, 1578), E1v, E2r.
27. Ibid., E1v.
28. Edward Coke, *Le Quart Part des Reportes del Edward Coke* (London, 1604), B2v.
29. Edward Coke, *The First Part of the Institutes of the Laws of England* (London, 1628), 379.
30. Francis Bacon *The Major Works*, ed. Brian Vickers (Oxford: Oxford University Press, 2002), 446.
31. The best primary sources for the Quarter Sessions are William Lambarde, *Eirenarcha: or the office of the justices of the peace* (London, 1581); and Michael Dalton, *The Countrey Justice* (London, 1618). For the Assizes, see J. S. Cockburn, ed., *Calendar of Assize Records*, 11 vols. (London: Her Majesty's Stationery Office, 1975–1985); Cockburn, *A History of English Assizes, 1558–1714* (Cambridge: Cambridge University Press, 1972); Cockburn, "Early Modern Assize Records as Historical Evidence," *Journal of the Society of Archivists* 5 (1975): 215–31.
32. Lambarde, *Eirenarcha*, 57–8, 455.
33. Ibid., 286.
34. Ibid., 294–5.
35. Ibid., 304, 308.
36. Dalton, *Countrey Justice*, 4–6, 13–17, 23–7.
37. Richard Bernard, *The Isle of Man, or, The legall proceedings in Manshire against sinne* (London, 1627), 129–30.
38. Hutson, *The Invention of Suspicion*, 43.
39. See further, chapter 4 of my book, *Shakespeare's Legal Ecologies: Law and Distributed Selfhood* (Evanston: Northwestern University Press, forthcoming 2017).
40. Stephen Guazzo, *The Civile Conversation* (London, 1581), 4–5.
41. Immanuel Kant, *Critique of Judgment*, trans. Werner S. Pluhar (Indianapolis: Hackett Publishing Company, 1987), 160.
42. Hannah Arendt, "The Crisis in Culture: Its Social and Its Political Significance," in *Between Past and Future: Eight Exercises in Political Thought* (Harmondsworth: Penguin, 1993), 197–226.
43. Ibid., 221.

44. Ibid., 222. For more of Arendt's work on judgment, see "Truth and Politics," in *Between Past and Future*, 227–64; "Personal Responsibility Under Dictatorship" and "Some Questions of Moral Philosophy," in *Responsibility and Judgment*, ed. Jerome Kohn (New York: Random House, 2003), 17–48, 49–146; *The Life of the Mind* (San Diego: Harcourt, 1978), 69, 93–5, 193. In addition to the two completed volumes of *The Life of the Mind* – "Thinking" and "Willing" – Arendt had intended to produce a third, on "Judging." She died before she was able to complete this section but much of the raw material for it can be found in the appendix to the Harcourt edition (255–72), "Judging: Excerpts from Lectures on Kant's Political Philosophy."

Part I

Staging Judgment: Deliberation in the Plays

Chapter 1

Preventive Justice in *Measure for Measure*

Virginia Lee Strain

This chapter elaborates two major historical and legal distinctions as they relate to Shakespeare's *Measure for Measure*. Beginning with the character Barnardine, I demonstrate the way his fictional case refracts, and must be ethically understood through, the gap that persisted between the formal law and the so-called life of the law – not the spirit, or the law's or legislators' intentions, but the life of the law as it was embodied in the practices of early modern communities.[1] The gap between the letter and the life enlarged the terrain of legal judgment far beyond technical questions of fact and law and brought the results of the legal system closer to social notions of justice. An understanding of the differences between punitive law as it was represented in the statute books and as it was practiced facilitates a much more nuanced evaluation of the decision by Shakespeare's Duke to pardon the murderer Barnardine, as well as others in the play.

The life of English law was overseen primarily by Justices of the Peace, whose responsibilities included not only punitive justice but also preventive justice – the second major distinction that I treat. Preventive justice included all the deliberation and activity that took place in lieu of, before, after, and even sometimes during trials, to inhibit crime or minimize its consequences. In early modern England, maintaining social order or "keeping the peace" was not only considered a more effective and just strategy than punishing those who had broken the law, but it also engaged much more of the magistrate's time and effort. Yet in legal studies no less than cultural studies, preventive justice has received scant attention.[2] If we over-identify justice with trials, and over-identify trials with the goals of conviction and punishment, a study of the principles and practices of preventive justice offers a new focus for a cultural study of the law that brings with it a distinct operational ethics. The second section of this chapter unpacks the history of preventive justice to provide a new historical, legal, and ethical context with which to evaluate Shakespeare's magistrates.

The historical picture of the law that I sketch below is necessary to combat the nearly universal assumption, in *Measure for Measure* and Shakespeare criticism, that the common law did not accommodate so-called equitable or merciful conflict resolutions; that it resembled, in effect, Angelo's depiction of the law as identical with its letter. Two arguments in particular perpetuate this absolute and incorrect distinction. It is inscribed in studies that differentiate the Duke, a sovereign, from his deputies, the representatives of the law. There is firm consensus that, through the Duke's divestment of power in the opening scene and his resumption of power in the final scene, the play is structured by the topic of sovereignty. The dramatization of the transfer of power has frequently elicited comparisons with the succession crisis and James I's recent installation. According to this argument, for mercy and/or equity[3] to be exercised, the law must be overridden by a superior authority; it is this power to override the law that becomes the public sign of the Duke's legitimacy as sovereign ruler in the final scene.[4] Yet neither the problems the Duke addresses nor the strategies he employs are especially monarchical. The transfer of power, including the substitutions and metaphors that it entailed, was the enabling and repeating mechanism of magistracy throughout the country. For instance, the commission of the peace (discussed below) was redrafted at least twice a year. Commissioning and re-commissioning were a regular feature of the country's legal-political hierarchy throughout which the sovereign's absence was the rule rather than a source of anxiety. To argue that Vincentio attempts to "refound the state" in the final scene, as Andrew Majeske does, begins to sound excessive even though it is in agreement with a decades-long tradition that has embraced the Duke's legal-theatrical spectacle as a significant juncture in the relationship between Renaissance drama and politics.[5]

The division between law and mercy or equity is also upheld in readings that distinguish between the jurisdictions of the common law and the so-called equity courts. Most recently, David Bevington has argued that "Shakespeare invites special sympathy for a middle position in the legal tangle that afflicts the citizens of Vienna" which Bevington dubs "equity." Defining equity as "a body of legal opinion designed to enlarge, supplement, or override narrow and rigid systems of law," he mistakenly claims that this was historically "embodied in the Elizabethan and Jacobean courts of Chancery *as opposed to the common-law courts*" (emphasis mine).[6] The Chancery, in fact, did not deal with the criminal and practical governing questions that are the focus of *Measure for Measure*; instead, its jurisdiction pertained chiefly to property and uses.[7] More importantly, as Lorna Hutson has made clear, common law judges negotiated between the letter of the law and the spirit through the sixteenth-century principle of statute interpretation that equitably equated the original lawmaker's intentions with the common good.[8] Whatever the relationship between the common law and equity courts at any given moment, the common law judges understood that their work had an ethical foundation and function that was related to, but not identical with, the letter of the law.

These two critical traditions maintain a categorical or jurisdictional difference between the Duke and his deputies by upholding a division between law and equity/mercy that was more functional in ideology than practice. My intention, instead, is to compare the magistrates in Shakespeare's play by analyzing their respective relationships to the operational ethics of punitive and preventive justice. When it comes to marrying formal law with social needs and values, I argue that the Duke's superiority is a function of degree, not kind; it is a function of his reformed or exercised judgment rather than sovereignty. My interest is not equity per se, but the legal labour and thought on behalf of the social and Christian order that is rendered invisible in most readings because the historical and legal categories that I privilege have failed to enter the critical discourse. As N. W. Bawcutt writes, critics "are tempted . . . to see [the play] as . . . an intellectual treatise in dramatic form."[9] The result is a prevalent belief that, in Huston Diehl's words, "Shakespeare seems far less interested in details of the English legal system . . . than in exploring the relation between law, broadly defined, and the problem of knowing and judging."[10] On the contrary, the problems of knowing and judging spring directly from, and are addressed by, the "details of the English legal system." I start from the premise that Shakespeare's relationship to ideas was not that of a treatise-writer but a theater-writer, meaning that his ideas had to be worked out in an embodied way; that this was no less true of the law; and that, in the theater and in the law, strategies of resolution and irresolution were both deployed for ends that included but exceeded the perspective and interests of individual characters or subjects. If not precisely realistic, the play is nonetheless mimetic of the law's historical complexion.

Barnardine and the Life of the Law

[James Hind] was convicted of Man-slaughter, and . . . yet was allowed his Clergy, but when he came to his Booke he could not read . . . so he was condemned, and sentence passed on him to dye; But the next morning . . . my Lord, he was pleased to pardon him for that time, and that offence, so left him a Prisoner in Reading Goale upon the account of high Treason against the State, where he yet remains; but it is not probable that for any thing he hath yet done, he will by an untimely death be brought to his End.[11]

Barnardine would never have been put to death. Historically, that is, a figure like Barnardine, the perpetually drunk and hilariously uncooperative prisoner convicted of murder in Shakespeare's *Measure for Measure*, would not have been executed in early modern England, for several reasons. As Cynthia Herrup explains, "Although most tried crimes were felonies and most indictments for felony resulted in capital convictions, relatively few convicts were condemned to die and even fewer were actually executed."[12] The available statistics suggest that 10 percent of those convicted of capital offenses found their way to the gallows.[13] Despite the letter of the law, there was a major gulf between a conviction and the fate of a convict. This was mostly an uncontroversial state of affairs; it was the largely positive outcome (i.e. fewer people died) of the traditional organization of local justice through which the nature of an offense was weighed against social realities and moral and social values (what legal path would best promote Christian principles and the community). In early modern England, like today, not every murderer was thought to deserve death. Beyond questions of guilt, the community that engaged in the stages of the criminal law process, from investigation to conviction, determined whether a lawbreaker was a "criminal" or "simply [an] errant [Christian brother]." Criminals were "recognized . . . by their fondness for crimes of profit, their calculated approach to illegal activity and their lack of remorse once they were taken into custody."[14] Herrup's study of Sussex legal records reveals that "[n]o category of offences invariably brought execution or leniency; mitigation varied with the nature and circumstances of specific crimes."[15] Despite a criminal code in which many offenses were assigned the same harsh punishment, traditions of "alternatives to formal prosecution" and for "the avoidance and mitigation of punishment" lent "a graded character" and flexibility to the law in practice.[16] Instead of the formally graded system of punishments that exists today, early modern English criminal law possessed an informally graded collection of mitigations that was activated at the judge's and the community's discretion.

The distinction between "criminal" or "errant [Christian brother]" seems to be asserted by Shakespeare's Provost, when he compares his two prisoners, Claudio the fornicator and Barnardine the murderer, who are scheduled to be executed on the same day: "Th'one [Claudio] has my pity, not a jot the other, / Being a murderer, though he were my brother."[17] The Provost's lines form a private response to the death sentences, issued by the deputy Angelo, that collapse the moral distinction between the two convicts. According to Richard Strier, the similar treatment of each prisoner is a sign of dysfunction: "If the legal system [of Vienna] were working at all . . . it would differentiate clearly between the legal situations of Claudio and Barnardine."[18] Yet the actual early modern legal system did function without extensive formal differentiation among the punishments for crimes. Strier misidentifies an administrative problem as a systemic one. If the legal system of Vienna is not working, it is not because of the statutory equation of each prisoner, but because of the judges. The offenses of fornication and murder are repeatedly contrasted in the play to highlight the need for proportionality in punishment, but that criticism is lodged at Angelo's judgment, not at the so-called fornication law nor at the legal system; no one but Pompey the bawd comes close to proposing that the actual law be altered.[19] The Provost does "differentiate clearly between the legal situations of Claudio and Barnardine," and, importantly, that differentiation did not, in legal practice, have to implicate a binary punitive logic of life and death. Having no pity for Barnardine (not feeling sorry for him or his fate) is a far cry from wishing for his execution.

While murder in the abstract represents, in the play, a serious crime warranting serious attention, the introduction of the character Barnardine upsets any clear moral scheme that would send all murderers to the gallows. Greenblatt asserts that "no one is concerned about shortening by a few hours the wretched Barnardine's wretched life,"[20] but clearly Shakespeare was determined to save him for at least another two hours, presumably because the playwright felt that the theater audience would respond more favorably if he lived. The playwright saves his prisoner by doubling down on the plot device of the head-trick, through which a deceased pirate's head substitutes for Barnardine's, which was supposed to substitute for Claudio's. Barnardine's life is thereby saved at the cost of making him entirely superfluous to the main plot; he is thus also saved from the cutting-room floor.

Nor is the murderer's execution simply delayed: the Duke pardons him in the final scene. We need to take seriously Shakespeare's preservation of this superfluous character as a form of social tolerance, a social verdict that underwrites the Duke's pardon. While the Duke, like Prospero, has frequently been likened to a playwright, orchestrating human action and outcomes onstage, here it is possible to reverse the direction of the comparison: the playwright is magisterial in his efforts to save Barnardine.

If Barnardine does not elicit our pity, he certainly generates a sense of forbearance. His comebacks transform the disguised Duke's and officers' commands into rhetorical appeals and are exactly calculated to elicit cheers from an early modern audience. "I swear I will not die today for any man's persuasion" (4.3.53), he declares, before marching or stumbling back to his cell. Drunk and stubborn, Barnardine nevertheless does not show signs of being a confirmed murderer in the way that Mistress Overdone is a confirmed bawd ("Double and treble admonition, and still forfeit in the same kind" [3.1.427–8]). Conal Condren, Stephen Greenblatt, and Andrew Majeske claim that the text presents Barnardine as an "unrepentant murderer," but that is not what we are told or shown.[21] The Provost reports that the prisoner has finally, after nine years, been convicted of murder; his crime is "Most manifest, and not denied by himself" (4.2.133), that is, Barnardine now simply admits to it. A lack of repentance, moreover, is an entirely inadequate concept to cover Barnardine's condition of extreme apathy toward both life and death after nine years in prison: "A man that apprehends death no more dreadfully but as a drunken sleep; careless, reckless, and fearless of what's past, present, or to come; insensible of mortality, and desperately mortal" (4.2.136–9). We know, too, that his case remained open for nine years because "His friends still wrought reprieves for him" (4.2.129). This detail is typically interpreted as more evidence of the legal system's corruption and malfunction. But such "friends" were an essential part of early modern criminal process, through whom the issue of the accused's character was raised. It was a far worse sign at law to be friendless. There is no indication that Barnardine's crime is part of a pattern of violence or that he is driven to crime for profit. He is designedly not the early modern felon *par excellence* who excited enough social and judicial disgust to bring on the death sentence.

Critics have found the Duke's pardons in the final scene repellent to the principle of justice because, like Angelo's death sentences, they seem to collapse the distinctions among offenders. "For Barnardine to be forgiven along with Claudio ... seems an abuse of justice on the part of the lenient Duke," concludes Richard Ide.[22] Every pardon, however, comes with a condition that addresses the malefactor's offense and circumstances. Barnardine is delivered into the hands of a spiritual community. The prisoner's fate speaks directly to the personal reform that he requires.[23] In crafting such an end for this character, Shakespeare seems to have been inspired on some level by the expression "benefit of clergy." Dating back to the twelfth century, "benefit of clergy" referred to the privilege through which "an accused person who could prove himself a clerk in orders would be handed over to the ecclesiastical authorities to be dealt with according to Canon law." The benefit of having your case removed from the temporal courts was that the Church courts did not have the power to execute. By the end of the fifteenth century, the privilege became "a regular means of escape from the mandatory death penalty" that was open to any man who could prove clergy through the test of literacy. Because a particular passage from the fifty-first Psalm was routinely used (the so-called "neck verse"), the unlettered who had memorized the text could also slip by.[24] The "most common mitigation of capital punishment in early modern England," benefit of clergy was thus a legal fiction that entailed a tolerated form of religious impersonation, a faint echo of the literal and figurative religious impersonations that course throughout *Measure for Measure*.[25] Barnardine is saved from the death penalty and removed from the temporal court system to a religious community to receive the benefit of a spiritual education at their hands, a conclusion far superior to prison, execution, or simply setting him free.[26] Most importantly, the prisoner's end shifts the focus from the question of his punishment to the question of his character and soul.

The question of Barnardine's character is deliberately left hanging in a way that gives structure but not determination to the future. His criminality is transformed into a potential rather than a certainty; it is forward- rather than backward-looking; not a matter of the past fact of his illegal action, but of whether or not he goes on to establish a pattern of anti-social behavior. The new future is liberating but also a test. We are invited to recall the opening Act, in which the Duke explains to Friar Thomas that Angelo's governance will test the magistrate's virtue. The play's resolution introduces a new beginning for Barnardine that is necessarily left unresolved. The convict is partially shielded from the temptations of "too much liberty" (1.2.114) by the addition of a preventive measure, the effectiveness of which is also to be determined. The friars offer an environment more conducive to personal reform than either Vienna or the prison. We know little about Barnardine except his crime and that he is "A Bohemian born, but here nursed up and bred, one that is a prisoner nine years old" (4.2.130–1). The signification of "here" pivots between Vienna (in contrast to Bohemia) and prison (where he is "nine years old"). Unlike fornication, which is tied to fallen human nature throughout the play, Shakespeare links the murderer's setting or circumstances to his degeneracy, implicating both the city and the legal system in Barnardine's spiritual decay. He has effectively already served a nine-year prison sentence for his crime (another good reason not to execute him), which has proven to be more than enough time to warp his personality. His state of perpetual drunkenness, somewhere between waking and sleeping, is emblematic not merely of a degenerate individual, but of the liminal, almost purgatorial, world of the prison, in which, in early modern England, prisoners were typically awaiting trial, awaiting sentencing, awaiting punishment, suspended between life and death, rather than serving sentences in our modern sense. The Duke's pardon replaces the negative indeterminacy of prison time with a future inscribed with the potential for reform.

By deferring the question of Barnardine's character and his criminality, the Duke decides not to punish irrevocably, at least not yet. Strier argues that a basic thrust of the play concerns the "fundamental [question] of whether judgment – in the sense of assigning punishment for offenses against the law – is in itself a desirable thing. If the answer to this question is negative, then it is hard to see how there can be a legal system."[27] The answer to that question, I argue, is provided by the legal culture in which the play was written: punishment and the question of punishment are best circumnavigated, if at all possible. While the law may have a monopoly on punitive justice, the instrument of the law should not be mistaken for its end, especially in the early modern period when the law's social function was so much more diffuse. Punishment was the last resort in a system devoted to conflict resolution and the restoration of social order. Most of the time (then and today, in fact) the pragmatic response to punishment and to ethical perplexities in the law was to avoid them, to work around them, rather than bring conflicts to a head and risk decrees and innovations that could threaten both subjects and the system. Hard cases, it has been said for centuries, make bad law. The Duke's treatment of Barnardine, its complexities and legal cultural resonances, illustrates that, between execution and pardon, there were a range of punishments and mitigation tactics that were more or less effectively administered depending on the quality of the engagement and judgment of magistrates and the local community. Far from representing a disappointing return to the lax state of the law at the opening of the play, the Duke's improvised resolution re-imagines and enormously expands the potential content of the life of the Viennese law.[28] To put this another way, the Duke replaces the punitive justice that he lauds in the opening Act with a much more labor-intensive preventive justice by the final scene. He thereby re-opens the future not only for those he pardons, but for the city as a whole.

As the example of the Duke suggests, preventive justice relies heavily on the individual judge's discretion. The avoidance of punishment and legal-ethical questions taxes and tests the judgment of the magistrate in a much more imaginative way than applying the strict letter of the law. Preventive justice was nevertheless the prerogative not of a sovereign power but of the Justices of the Peace who were commissioned to "keep the peace" throughout the kingdom. The next section historicizes the Justice's preventive role and reasoning in greater detail. Against this picture of the law in practice, Angelo's inadequacies as a magistrate come into sharp focus.

Preventive Justice and the JPs of Vienna

In the cases of the two convicts of *Measure for Measure*, Shakespeare is careful to present us with the two basic forms of legal issue: Barnardine's case raises a question of fact (was a crime committed and by whom), and Claudio's case raises a question of law (he admits to the act with which he is charged but challenges its definition as a crime). Yet we never see these issues come to trial onstage; we are never left in any suspense about the facts, a verdict, or sentencing.[29] For most of the play, instead, Shakespeare forces us to evaluate the quality of legal administration and judgment in Vienna on other grounds. The dramaturgical choice to marginalize trials reproduces the historical organization of legal labor that can be tracked in manuals for Justices of the Peace (JPs). Printed numerous times in the later sixteenth and seventeenth centuries, William Lambarde's *Eirenarcha: or Of The Office of the Iustices of Peace* provided an account of the structure of local governance that was likely known to a great number of literate men in the period, most of whom were expected to play some kind of role within the legal system.[30] Lambarde's text reflects the bifurcation of the JP's duties into policing and judicial functions. Book One, devoted to the history of JPs and their jurisdiction out of session, is slightly longer than Book Two, which is devoted to the work of JPs in their courts, the Quarter Sessions, which convened for a few days four times a year. To the early modern mentality, the work out of session – involving year-round surveillance, administration, and investigation – took practical and ethical priority over trials and punishment. Lambarde writes that "our law is no lesse carefull this waye to conserue the Peace, both by staying them that doe any waye aduenture towardes the breache thereof, and by punishing them that doe actuallye enter into the very violation of the same."[31] In *The Covntrey Ivstice, Conteyning the practise of the Ivstices of the Peace out of their Sessions*, Michael Dalton puts even more pressure on the role of prevention:

> The conseruation of this Peace (and therein the care of the Iustice of Peace) consisteth in three things, *viz.*
>
> 1 In preuenting the breach of the Peace (wisely foreseeing and repressing the beginnings thereof) by taking suertie for the keeping of it, or for the good behauiour of the offendors, as the case shall require.
>
> 2 In pacifying such as are in breaking of the peace . . .
>
> 3 In punishing (according to Law) such as haue broken the Peace.
>
> But of the three, the first, the preuenting Iustice, is most worthy to be commended to the care of the Iustices of Peace.[32]

The dual yet unequal focus of the criminal law on prevention and punishment is institutionalized in even more adamant terms by William Blackstone in the eighteenth century, who contends that "preventive justice is, upon every principle of reason, of humanity, and of sound policy, preferable in all respects to punishing justice." Concern for prevention, moreover, distinguished the English legal system itself: "it is an honour, and almost a singular one, of our English laws."[33]

Despite its centrality to governance across periods, preventive measures have only recently begun to be gathered and examined collectively within legal studies. Carol S. Steiker reported in 1997 that

> courts and commentators have had much less to say about the . . . topic of the limits of the state not as punisher (and thus necessarily as investigator and adjudicator of criminal acts) but rather as preventer of crime and disorder generally. Indeed, courts and commentators have not yet even recognized this topic as a distinct phenomenon either doctrinally or conceptually.[34]

This lacuna in scholarship is all the more troubling in the post 9/11 world in which preventive security measures are putting increasing pressure on the definitions of our most basic political concepts. In their major 2014 study, Andrew Ashworth and Lucia Zedner write,

> The place of preventive endeavour among the very foundations of state authority is one of the key questions of contemporary political theory. It is also central to contemporary legal theory, in that we cannot properly understand what obligations citizens owe to each other and to the state until we establish what the role of the state itself entails.[35]

Part of Ashworth and Zedner's argument, however, is that the contemporary perception of "a shift of emphasis [in policy] from punishment to prevention" in the wake of 9/11 is mistaken. As evidence of prevention's historical importance, they cite the English statute of 1361 that established the Justice of the Peace's "power to bind a person over to keep the peace."[36]

Binding over entailed, as Lambarde writes, "An acknowledging of a bond to the Prince, taken by a competent Iudge of Recorde, for the keeping of the Peace."[37] Steve Hindle unpacks the process at greater length:

> Binding over refer[ed] to a magistrate's power to bind an individual in a fixed sum, or recognizance, and for a fixed period, to keep the peace and/or to be of good behaviour irrespective of conviction for a criminal offence. If the person bound over was subsequently found to have breached the peace and/or failed to be of good behaviour during that period, he or she was liable to have the recognizance "estreated" or forfeited to the crown.

A broad range of socially unacceptable behaviors beyond strictly criminal activities could result in warrants to keep the peace or for good behavior ("good abearing" in Lambarde), so that this "almost infinitely adaptable apparatus of containment" "operated as an early modern 'sus law' [i.e. a 'stop and search' law] with all the discretion and flexibility that implies." Binding over helped a community establish who was a lawbreaker and who was a criminal. Hindle concludes that "[t]he practice has underpinned the structures of authority in English society for almost ten centuries."[38]

While preventive justice played an essential role in law and governance at the local level in early modern England, its extent and effectiveness were entirely dependent on the personal initiative and discretion of the JP. The dangers of the discretionary power wielded by independently directed justices must be weighed against the pitfalls of the alternative. The average subject preferred the JP's preventive interventions to a formal trial: "To the actual or potential victim of crime, swearing the peace offered protection without the trouble and charge of indictment for assault or civil litigation."[39] There were and are many drawbacks to both criminal and civil trials. They not only put complainants or plaintiffs and defendants (their bodies, souls, property, finances, and time) at risk, but they also always test the law's coercive force and coherence.[40] Thanks in no small part to the literary tradition, as well as the nature of historical legal records, however, we understand the trial as the epitome of the Anglo-American legal system at work. In fact, whether in sixteenth-century England or twenty-first-century America, trials function more like the visible tip of an iceberg: most of the law happens elsewhere. In early modern England, both civil cases and "many criminal cases were settled out of court."[41] Even when a trial was begun, an issue did not have to end in a decision.[42] The formal apparatus of law seems to have been engaged frequently "in the hopes of bringing on a properly regulated mediation."[43] Far from exemplifying justice at work, then, a trial and a final decree can be characterized as the failure of every other method and stage of conflict prevention and resolution. This reorientation toward trials explains an apparent peculiarity of the trial that concludes *Measure for Measure*. The Duke has surreptitiously prevented Angelo from committing sexual assault and homicide – no crime has taken place – so that conviction and punishment must never have been his intention in staging a trial in the first place. Instead, the trial is used as a forum for the public exposure of Angelo's character, for socio-political shaming and regulation.

If trials have dominated the cultural imagination of legal practice, trial judges have come to exemplify legal judgment. Ronald Dworkin is responsible for this figure's most famous contemporary description as "an imaginary judge of superhuman intellectual power and patience" named Hercules.[44] That "superhuman intellectual power and patience" that seems to set the judge apart and to legitimize his or her authority, however, is measured in trial by the extent of the judge's self-abnegation, by his or her adoption and expression of externally imposed rules for professional deliberation and conduct. Paul Kahn explains that "the subject who perceives and articulates law – paradigmatically the judge . . . must be a person without a unique subjectivity, if the rule of law is to appear different from the rule of men."[45] In the early modern period, similar results were achieved through the concept and discourse of "artificial reason," through which judges arrived at the professional tradition of interpreting and applying the law. Judicial deliberation and decisions were legitimized not as the letter of the law, but as giving voice to the common law tradition; thus, these figures were dubbed the "oracles of the law."[46] The potential contribution of the judge's personal discretion was further minimized in trial, in England, by the way that multiple judgments were consulted across the bench (judges rarely sat alone in most courts) and through the grand and petty juries that made non-professionals responsible for presentment, evidential reasoning, and conviction.[47]

The impersonal justice represented by trials and trial judges is in stark contrast with the pragmatic, makeshift reasoning required of local magistrates out of court, when they resorted to their own discretion and knowledge of local affairs. "As local gentlemen, justices were natural arbitrators in the community," writes Herrup. They "examined, admonished, bonded, and committed people who seemed to threaten the local peace. They tried to settle disagreements without resort to litigation or indictment."[48] These functions, Dalton explains, were "done by them out of their Sessions, and sometimes priuately, and peraduenture vpon the sudden, without the aduice or association of any other."[49] "[A]ny one Iustice of the Peace," writes Lambarde, "is sufficiently armed with auctoritie (out of the Sessions) to preuent the breache of the Peace." So, he reasons, "ought hee both to employ his witte, and to vse his auctoritie, to preuente the Breache of the same."[50] In an office of divergent and sometimes even conflicting responsibilities, the JP needed above all the qualities of prudence and responsiveness to provide justice that was at once highly personal and impartial. The expansive early modern understanding of magistracy that I have depicted here is pointedly introduced in the opening of Shakespeare's comedy.

Instead of initiating a "consistent critique of absolutism," I argue that the opening scene of *Measure for Measure* evokes the ethos of local justice and governance by characterizing Escalus and Angelo as JPs.[51] The two deputies of Vienna conform to specific types of Justices who were organized through the commission of the peace. The commission listed the highest ranked JPs first in the catalogue of country gentlemen that it named to office. Certain JPs were then also chosen for the "quorum." As Lambarde explains, "These of the *Quorum*, were . . . chosen, specially for their learning in the lawes of the Realme."[52] Two potentially competing forms of authority, socio-political status and professional expertise, needed to be nego-tiated when JPs worked together, as they were frequently required to do. In *Measure for Measure*, the Duke's first speeches pointedly establish Escalus as the more learned and experienced magistrate, while Angelo is given a higher rank. The Duke commends Escalus's knowledge in his opening lines:

> The nature of our people,
> Our city's institutions, and the terms
> For common justice, you're as pregnant in
> As art and practice hath enriched any
> That we remember. (1.1.10–14)

Escalus is widely understood as a foil for Angelo's strict enforcement of the law. He is either the voice of equitable moderation or of the broken system's leniency.[53] Instead, I'd like to suggest that Escalus's arguments and actions are motivated from within his experience and sense of duty as an officer, from inside the operational and pre-ventive ethics of legal administration. It is the deputy distinguished for his learning and experience who advocates for consideration of Claudio's circumstances. He represents a tradition of legal practice that had more ethical and professional weight than the letter of the law. When asked how he thinks Angelo will fare in the Duke's place, Escalus's decorous response exclusively references social rank rather than governing ability: "If any in Vienna be of worth / To undergo such ample grace and honour, / It is Lord Angelo" (1.1.23–5). The office of JP was actively sought in the period by local elites more interested in the social status that the position conferred or con-firmed than in undertaking its responsibilities. If we miss the hints in the opening scene, Angelo's rejection of the suddenly dowerless Marianna places him in the ranks of the socially ambitious gentry. He is not the first aspirational Puritan to be publicly exposed in a Shakespearean comedy. Through the differences between these two deputies, Shakespeare's efficient dramaturgy manages to represent the personnel breadth of a commission of the peace with the small-est number of actors possible.

The Duke's commission imposes on the inexperienced and proud Angelo a form of rule that embraces the law's most extreme puni-tive measure as a form of prevention. He puts the deputy in charge of imposing a forgotten law that punishes fornicators with death in the belief that this policy change will establish a powerful new deter-rence for a generally degenerate city.[54] Legal punishment was and still is defended as a deterrent, and therefore as a part of preventive justice. As Blackstone writes, "all punishments inflicted by temporal laws conduce to one and the same end, of preventing future crimes, whether that be effected by amendment, disability, or example."[55] Angelo's main defense of capital punishment – the ultimate disabling measure – is its exemplary value for the individual and the community.[56] The deputy justifies Claudio's death sentence as a way of preventing the offender himself from inevitably perpetrating future offenses. So thoroughly exemplary or representative is the individual incident that every man who breaks the law is a criminal who requires execution: "[I] do him right that, answering one foul wrong, / Lives not to act another" (2.2.104–5). Angelo invests exemplarity not with the rhetorical power of persuasion, and not even with the positive law's power of coercion, but with logical necessity. The projection of this hypothetical future of criminality, however, contrasts too sharply with the other version of Claudio's future offered at the beginning and confirmed at the end of the play: it is most likely that he and Juliet will get married, obtain the withheld dowry, and live happily ever after per romantic comedy convention. Both probability and literary genre push back against Angelo's narrow assessment of Claudio's character which derives from a deductive process that never considers the offender's manifest character. As an instrument of prevention, execution is justified by a deterministic interpretation of human behavior and nature. It attributes to offenders a specific future that warrants a radical intervention in their present lives. Angelo's punitive-preventive justice thus contrasts structurally with the Duke's clandestine measures that preserve human life by maintaining and instrumentalizing the uncertainty of the future.

Claudio's execution is also supposed to provide another form of preventive exemplarity through which the law and the community intersect. According to the deputy, this lawful death will establish a new pattern of behavior for other would-be criminals: "future evils . . . Are now to have no successive degrees" (2.2.96–8). This was the Duke's original intention in resuscitating the fornication law. Instead of deterring fornication, however, Claudio's case – his crime and his fate – becomes or represents the norm. At the prison, for example, Pompey delivers a soliloquy that catalogues the numerous clients of Mistress Overdone who are now locked up thanks to the new policy (4.3.1–17). They have obviously paid no attention to Claudio's case and sentence that were publicized at Angelo's special command (we first see the offender as he is being marched around the city by the Provost [1.2.105–8]). Shakespeare's Vienna looks well on its way to confirming Pompey's prophecy: "If you head and hang all that offend that way but for ten year together, you'll be glad to give out a commission for more heads" (2.1.217–19). Execution proves an ineffective deterrent when basic human nature is at stake. This point was powerfully made nearly a century earlier in Thomas More's *Utopia*. Raphael Hythloday expresses outrage over the immorality and irrationality of the English law that classifies theft as a felony punishable by death when thieves are forced to steal for sustenance as a result of socio-economic forces.[57] While human nature is not effectively regulated through legal punishment, magistrates nevertheless had an obligation to find or shape extra-legal solutions to disorders that upset the common peace, as the principles and history of preventive justice make clear. Angelo's understanding of the law and magistracy, however, is far too limited for him to perceive the extent of his duty to the community.

By collapsing preventive justice into the punitive realm so entirely and irrevocably through capital punishment, Angelo limits the magistrate's function to the mere oversight of trials and to sentencing by the letter. "It is the law," he tells Isabella, "not I, condemn your brother" (2.2.81). He presents himself as bound to his office, as much a prisoner to the law as Claudio: "Look what I will not, that I cannot do" (2.2.53). The magistrate's character, therefore, even if it is criminal, has no bearing on the application of the law: "What knows the laws / That thieves do pass on thieves?" (2.1.22–3). Through this absolute division between office and officer, the law's impartiality is guaranteed, and the judge himself is subject to the same judgment: "When I that censure him do so offend, / Let mine own judgement pattern out my death, / And nothing come in partial" (2.1.29–31). The deputy's ethic of impartiality seems like a legal necessity or at least logical in light of his own subsequent actions. The single character in the play who actually conforms to Angelo's model of criminal nature is Angelo himself. But his fate equally demonstrates that even the letter of the law is subject to the judge's desires. Having, he believes, coerced Isabella into sex in exchange for Claudio's pardon, Angelo decides to go ahead with the death sentence to prevent the brother's future revenge on behalf of his sister's violated honor. Impartial legal execution morphs into homicide, and "One foul wrong" leads logically and quickly into another, greater offense. The sentence that had seemed to Angelo to be impervious to judicial interference is corrupted.

An entirely impersonal administration of the law that would guarantee an impartial justice is impossible. The modern Anglo-American legal system attempts to compensate for this by populating legal offices with strangers. In the case of a local magistrate in early modern England, however, ignorance of the community and individual litigants or defendants did not signify judicial impartiality so much as negligence. Justices, if they were doing their jobs, spent most of their time out of court deliberating the best strategies for enacting social policies and preventing the kind of conduct and situations that would lead to trial. The threat of undue, self-interested, or profit-driven magisterial interference in local affairs was socially tolerable, moreover, in comparison with an impartial practice of judgment that would have led so easily to executions. In the play, Angelo is saved from a life of crime by the Duke's preventive maneuvering, which, to use Blackstone's term, disables Angelo from carrying out his illicit designs. Long before any question of a merciful pardon arises, Angelo's "act [does] not o'ertake his bad intent" (5.1.453) because of the Duke's ingenuity, his wit and resourcefulness joined with a willingness to investigate. If Angelo and the Duke begin the play on the same page, their courses diverge quickly. The one embraces a punitive plotline; the other finds himself on a new and improvised preventive path that reforms his own approach to governance. It is through the pragmatic and shifting demands of preventive justice that the Duke is able to transition from a magistrate who "ever loved the life removed" (1.3.8) and "contended especially to know himself" (3.1.488–9) to one who, in Condren's words, "exemplifies the active life, busying himself about the city."[58] His reserved nature need not have changed, simply his orientation to his office. The Duke's actions in disguise take to a comical extreme the preventive energy, ethics, and logic of early modern law.

Shakespeare's representation of the life of the law, especially its mitigating improvisations, puts pressure on the categorical difference between life and stage comedy. The further away Vienna moves from the letter of the law, that is, the closer it gets to early modern English legal culture. The makeshift resolution that the Duke manages for his city has a powerful affinity with the legal value of social harmony, or "peace," that Dalton defines in his treatise for local magistrates:

> Peace in effect . . . is the amitie, confidence, and quiet that is betweene men; And he that breaketh this amitie or quiet, breaketh the Peace. Yet, Peace (in our Law) most commonly is taken for an abstinence from actuall and iniurious force, & offer of violence; and so is rather a restraining of hands, then an vniting of minds, And for the maintenance of this Peace chiefly, were the Iustices of Peace first made.[59]

Impressively realistic, this definition of peace concedes the improbability of actual changes of heart among bickering neighbors. It shapes standards for social maintenance based on mutual interest rather than the realization of abstract ideals or individual preferences. Such a peace, moreover, is the jurisdiction of magistrate and playwright alike. At the end of Shakespeare's comedy there is a uniting of hands in multiple marriages regardless of a "vniting of minds." As well as providing the conventional ending of a comedy, this is a legal resolution, an arbitrated or imposed resolution that prioritizes the common good and peace over individual desire.

Notes

1. Although the "living law" is a metaphor that has persisted for centuries, John C. Higgins prefers Raymond Williams' notion of the "lived hegemony" to describe the "set of practical and discursive negotiations of political authority" that occurred in the name of "justice, mercy, and equity." John C. Higgins, "Justice, Mercy, and Dialectical Genres in *Measure for Measure* and *Promos and Cassandra*," *English Literary Renaissance* 42 (1992): 273, 293.

2. Surveillance is certainly a part of preventive justice and *Measure for Measure*, but it has been treated nearly exclusively from a late twentieth-century perspective. See especially the now classic study by Jonathan Dollimore, "Transgression and Surveillance in *Measure for Measure*," in *Political Shakespeare: New Essays in Cultural Materialism*, ed. Jonathan Dollimore and Alan Sinfield (Ithaca: Cornell University Press, 1985), 72–87.

3. The distinction between equity and mercy is, of course, important, but for the purposes of this point, it isn't. Both terms are presented in binary opposition to the law in a great deal of criticism on the play.

4. Political theology readings of early modern literature and especially Shakespeare have proliferated since the turn of the century. See especially Debora Kuller Shuger, *Political Theologies in Shakespeare's England: The Sacred and the State in Measure for Measure* (Basingstoke: Palgrave Macmillan, 2001); and Richard Wilson, "'As mice by lions': Political Theology and *Measure for Measure*," *Shakespeare* 11 (2015): 157–77.

5. Andrew Majeske, "Equity's Absence: The Extremity of Claudio's Prosecution and Barnardine's Pardon in Shakespeare's *Measure for Measure*," *Law and Literature* 21 (2009): 169.

6. David Bevington, "Equity in *Measure for Measure*," in *Shakespeare and The Law: A Conversation Among Disciplines and Professions*, ed.

Bradin Cormack, Martha C. Nussbaum, and Richard Strier (Chicago: University of Chicago Press, 2013), 164.

7. See J. H. Baker, "The Court of Chancery and Equity," in *An Intro-duction to English Legal History*, 4th ed. (Oxford: Oxford University Press, 2007), 97–116.

8. See Lorna Hutson, "Not the King's Two Bodies: Reading the 'Body Politic' in Shakespeare's *Henry IV, Parts 1 and 2*," in *Rhetoric and Law in Early Modern Europe*, ed. Victoria Kahn and Lorna Hutson (New Haven: Yale University Press, 2001), 166–98; and *The Invention of Suspicion: Law and Mimesis in Shakespeare and Renaissance Drama* (Oxford: Oxford University Press, 2012), 50–5. On equity and Shake-speare or *Measure for Measure*, see also Higgins, "Justice"; Majeske, "Equity's Absence"; Stacy Magedanz, "Public Justice and Private Mercy in *Measure for Measure*," *Studies in English Literature, 1500–1900* 44 (2004): 317–32; B. J. Sokol and Mary Sokol, "Shakespeare and the English Equity Jurisdiction: *The Merchant of Venice* and the Two Texts of *King Lear*," *The Review of English Studies* 50 (1999): 417–39; and Eric V. Spencer, "Scaling the Deputy: Equity and Mercy in *Measure for Measure*," *Philosophy and Literature* 36 (2012): 166–82. See also Mark Fortier, *The Culture of Equity in Early Modern England* (Alder-shot: Ashgate, 2005).

9. N. W. Bawcutt, introduction to *Measure for Measure* (Oxford: Oxford University Press, 1991), 42.

10. Huston Diehl, "'Infinite Space': Representation and Reformation," *Shakespeare Quarterly* 49 (1998): 403.

11. George Fidge, *VVit for mony being a full relation of the life, actions, merry conceits, and pretty pranks of Captain Iames Hind the famous robber both in England, Holland, and Ireland: With his new pro-gresse through Berkshire, Oxfordshire, and adjacent counties begun on Monday the first of March, 1651, with the judges of the assize for that circuit* (London, 1652), C8v.

12. Cynthia B. Herrup, "Law and Morality in Seventeenth-Century England," *Past and Present* 106 (1985): 102; and *The Common Peace: Participation and the Criminal Law in Seventeenth-Century England* (Cambridge: Cambridge University Press, 1989), 197. "Throughout the period," confirms J. A. Sharpe, "the criminal law was harsh, and becoming harsher; likewise, throughout the period its full harshness was being applied increasingly sparingly"; *Crime in Early Modern England*, 2nd ed. (London: Routledge, 2013), 99. Higgins, "Justice", recounts the statistics related to early modern executions as evidence of their cultural impact. While the early moderns certainly executed more people than we do today, executions nevertheless resulted from a small percentage of cases. Higgins and Peter Lake turn to murder pamphlets as evidence of the cultural intolerance for capital crimes, but this approach ignores the fact that the genre's material is *sensational* and that its zealous

moralism is calculated to rhetorically legitimize the printing and consumption of gruesome tales. See Peter Lake, "Ministers, Magistrates and the Production of 'Order' in *Measure for Measure*," *Shakespeare Survey* 54 (2006): 165–81.

13. J. S. Cockburn, *A History of English Assizes, 1558–1714* (Holmes Beach, FL: Wm. W. Gaunt & Sons, 1986), 131; Sharpe, *Crime in Early Modern England*, 97.

14. Herrup, "Law and Morality," 110, 113. On the problem of the definition of crime, see Sharpe, *Crime in Early Modern England*, 5–10. On "Calvin's premise that the law exists not to control the dangerous behavior of a few but to reveal everyone's imperfections," see Diehl, "Infinite Space," 406.

15. Herrup, "Law and Morality," 113.

16. Sharpe, *Crime in Early Modern England*, 63; Baker, "Court of Chancery," 512; Higgins, "Justice," 272.

17. William Shakespeare, *Measure for Measure*, in *The Norton Shakespeare*, 3rd ed., ed. Stephen Greenblatt et al. (New York: W. W. Norton, 2015), 4.2.55–6. References are to Act, scene, and line. All subsequent citations are to this edition. The Provost clearly means "brother" in the sense of the family relation, but the term has, as Herrup uses it, the further sense of Christian brotherhood, according to which standards, of course, Barnardine is the Provost's brother. On universal siblinghood and the play, see Marc Shell, *The End of Kinship*: Measure for Measure, *Incest, and the Ideal of Universal Siblinghood* (Stanford: Stanford University Press, 1988). On the connotations of "pity" in legal discourse, see Higgins, "Justice."

18. Richard Strier, "Shakespeare and Legal Systems: The Better the Worse (But Not Vice Versa)," in *Shakespeare and The Law: A Conversation Among Disciplines and Professions*, ed. Bradin Cormack, Martha C. Nussbaum, and Richard Strier (Chicago: University of Chicago Press, 2013), 189.

19. Shuger, *Political Theologies*, 9.

20. Stephen Greenblatt, *Shakespeare's Freedom* (Chicago: University of Chicago Press, 2009), 10.

21. Majeske, "Equity's Absence," 177; Greenblatt, *Shakespeare's Freedom*, 8–9; Conel Condren, "Unfolding 'the properties of government': The Case of *Measure for Measure* and the History of Political Thought," in *Shakespeare and Early Modern Political Thought*, ed. David Armitage, Conal Condren, and Andrew Fitzmaurice (Cambridge: Cambridge University Press, 2009), 169.

22. Richard Ide, "Shakespeare Revisionism: Homiletic Tragicomedy and the Ending of *Measure for Measure*," *Shakespeare Studies* 20 (1987): 119. The Duke's pardons are also naturally the focus of discussions on mercy and equity. Majeske, "Equity's Absence," argues that the Duke's pardons exceed justice by offering mercy, a religious principle that grants

forgiveness regardless of merit. Magedanz argues the reverse, making the case for the Duke's equity against mercy, and defining equity as "a reasoned quality that regards the totality of circumstances around an action in weighing judgment on that action" ("Public Justice," 327). She tracks the way the Duke's final judgments "ha[ve] some subtle interactions with the main characters' situations" (327).

23. Here, Shakespeare is again following a pragmatic and ethical legal tradition. Herrup reports that, "In many cases punishment as well as mitigation was geared specifically to both the crime and the defendant" ("Law and Morality," 121).

24. Baker, "Court of Chancery," 513–15.

25. Herrup, *The Common Peace*, 48–9.

26. Do the friars, like the Sisters of St. Clair, represent a "more strict restraint" (1.4.4) than the prison? A reader might also argue that the Duke facilitates Barnardine's removal from prison to a form of religious sanctuary, where, in practice since the middle ages "thieves and murderers could take refuge and thereby gain immunity even against the operation of criminal justice." In "private or special sanctuaries, usually in large monastic houses . . . criminals could take permanent refuge" (Baker, "Court of Chancery," 512–13). Several of the characters in Shakespeare's comedy evoke the practices most common for skirting capital punishment, in addition to Barnardine's benefit of clergy or sanctuary. Juliet's case recalls the "benefit of womb," through which women accused of felony could claim to be pregnant and receive a reprieve from execution at least until the child was born. A jury of matrons had to be called by Assize judges to investigate and prove the fact of pregnancy (Sharpe, *Crime in Early Modern England*, 97). Far from doubtful, and therefore unlike Doll Tearsheet's pillow pregnancy in *2 Henry IV*, Juliet's pregnancy is writ large enough to be a clear proof of the crime of fornication. Her stomach sends everyone to jail instead of saving them from it. Meanwhile, Lucio and his friends in 1.2 discuss soldiers, sailors, and pirates, recalling the practice of "pardon[ing] on condition that [the suspect or convict] entered military or naval service." Even Pompey's fate as a hangman's assistant recalls historical legal practice: "At York, and possibly other assize towns," Sharpe explains, "it was apparently customary in the mid seventeenth century to reprieve a convicted felon on condition that he acted as hangman" (*Crime in Early Modern England*, 97). The play is infused with clear and confused refractions of the culture of the criminal law of the time and especially of its forms of mitigation.

27. Strier, "Shakespeare and Legal Systems," 184.

28. Jennifer R. Rust argues, alternatively, that "Barnadine vividly demonstrates how the Duke simultaneously fails as both a pastoral and political governor." "'Of Government, the properties to unfold': Governmentalities in *Measure for Measure*," in *Rethinking the Secular*

in the Age of Shakespeare, ed. Katherine Steele Brokaw and Jay Zysk (forthcoming).

29. On the non- or misrepresentation of jury trials onstage in early modern drama, see Holger Syme, "(Mis)representing Justice on the Early Modern Stage," *Studies in Philology* 109 (2012): 63–85; and Derek Dunne, "Re-assessing Trial by Jury in Early Modern Law and Literature," *Literature Compass* (forthcoming).

30. Herrup points out that because of inflation over the course of the sixteenth century, the lower ranks of yeomen, as well as the gentry, would have met the income requirements for a range of offices (Herrup, *The Common Peace*, 205). On the participatory nature of early modern English law and its relation to the development of Renaissance drama, see Hutson, *The Invention of Suspicion*.

31. William Lambarde, *Eirenarcha; or, Of The Office of the Iustices of Peace, in two Bookes; Gathered 1579. and now reuised, and first published, in the 24 yeere of the peaceable raigne of our gratious Queene Elizabeth* (London, 1582), 133. The two-book structure that I emphasize here is not retained in all of the editions of this text from the sixteenth to the seventeenth century.

32. Michael Dalton, *The Covntrey Ivstice, Conteyning the practise of the Ivstices of the Peace out of their Sessions* (London, 1618), 7.

33. William Blackstone, *Commentaries on The Laws of England in Four Books*, notes by Edward Christian (Portland: Thomas B. Wait, & Co., 1807), 251.

34. Carol S. Steiker, "Supreme Court Review, Foreword: The Limits of the Preventive State," *The Journal of Criminal Law & Criminology* 88 (1997–98): 774. Some work has been done on the concept and history of "criminal equity." See Fortier, *Culture of Equity*, 81–3.

35. Andrew Ashworth and Lucia Zedner, *Preventive Justice* (Oxford: Oxford University Press, 2014), 9–10.

36. Ibid., 27, 4.

37. Lambarde, *Eirenarcha*, 83.

38. Steve Hindle, *The State and Social Change in Early Modern England, 1550–1640* (Basingstoke: Palgrave Macmillan, 2000), 114, 101, 97.

39. Ibid., 101. See also Sharpe, *Crime in Early Modern England*, 64.

40. On the disincentives to prosecution, see Sharpe, *Crime in Early Modern England*, 64; and Hindle, *State and Social Change*, 95.

41. Sharpe, *Crime in Early Modern England*, 65.

42. Tim Stretton, *Women Waging Law in Elizabethan England* (Cambridge: Cambridge University Press, 1998), 82.

43. Sharpe, *Crime in Early Modern England*, 65. John Manningham, a barrister of the Middle Temple, noted in his diary from 1602 that "Two poore men being at a very doubtfull demurrer in the Kings benche, the Justices moved that they would referr the matter to some indifferent men that might determine soe chargeable and difficult a controversy."

Diary of John Manningham, of the Middle Temple, and of Bradbourne, Kent, Barrister-at-Law, 1602–1603, ed. John Bruce (New York: AMS Press, 1868), 129.

44. Ronald Dworkin, *Law's Empire* (Cambridge, MA: Belknap Press of Harvard University Press, 1986), 239.
45. Paul W. Kahn, *The Cultural Study of Law: Reconstructing Legal Scholarship* (Chicago: University of Chicago Press, 2000), 77.
46. See Virginia Lee Strain, "*The Winter's Tale* and the Oracle of the Law," *English Literary History* 78 (2011): 557–84.
47. See John H. Langbein, "Bifurcation and the Bench: The Influence of the Jury on English Conceptions of the Judiciary," in *Judges and Judging in the History of the Common Law and Civil Law: From Antiquity to Modern Times*, ed. Paul Brand and Joshua Getzler (Cambridge: Cambridge University Press, 2012), 67–82. For an expanded account of the representation, in legal writing and revenge drama, of the role of impartiality in trial judges, see Derek Dunne, "'Partialitie in a Iudge, is a Turpitude': Partial Judges and Judicious Revengers in Early Modern English Drama," in *The Emergence of Impartiality*, ed. Kathryn Murphy and Anita Traninger (Boston: Brill, 2014), 171–88.
48. Herrup, *The Common Peace*, 54.
49. Dalton, "Epistle" to James Lee and Thomas Spencer.
50. Lambarde, *Eirenarcha*, 82, 86.
51. Jean Howard, "*Measure for Measure* and the Restraints of Convention," *Essays in Literature* 10 (1983): 156.
52. Lambarde, *Eirenarcha*, 55–6.
53. Escalus's greatest defender is perhaps Bevington. Strier registers skepticism about the magistrate's role as a model of judgment, primarily because he "turns out to be a rather minor character" (Strier, "Shakespeare and Legal Systems," 184). But Escalus's counterpart in George Whetstone's *Promos and Cassandra*, Ulrico, stands out as the single uncorrupt magistrate in the play even though his part is equally small. Escalus's value is confirmed in the fact that he, the Provost, and Isabella are promised promotions or rewards by the Duke in the final scene.
54. On the historical problem of such forgotten laws that appear repeatedly in early modern literature, see Virginia Lee Strain, "The Ensnared Subject and the General Pardon Statute in Late Elizabethan Literature," in *Taking Exception to the Law: Materializing Injustice in Early Modern England*, ed. Donald Beecher et al. (Toronto: University of Toronto Press, 2015), 100–19.
55. Blackstone, *Commentaries*, 251–2. For a discussion of Blackstone's contribution to the principles of preventive justice, see Markus D. Dubber, "Preventive Justice: The Quest for Principle," in *Prevention and the Limits of the Criminal Law*, ed. Andrew Ashworth, Lucia Zedner, and Patrick Tomlin (Oxford: Oxford University Press, 2013), 47–68.

56. Special issues on exemplarity in the *Journal of the History of Ideas* 59 (1998) and *Law & Literature* 25 (2013) were especially helpful in thinking through this quite compact treatment of Angelo's argumentation.
57. Sir Thomas More, *Utopia*, revised edition, ed. George M. Logan and Robert M. Adams (Cambridge: Cambridge University Press, 2002), 15–16.
58. Condren, "Unfolding 'the properties of government'," 173.
59. Dalton, *The Covntrey Ivstice*, 6.

Chapter 2

Believing in Ghosts, in Part:
Judgment and Indecision in *Hamlet*
Vivasvan Soni

Within the contemporary humanities, and particularly in the many varieties of critical theory that have dominated its interpretive lexicon for some years now, the "critique of subjectivity" has acquired the status of *doxa*.[1] There are many reasons for this critique, whether it be the putative indemonstrability of consciousness;[2] the promethean overvaluation of the subject's capacities for agency; the converse fear of solipsism and impotence; the anthropocentrism thought to be implicit in the category of subjectivity; the suspicion of a liberal conception of autonomy that supposedly severs the subject from its social world;[3] the assumption that consciousness is a mere epiphenomenon structured or even conditioned by material forces such as desire, affect, the body, history or the economy; the refusal of transcendence; and the denial of freedom. The list could no doubt be extended indefinitely. I am not suggesting that we jettison this critique entirely, nor do I mean to impugn all of the reasons behind it. Each one will need to be re-examined carefully, a task that cannot be undertaken here. But when the critique takes radical form, as it so often does, striving to eliminate from analysis any element of subjectivity or interiority, then we risk losing or rendering unintelligible some of the most basic concepts that make sense of the human and moral world, chief among them concepts such as agency, responsibility, and judgment.[4] In particular, there can be no account of judgment that does not make reference both to subjectivity and to the milieu of *ideality* in which it operates.

If the category of subjectivity has come to seem so troubling, and Hamlet has at least since the late eighteenth century become one of the emblematic figures for subjectivity and interiority,[5] it should not surprise us that critics such as Walter Benjamin and Margreta de Grazia have sought to rescue the play from the imputation that it is emblematic of the modern concerns with subjectivity, interiority, and the danger of inaction that invariably seems to accompany them.[6] Yet despite these revisionist interpretations, it is difficult not to see Hamlet as someone who is obsessed with his own subjectivity and the metaphysical problem of subjectivity more generally.[7] One of the distinctive features of subjectivity is that it finds itself homeless, radically out of joint with its world: this is the price it must pay for its transcendence. An abyss opens up between subject and object, spirit and matter, mind and world, god and animal, and perhaps above all, between intention and the achievement of ends. This abyss plagues Hamlet throughout the course of the play, as he worries about the incommensurability between his bodily existence and his capacities of thought.[8] "What a piece of work is a man! How noble in reason, how infinite in faculties, . . . in action how like an angel, in apprehension how like a god! . . . And yet to me, what is this quintessence of dust?" (2.2.265–9).[9] Writing to Ophelia, he signs his letter: "Thine evermore, most dear lady, whilst this *machine* is to *him*, Hamlet" (2.2.122, my emphasis), implying that his self is not to be conflated with the machine that is his body. And later, when reflecting on Yorick's skull, Hamlet wonders at how two of the great actors on the world stage, Alexander and Caesar, can be reduced to the crudest forms of matter once their spirits have fled: "Why may not imagination trace the noble dust of Alexander till 'a find it stopping a bunghole? . . . Imperious Caesar, dead and turned to clay, / Might stop a hole to keep the wind away" (5.1.182–92). Indeed, we might view the play in its entirety, bookended as it is by the ghost of Hamlet's father (spirit without body) and Yorick's skull (body without spirit), as being haunted by the split that leaves the subject homeless in the world, a ghost forever wandering abroad at night.[10]

But why should it be necessary to rehearse a reading of the play that is already well established, even if it has been vigorously contested in the twentieth century? First, it will allow us to recognize the play's persistent concern with judgment, an aspect that is not usually remarked yet is arguably one of its most central motifs. Second, it will allow us to understand differently why delay and indecision trouble Hamlet, without reducing the play to representing "a heavy deed placed on a soul which is not adequate to cope with it"[11] or Hamlet to "a person, in whose view the external world, and all its incidents and objects, were comparatively dim, and of no interest in themselves, and which began to interest only, when they were reflected in the mirror of his mind."[12] There are many ways of conceiving judgment, but in the context of *Hamlet*, what is most important is that judgment is the process by which a subject, always unhinged from the world (madness), strives to bind itself to the world again (*re-ligare*), without collapsing itself back into the world (death). Judgment is the ever-tenuous bond that links subject to object, spirit to matter, mind to world, intention to action and god to animal in us. It maintains the distance necessary for reflection, while reaching out to touch the world, to engage it and inhabit it.[13] For this reason, it is always a difficult, incomplete, and imperfect process, an ongoing labor, which if we refuse will end in madness, inaction or solipsism ("poor Ophelia, / Divided from herself and her fair judgment, / Without the which we are pictures or mere beasts" [4.5.83–5]), and if we succeed too well will end in death ("Oh, that this too, too solid flesh would melt, / Thaw, and resolve itself into a dew" [1.2.129–30]). Somewhere between these extremes, then, we must hold ourselves separate from the world yet tether ourselves to it by multiple filaments of judgment if we are to judge well and live well.

Rather than viewing *Hamlet* as merely a play about subjectivity, interiority, and indecision and about a protagonist paralyzed by the abyss that divides him from the world in which he wants to act – or conversely, as a play that has nothing whatsoever to do with subjectivity – I propose that we read it as an extended meditation on judgment in its many guises. I say "meditation" because it is not clear to me that the play offers any easily codifiable lessons or insights about judgment.[14] Yet it invites us, often explicitly, to think about judgment in myriad forms, in nearly its every scene. Indeed, I will make the case that there is hardly another issue that runs more consistently through the play than this one. If this is so, then it also should not surprise us that delay and indecision become prominent concerns for Hamlet at various moments, without these having to govern our reading of the play in its entirety. Because judgment is never an automatic process, but requires effort and labor which take time, the worry about delay and indecision can never be far off for a judging subject. Not only does the work of judgment take time, but every judgment is doubled by a second judgment about when the right time is to end reflection and make a decision, embedding the question about delay as a *possible* question within every judgment. Judgment is the thinking of finitude, and as such, time will be of the essence.

Before we proceed to analyze aspects of *Hamlet*'s treatment of judgment in more detail, it is worth pausing to recognize how pervasive its concern with judgment is in scene after scene. The appearance of the ghost in Act 1 not only raises the epistemological question of how we assess the value of sensory evidence (1.1.25–6, 58–60, 169) but also the question of the necessity of fictions for constituting our resolutions, perhaps the most important form of judgment, as we will see in a moment (1.5). Act 1.2 begins with Claudius's misguided interpretation of Aristotelian *phronesis*, which places discretion in a mean (1.2.1–16). This is countered by Hamlet's forceful judgment that it is too soon to end the work of mourning and inappropriate to couple it with marriage (1.2.150–8). Picking up on the theme of common sense from Act 1.2 (1.2.98–9), Act 1.3 asks us to reflect on the emptiness of proverbs without a capacity of judgment to implement them (1.3.35–42, 57–79), while Laertes also explains to Ophelia how Hamlet's ability to exercise his judgment in choosing a marriage partner is constrained (1.3.14–27). The encounter between Ophelia and Hamlet in Act 3.1 is staged as an occasion for Claudius and Polonius to judge Hamlet's behavior (3.1.34), and at the very heart of the play, the *Mousetrap* will provide Hamlet and Horatio an opportunity to judge Claudius's guilt together: "Give him heedful note, / For I mine eyes will rivet to his face, / And after we will both our judgments join / In censure of his seeming" (3.2.77–80; see also 3.2.268–9). In fact, the play-within-the-play, by "hold[ing] ... the mirror up to nature" and reflecting Claudius's deed back to him (3.2.20), awakens his conscience or capacity to judge his own actions (3.2.252; 3.3.42–3). Likewise, Act 3.4 twice interrogates the genesis of conscience through conversation and the capacity for self-division, in both Hamlet and Gertrude (3.4.90–2, 111–14, 159), even as it questions Gertrude's judgment in stooping from old Hamlet to Claudius (70–2). In Act 4, the play draws attention to the political register of judgment, when Claudius talks of the "distracted multitude, / Who like not in their judgment, but their eyes" (4.3.4–5) and the messenger reports on the people's rebellious choice of Laertes as king (4.5.102–8). Hamlet's conversation with the gravediggers, as humorous as it is, contains a profound lesson about the importance and necessity of judgment for interpreting language. Without judgment, the infinite play of wit can carry off the meaning of even the most quotidian expressions ("Whose grave's this, sirrah?" [5.1.104]).[15] However straightforward the use of language may appear, some work of judgment is always required to render it intelligible. Even the concluding scene of swordplay is staged as a scene of judgment. Not only does the king introduce the fencing match by implicating the spectators' judgment ("Come, begin. / And you, the judges, bear a wary eye" [5.2.246–7]), but Hamlet also actively summons us along with Osric to judgment after the first hit ("Judgment?" [5.2.252]). Although the carnage of the last scene can hardly be a model for anything but failed judgments, it nevertheless finds Hamlet appealing for judgment and Horatio referring to the "accidental judgments" that have just transpired (5.2.356), "judgments" stripped of the cognitive process that makes them judgments and reduced to arbitrary decisions and outcomes. And finally, let us remember that if *Hamlet* means to rewrite the genre of the revenge tragedy, one of the things that separates the merely reactive deed of revenge from justice and forgiveness is the work of judgment.[16] It would seem incontrovertible, then, that questions of judgment structure the play from start to finish.[17]

Let us begin by thinking about the role of the ghost in the play. The ghost has long been considered one of the most memorable and sublime effects in *Hamlet*,[18] and has continued to fascinate in readings by Derrida and Greenblatt.[19] Prior to his encounter with the ghost, Hamlet is appalled by his mother's over-hasty marriage to Claudius, but has as yet no thought of revenge for a murder he does not suspect. The ghost precipitates Hamlet's decision to avenge his father, which sets in train the subsequent events of the plot.[20] In other words, the ghost is an essential element in Hamlet's judgment, his resolving on a course of action. But what is the significance of the ghost in this context?[21] In what way might it be said to be necessary for enabling Hamlet's judgment, and perhaps judgment in general?

Before we can understand how the ghost functions, we must first understand what it is. In *Specters of Marx*, Derrida has already called our attention to the dubious ontological status of the ghost, an apparition without substance, neither fully present nor entirely absent, a shadowy existence that both is and is not, neither of this world nor something transcendent:[22] "For it is as the air invulnerable" (*Hamlet*, 1.1.149). But if we are to credit the existence of such things, and take them seriously, some translation is necessary, because *surely* we do not expect to encounter ghosts roaming abroad in the world anymore.[23] In the play, the ghost is, first and foremost, a story, a ghost-story we might say. It circulates like a rumor, an inkling that something is wrong or indeed "rotten in the state of Denmark" (1.4.90). It does not undertake to perform any significant deed nor does it offer to do violence to anyone. It simply enjoins Hamlet to remembrance, and its action, if it can be said to act, comes in the form of telling its story (1.5.9–91). "I am thy father's spirit," the ghost tells Hamlet (1.5.9), and this should be taken literally: it is only as stories that the spirits of the dead live among us (see also 1.2.184–5), and indeed it is in stories and language that we exist for each other and interact with each other as more than just material bodies. If the word "spirit" can have any meaning for us today, and nothing seems less certain, it lies in the capacity of language to transcend, however improbably and imperfectly, the forms of its material embodiment.

When I claim that the ghost is a "story," I do not mean this in a demystifying or reductive sense, as if to say: "Don't be afraid of ghosts; they're just stories without effect." Rather, I want to understand what it means to think of stories as ghosts, with all the fear, the apprehension, the thrill, the uncertainty, and the responsibility that goes along with them. The ghost is not a mere yarn, as we might think of a bad novel, something we read for amusement, put down when we're done and never give a second thought to. No, it gets inside of us, troubles us, provokes us. The story acts in a profound way in the play, and that in itself is something that should make us tremble. After one has heard a harrowing story like this, there is no going back to the world as it was. The world looks different.[24] Whereas before this, Hamlet might have been aggrieved at Gertrude's marriage and at losing the throne, now the accusation of murder hangs in the air and a sinister taint haunts Claudius's actions, however uncertainly at first. We see *through* the ghost, and the very appearance of the world is transformed. But it is not simply an epistemological question of the world appearing in a different light. One cannot listen to a story like this and not *do* something about it. It demands action (1.5.6–7). Even the refusal to act, after the story has been told, becomes as weighty as revenge. The ghost places a burden on Hamlet, to judge, resolve, and act. Its "questionable shape" calls forth the question "What should we do?" (1.4.43, 57) rather than questions of identity like "Who or what am I?"[25] It brings to light the burden of judging as an inescapable and singular responsibility.

Judgment is usually conceived as a matter of subsuming particulars under some rule, but what interests me is the way in which judgment is not reducible to a practice of empirical verification, but requires and is predicated on certain kinds of fiction, like the ghost.[26] The value of a naive empiricism is called into question from the very beginning of the play. After Horatio first sees the ghost, Barnardo asks him: "How now, Horatio, you tremble and look pale. Is not this something more than fantasy?" to which Horatio replies "Before my God I might not this believe / Without the sensible and true avouch / Of mine own eyes" (1.1.55–9). A skeptical audience might be forgiven for being amused at the empirical attestation of ghosts here. After all, neither we nor Horatio have any idea what we have just seen. From the beginning, the existence and status of the ghost are framed more as a matters of faith and belief than of fact (1.1.25–6). But more to the point is Hamlet's jesting but entirely appropriate refusal of the evidence of his senses in favor of his judgment when he first meets Horatio:

> Hamlet: But what, *in faith*, make you from Wittenberg, Horatio?
> Horatio: A truant disposition, good my lord.
> Hamlet: I would not hear your enemy say so,
> Nor shall you do my ear that violence
> To make it *truster* of your own report
> Against yourself. *I know* you are no truant (1.2.168–73, my emphasis)

Hamlet will not believe the evidence of Horatio's own testimony or his senses. His interpretation of Horatio's character makes the obvious explanation implausible; his judgment tells him that there must be another explanation for this situation, a different story that will account for the same facts. In fact, what is framed in terms of knowledge ("I know . . .") and faith ("truster") is neither; somewhere between these, it is a matter of judgment, using a *fiction* of character to *evaluate* empirical evidence.[27] It is not that we must be oblivious to the empirical. Horatio, after all, stands before Hamlet's eyes, and it is this fact that stands in need of explanation. But the empirical is not self-explanatory, and it requires an exercise of judgment to be able to seek out an adequate account, a judgment that is not an unquestioning belief or dogmatic opinion. This judgment is impossible without stories and fictions.

On the face of it, the ghost's narrative is an entirely different matter. The story of old Hamlet being poisoned while asleep in his orchard is in principle subject to empirical verification, by a witness, say, or the appropriate forensic techniques. But, within the play, these are unavailable. Old Hamlet's body is presumably moldering in the grave, and the event of the murder has only one living witness, the accused, who is unlikely to collude in his own conviction (although he does confess in the presence of the audience in Act 3.3). The crucial evidence is effectively beyond reach. The story of old Hamlet's murder circulates like an unverifiable rumor, and the problem of its evidentiary status is exacerbated by its uncertain provenance ("Be thou a spirit of health or goblin damned" [1.4.40]). And yet the ghost's story is not one that can simply be ignored because we do not have all the facts; it requires action. There is possibly a usurper and a criminal on the throne of Denmark, and something needs to be done. Now it may appear that the lack of evidentiary completeness is an accident of this particular situation, and could be remedied. But I want to suggest that every situation of judgment is structured in precisely this way: there is insufficient evidence; or there is not enough time to gather all the evidence; or the very procedures for establishing what counts as evidence are contested; or determining which facts matter depends on the narratives that establish their ranked importance. The ghost leads; it shapes the reading and interpretation of the facts. "Whither wilt thou lead me?" asks Hamlet, "Speak, I'll go no further" (1.5.1). The words of the ghost move Hamlet, make it possible for him to go on, to take action. The situation of judgment Hamlet confronts is structurally identical to the one that confronts us every time we are compelled to make a judgment. It is a condition of our finitude, and judgment is the mode of cognition called for under such conditions.

Why finitude? Because it is not only a question of limitation, but, among other things, a question of time, of death, and of mourning (*Trauerspiel*).[28] The play stages one of its earliest scenes of judgment, Act 1.2, precisely as a question of time and mourning. Hamlet, when we first meet him, is in mourning for his father's recent death, and troubled by the impropriety of his mother's "hasty" marriage. In this situation, Claudius liberally advises Hamlet to cast off his mourning airs. His advice, as trite as it is irrefutable, is a model of prudence, measure, and judgment, as is his earlier speech about balancing the imperatives of grief and celebration as though he were seeking an Aristotelian mean (1.2.1–16):

> 'Tis sweet and commendable in your nature, Hamlet,
> To give these mourning duties to your father,
> But you must know your father lost a father,
> That father lost, lost his, and the survivor bound
> In filial obligation *for some term*
> To do obsequious sorrow. But *to persever*
> In obstinate condolement is a course
> Of impious stubbornness (1.2.87–94, my emphasis)

Yet there is little in the play that grates as much as these two speeches. Why? It cannot only be Claudius's insincerity, which we discover later. Rather, it is a question of time and timing – the appropriate time for mourning – and this can only ever be a matter of judgment. How long is it appropriate to remain in mourning for? On the one hand, though it would be right to do so, we cannot mourn forever. That would be paralyzing and debilitating. On the other hand, to refuse to mourn at all would be, as Hegel shows, to refuse the imperatives of the cultural process by which we turn the dead matter of the body into an enspirited being, by raising it up into our memory against the "corruptions of the grave."[29] Somewhere between these extremes must lie the time of mourning, but where? Is it a day, a week, a month, a year? It is not just that nobody is empowered to decide this question in the abstract, but the very laying down of a rule is arbitrary and will always seem inappropriate. And yet I think it would be safe to hazard that a day or a week would be too short, and if we did not live in a culture of efficiency, even a month or two. But beyond this, it is a question of judgment. If there is miscalculation and even poor judgment in Claudius's speech to Hamlet, then, it lies not in any of the abstract propositions he offers – all of which are, as I have said, irrefutable – but rather in the very act of staging prudence and calculation to one who is recently bereaved. Claudius reads the situation badly, and judgment is always dependent on the specificities of situation. His very performance of the forms of good judgment in this case is a demonstration of his bad judgment, namely his refusal to take account of Hamlet's emotional state. Indeed, in this context, nothing could be more callous than his "think of us / As of a father," even if the sentiment were well-intentioned.[30]

Another way of putting the problem would be to say that judgment cannot be performed by a mere adherence to the forms, or that it can only be performed in the way that Hamlet advises the actors to act: "let your own discretion be your tutor" (3.2.17). The advice is at once empty and profound. It says that good judgment cannot be *reduced to* following a set of rules, since following rules can be a way of avoiding the obligation of judgment.[31] Indeed, the rest of Hamlet's advice to the players – and *advice* is precisely the mode in which judgment is communicated – will be found to be empty in precisely this way (e.g. "Suit the action to the word, the word to the action . . ." [3.2.15–31]). It says nothing and is irrefutable at once, and cannot really be used as a manual to train an actor. It only makes sense when uttered to an actor who already has some understanding of his or her craft, and knows through long practice more or less what is meant here.

The argument between Hamlet and Claudius about when to end mourning is an argument not only about the right judgment (would it be appropriate to stop mourning old Hamlet) but also about the right time to make a judgment (is *now* the time to be done with mourning). The argument brings to light an important feature of judgment: any act of judgment always requires a second judgment about when is the right time to pass judgment. In the case of Hamlet and Claudius, the question concerns among other things the emotional constitution of human beings and the temporal unfolding of the work of mourning. But it could also be a question of when we have sufficient information to make an informed decision, or whether the situation is urgent enough that we have to judge despite the insufficiency of our knowledge. In logical terms, this doubling of judgment quickly leads to an infinite regress, which might be thought to paralyze judgment altogether. But in practice, it is rare that we are paralyzed by such a regress. Rather, we make judgments all the time about when it is right to raise the question about the time of judgment and when not, as well as how many of these nested questions it makes sense to raise. What this reveals, again, is that judgment is not a practice of algorithmic calculation, but rather of reasoned deliberation that requires the capacity to step outside these infinite temporal loops and survey them from afar. Without some capacity for transcendence, however limited, the subject would remain trapped in endless trains of thought, unable to resolve. But judgment allows us to begin with the *end*, the demands of the particular situation, and to decide within the constraints and parameters specified by the situation. Judgment is always guided by the end, and the ability to discern the end is crucial to the work of judgment. It is in this sense of *having the end in view* that we speak of "critical distance" or judging from afar, not in the sense of being abstracted or detached from the situation and attaining an "impartial" perspective, whatever that might mean.[32]

The scene in which Hamlet refuses to kill Claudius while he is praying highlights once again the crucial question of the time of judgment and action, and their relation to ends. Hamlet has already resolved to kill Claudius in order to avenge his father, but this does not end the need for judgment. Poised on the brink of action, sword raised, Hamlet pauses to reflect on whether performing the deed *now* (killing Claudius) will achieve its end (revenge), and he concludes that it will not (3.3.73–96). It would be wrong to speak of either delay or indecision in this instance, though both Hamlet and the ghost make this an issue in the following scene (3.4.107–12). Rather, Hamlet makes a judgment here, that now is not the right time to act and execute his judgment, and he gives reasons for his judgment which, horrific as they are, make sense of his decision and give priority to the ends shaping his action.[33] The reasons that ground a judgment are never absolute or it would not be a judgment, and we can always oppose to them other reasons. We might argue that Hamlet's desire to send Claudius to hell exceeds the ghost's mandate or that Hamlet secretly lacks the necessary resolve to perform the deed and is rationalizing his irresolution or, with the benefit of hindsight, that if Hamlet had killed Claudius at this moment, many unnecessary deaths might have been avoided. But it remains the case that Hamlet makes a judgment here, one that can be distinguished both from an arbitrary decision and from hesitation, delay, and indecision.[34] Hamlet's resolution to kill Claudius does not immunize him from having to make judgments throughout the play, especially about the right time to execute his judgment.

Until now, I have spoken somewhat polemically of subjectivity, interiority, transcendence, and the fictions that constitute the realm of ideality and "spirit," as preconditions for the capacity of judgment. The worry about such language, reflected in two other iconic texts from the period (Descartes' *Meditations* and Cervantes's *Don Quixote*), is that it can give rise to an account of judgment that is subjective, solipsistic, disconnected from the world, and very nearly deranged.[35] *Hamlet* may court such a reading at times, as it ponders the question of madness in Hamlet and Ophelia, but ultimately it insists that the horizon of community and common sense (*sensus communis*) can never be far away for a judging subject. If as I have suggested judgment is the way that the subject reaches out and touches the world, it does so first in the mode of deliberation with others. At least four times, at the heart of the play, judgment takes place in conversation with others and in view of others: when Hamlet and Horatio get together to judge Claudius's reaction to the play; when Claudius judges himself after the play; and when Hamlet visits Gertrude in her chamber, and they each find themselves divided by the voice of another. The play seems to insist that the capacity for internal deliberation, so constitutive of the work of judgment, requires an ability to hear and even to internalize other voices, to such an extent that we may experience ourselves as multiple and divided from ourselves.

In Act 3.4, Hamlet, in all his cruelty, awakens Gertrude's conscience, and the ghost comes "to whet [Hamlet's] almost blunted purpose" (3.4.112). The scene appears to stage a double retreat into privacy and interiority, taking place in the queen's private bedchamber, where Hamlet says: "You go not till I set you up a glass / Where you may see the *inmost* part of you" (3.4.18–19, my emphasis). But the scene does not represent a flight into the solitude of the self. Not only does Hamlet converse with Gertrude, but she declares "O Hamlet, thou hast cleft my heart in twain" (3.4.159), and it is this self-division, mediated by Hamlet ("Oh, step between her and her fighting soul" [3.4.114]), that allows her to judge herself. In addition, in this scene, unlike in Act 1, the ghost can only be seen by Hamlet, making us wonder if it is not a manifestation of a self-divided Hamlet in conversation with himself. Even in the most secluded interiority, judgment can only take place if I am not entirely myself or more than one. If soliloquy is the outward representation of this inner conversation with myself,[36] then it can only properly be a *conversation* if I am already divided against myself or at least unsure in my inchoate multiplicity of where the path to my self lies.[37]

Hamlet wants to hold the mirror up to Gertrude in her closet,[38] but the *Mousetrap* performs the same function more publicly, allowing Hamlet to judge with Horatio of Claudius's guilt, and Claudius to judge himself in conversation with the play even when he seems most alone ("Oh, my offense is rank" [3.3.36]). Hamlet contrives the *Mousetrap* as a way of both pricking the conscience of the king and of assessing the status of the ghost and its narrative. The play-within-the-play is framed as an occasion of judgment, specifically, and even more of what the eighteenth century would call a *sensus communis* or common sense, a shared horizon of judgment. Moments before the play begins, Hamlet tells Horatio: "Give him heedful note, / For I mine eyes will rivet to his face, / And after *we will both our judgments join* / In censure of his seeming" (3.2.77–80, my emphasis). It is worth dwelling on the unprecedented strangeness of the scene of judgment that is being staged here. In order to judge the ghost who enables judgment, Hamlet employs the services of another fiction, the play-within-the-play. Imagine for a moment sending a suspected criminal to a theater which would stage a thinly disguised version of the purported crime in order to assess their guilt! Yet the *Mousetrap* reveals something important about judgment. There is no transcendent standard or infallible rule for judgment, because judgment always relies on fictions. Only a faith in fiction, or rather a *partial* faith, can enable judgment. Hamlet does not believe the ghost unquestioningly (2.2.509–26), but passing judgment on that which enables judgment requires yet another fiction and so on. There is no bedrock on which this process can rest, in order to ground judgment absolutely. Once again, as with the question about the right time for judgment, we discover a recursive structure to finite judgment. Every fiction can potentially be interrogated further, but the act of judgment will ultimately require faith in some fiction to terminate the interminable interrogation, at least temporarily. This is a partial faith, because even when it enables a judgment, it leaves itself open to further interrogation. The structure of finite judgment requires that we "believe in ghosts, in part," that we have faith in fictions that can nevertheless always be questioned. The notion of "believing in part" is taken from Horatio's response to Marcellus's story that cocks crow all night on Christmas Eve. "So have I heard," says Horatio, "and do in part believe it" (1.1.169). Is it possible to believe "in part" or is faith by its nature wholehearted? Whether it is possible or not, it is certainly *necessary* if there is to be anything like judgment. And if it is possible, one could hardly imagine a more difficult condition on resolution and action than this principle of always leaving open to question the very fictions, faith in which is the enabling condition of resolution and action itself.

Under these circumstances, how is it possible to ground a judgment? Hamlet bases his judgment of Claudius's guilt and the ghost's veracity ("I'll take the ghost's word for a thousand pound" [3.2.268–9]) in community, in a shared process of judgment with Horatio. He calibrates his judgment by Horatio's or uses Horatio's judgment as a check on his own. This is not to say that he is incapable of judging independently or autonomously. He judges for himself, but such judgments risk being arbitrary, wild, unpredictable, or unaccountable ("These are but wild and whirling words, my lord" [1.5.139]).[39] Even when one's judgments are opposed to the common sense of a community, it is only in the context of community that a judgment acquires salience, texture, and heft. Indeed, the very idea of autonomy only makes sense in the context of the community which makes it possible. To judge without reference to community at all, without any accountability to a community, would be madness. In fact, Hamlet's feigned or perceived madness makes visible the intimate and reciprocal relation between community and judgment. At the end of Act 1.5, Hamlet decides to "put an antic disposition on" (172), in order to mask his purpose of exacting revenge on Claudius. Hamlet can only appear mad by concealing the grounds of his judgment, the encounter with the ghost. This is why he must swear his companions to secrecy about this encounter. To those who are not privy to the secret, Hamlet's behavior appears unaccountable. Only within the community of those who "believe in part," those who have seen the ghost, do Hamlet's judgments and actions make sense.[40] As audience members who witness the scene with the ghost, we are structurally folded into this community. However much we may question the efficacy of Hamlet's actions, we can at least make sense of them and understand their purpose. To us, he is not mad, because and to the extent that we too "believe in part."[41]

And yet, as necessary as this community is, it is not an infallible ground for judgment any more than the ghost or the play are. Common sense proverbs offered as a guide to judgment are, we find

out repeatedly in the play, empty and still require judgment to implement. Community is both fragile and a fiction, like everything else
that grounds a judgment. A community constituted around a fiction,
as community must be, can never be insulated from participating in
a shared delusion. Though the fictive foundation of community does
not mean that it is always deluded, this is an ever-present risk.

The burden of judging under these conditions of finitude is tragic,
almost too much to bear.[42] Hamlet staggers under it for most of the
play.[43] If the subject is always homeless and out of joint with its
world, and only reaches out to engage the world through acts of
judgment, there is never a guarantee that these acts will reach their
mark or achieve their ends. They may remain "wild and whirling
words" swirling around in a cloistered and self-confirming interiority
with no exit, or they may strike randomly, drunkenly, or accidentally
in the dark at something hidden behind an arras, since their only
"ground" if they have any is unstable layer upon layer of fiction.
Indeed, we might read the ghost's underground machinations in Act
1.5 in just this way: it is at once the ground of his resolution, and
constantly shifting, never reliable. The ghost opens the abyssal space
of judgment before Hamlet, forcing him to judge at the same time as
it reveals the precariousness of the grounds of judgment. But even
when the grounds hold up, there is an immense gap between judgments and their execution, a gap that can never be bridged simply,
straightforwardly, or mechanistically. The Player King takes the point
too far when he says "Our thoughts are ours, their ends *none* of our
own" (3.2.200, my emphasis), for if it were true then action would
have no point. But he effectively calls our attention to the precariousness of judgment, as does Hamlet when he acknowledges how often
"our deep plots do pall" and recognizes that even good judgment, by
itself, does not suffice and needs something more ("There's a divinity
that shapes our ends, / Rough-hew them how we will" [5.2.8–10]).[44]

Confronted with the overwhelming difficulty and precariousness
of judgment, it is no wonder that Hamlet often dreams of escaping
the burdens and responsibilities of being a judging subject. It would
seem that we are back at the problem of Hamlet's infamous delay, as
a flight away from the mundane and determined world of actuality,
into the rich potentials of the inner world of thought where decisions
seem unnecessary. Hamlet himself hints at this interpretation of his
predicament in the "To be or not to be" soliloquy when he declares:[45]

> Thus conscience does make cowards of us all,
> And thus the native hue of resolution

It shows a restless / unsettled / discontented mind?

Is sickled o'er with the pale cast of thought,
And enterprises of great pitch and moment,
With this regard, their current turn awry,
And lose the name of action. (3.1.84–90)

Maybe, is he does only have one significant delay, the perceived delay shows the restless of his subjective view?

Subsequently, both the ghost and Hamlet accuse Hamlet of dither-
ing (3.4.107–14; 4.4.34), laying the grounds *within the play* for the
romantic reading of Hamlet as a prevaricator lost in the labyrinthine
worlds of his own interiority. But the only significant delay that we
witness is Hamlet's refusal to kill Claudius at prayer, for which there
are "good" reasons, that is to say reasons that are not hard to credit
given Hamlet's subsequent actions. Hamlet's delay at this moment,
though it may be one way of avoiding judgment itself, does not avoid
the *responsibility* of judgment. Indeed, if one wants to flee the burdens of judgment, then the retreat into subjectivity and interiority is
hardly likely to help, since that is precisely the site and source of the
problem, namely the endless agonizing about when is the right time
to make a judgment. Interiority does not provide a reprieve from
the burdens of judging, but exacerbates them. To be a subject, as
I have already argued, is nothing else than to be a judging subject,
to have the capacity for judgment in virtue of the limited transcendence afforded by one's interiority. Only subjects have this capacity
to judge. The only relief from the burden of judging, then, must lie
in the erasure of subjectivity itself; death, in short.[46] In order not
to have to judge, one must become completely continuous with the
material world, no longer out of joint with it, since this being-out-
of-joint is what imposes the burden of judging in the first place. It
is this desire for the erasure of subjectivity, the desire to become of
a piece with the world, that we find Hamlet expressing in some of
his most memorable words: "Oh, that this too, too solid flesh would
melt, / Thaw, and resolve itself into a dew" (1.2.129–30). "To die,
to sleep – / No more" (3.1.61–2). It is not this or that particular
judgment that Hamlet wishes he did not have to make; he wants,
rather, to be relieved of the capacity of judgment altogether and the
endless demand for judging that it imposes, recognizing full well that
only death can "end the heartache" of perpetual judging imposed by
being the kinds of being we are. Post-romantic readings of *Hamlet*,
like Benjamin's, which want to erase or ignore subjectivity and interiority in the play, are complicit with this desire of Hamlet's.

And yet, as much as Hamlet desires to efface this subjectivity
and interiority that bring with them the inescapable burden of judgment, he keeps remembering, being reminded, reminding himself

I disagree

Fortinbras Soliloquy is about how he has delayed

Q2 is.

Q1

Hamlet is decisive initially (believes Horatio, follows Ghost)

("Remember me" [1.5.91]), in a steady rhythm that punctuates the play, of the improbable persistence of this spirit or subjectivity, this ghost in the machine, even in the most extreme circumstances:[47] "To sleep, perchance to dream – ay, there's the rub" (3.1.66). If spirit is out of joint with the world, then it is not hard to imagine that it can detach itself and begin to wander abroad, as a ghost, not just in some metaphysical sense of an afterlife, but in some very mundane ways as we shall see in a moment. In this sense, something is very much "out of joint" and spirits other than old Hamlet haunt the play from beginning to end with their fictions. Despite their immateriality or perhaps because of it, spirits are not easy to get rid of. At the moments when Hamlet most wants to erase this spirit or subjectivity which enables judgment, it is because he recognizes that for all its fragility, its *almost* nothingness, it endures irresistibly: "it is as the air invulnerable" (1.1.149). It shapes judgment and action, and makes them possible. On a small scale, the fictions and ideality that are the element of subjectivity can move an actor to dramatic expression "for nothing," for ends that are purely fabricated: "Is it not monstrous that this player here, / But in a fiction, in a dream of passion, / Could force his soul so to his own conceit" (2.2.474–7)?[48] But what is true in microcosm is also true on the grandest stage of the world's theater. It is the ends we forge for ourselves, even when they are trivial and dangerous, that animate our judgments and actions with their spirit:[49]

> Examples gross as earth exhort me:
> Witness this army of such mass and charge,
> Led by a delicate and tender prince,
> Whose *spirit* with divine ambition puffed
> Makes mouths at the invisible event,
> Exposing what is mortal and unsure
> To all that fortune, death and danger dare,
> Even for an eggshell.
> . . .
> . . . to my shame I see
> Th'imminent death of twenty thousand men
> That for a *fantasy* and *trick of fame*,
> Go to their graves like beds . . . (4.4.47–63, my emphasis)

At moments like this, even when the insight cannot be sustained, Hamlet helps us to recognize that only through the ghostly almost-nothing of subjectivity, its fictions and fantasies, are judgment, resolution, and action possible. Without them, "that capability [large discourse] and godlike reason [would] fust in us unused" (4.4.39–40) and the "chief good and market of [our] time [would] be but to sleep and feed" (4.4.35–6).

compare Q1 + Q2

Nowhere is the necessity of the space of subjectivity and its ghostly transcendence more poignantly apparent than in Hamlet's encounter with Yorick's skull. Although Hamlet had desired to be reduced to matter in just this way, he is repulsed when he sees what it means for this desire to be realized, for the body to be stripped of its animating spirit ("My gorge rises at it" [5.1.68]).[50] And yet, despite appearances, Yorick has not been reduced to this skull. He has gone abroad. He is, if anywhere, in Hamlet's words and that "distracted globe" where "memory holds a seat" (1.5.96–7):[51]

> A fellow of infinite jest, of most excellent fancy. He hath bore me on his back a thousand times . . . Here hung those lips that I have kissed I know not how oft. Where be your gibes now, your gambols, your songs, your flashes of merriment that were wont to set the table on roar? (5.1.165–71)

In this case, the skull is less a memento of death than a memento of life. However much Hamlet wants to reduce himself to matter at various points, he keeps being reminded of the ghostly realm of subjectivity, the little difference that is almost no difference and yet not nothing, perhaps even everything. Even though Hamlet the materialist has difficulty discerning this difference ("Why may not imagination trace the noble dust of Alexander . . ."),[52] as many critics since have, the play and Horatio in particular bring it into view for us: "'Twere to consider too curiously to consider so" (5.1.185).

Even though he repeatedly reminds us of it, Hamlet resists the insight about subjectivity and agency, and the burden of judgment and action that comes with it, almost to the end. The work of judgment, I have been arguing, involves crafting and committing to ends, whose flimsy fictionality was so disturbing to Hamlet whenever he became aware of it ("even for an eggshell"). Hamlet begins the last scene of the play by casting doubt on this work and even speaking in favor of "indiscretion": "Rashly, / And praised be rashness for it – let us know / Our indiscretion sometimes serve us well, / When our deep plots do pall and that should learn us / There's a divinity that shapes our ends" (5.2.6–10). Having made the case for haste and even "rashness,"[53] Hamlet argues a short while later for a messianic waiting that evacuates any possibility of agency: "There is a special providence in the fall of a sparrow. If it be now, 'tis not to come; if it be not to come, it will be now; if it be not now, yet it will come" (5.2.189–92). The "we" of the earlier speech has vanished in favor of an impersonal agency ("it") that produces effects in ways that cannot be sounded. The puzzle of "If it be now, . . ." etc. reflects the inscrutable operation of a providence whose (il)logic rapidly loses us in a maze. Rather than try to make sense of it, we are urged to give up entirely the work of forging our own ends: "The readiness is all . . . Let be" (5.2.192–3). It may seem contradictory for Hamlet to be arguing one minute for haste and the next for endless waiting. But both positions are characterized by a suspicion of the work of fictioning ends, a renunciation of judgment, and a denigration of the labor of thought that lies behind both. Although birds often represent the transcendence of spirit (think, for example, of Shelley's skylark), in *Hamlet* they figure the ways in which the realm of spirit, thought, ideality, and judgment are bypassed, as though this were the only way to recover any possibility for "action." With the fall of the sparrow, the failure of the spirit's transcendence, providence replaces the onerous task of making our own ends. But earlier in the play, the wings of thought served as a figure not only for haste but for misunderstanding the difficulties of thought in favor of a more reactive vengeance: "Haste me to know't, that I with wings as swift / as meditation or the thoughts of love / May sweep to my revenge" (1.5.29–31). As the play and its many soliloquies have shown, there is nothing swift about meditation, and were it to be so, we would wonder whether any thought, reflection, or deliberation had taken place.

Haste and waiting. Two modes of "action" stripped of judgment. It is precisely in *both* these modes that Hamlet enters upon the catastrophe of the play, the final scene of swordplay, with predictably disastrous effects. He goes in with no plan. He will wait to see what happens, and then he will react rashly, as he did when he murdered Polonius.[54] Judgment, with its ability to relate us to ends and purposes, has been abandoned, as Horatio's subsequent description of the events underscores: "So shall you hear / . . . / Of accidental judgments, casual slaughters, / Of deaths put on by cunning, and for no cause" (5.2.354–7). This is what action without thought and judgment looks like: it is "casual" and without "cause" or purpose. "Accidental judgments" are not in fact judgments at all. They are the semblance of judgments, events and outcomes devoid of the thinking and deliberation – the invisible labor of subjectivity ("that within which passes show") – that would transform them into judgments. It is no wonder, then, that in the midst of these "casual slaughters," too late, Hamlet pleads for judgment (5.2.252).

But amid the blood and bodies more fitting for the battlefield than the court (5.2.375–6), matter reduced to its brute materiality, spirits still hover ("And in this harsh world draw thy breath in pain, / To tell my story" [5.2.322–3]) and a nearly indiscernible act of judgment transforms the world in ways that are at once profound and invisible:

> Laertes: Exchange forgiveness with me, noble Hamlet.
> Mine and my father's death come not upon thee,
> Nor thine on me. [*He dies*]
> Hamlet: Heaven make thee free of it. I follow thee. (5.2.303–6)

What does forgiveness change? At one level, nothing is different. Hamlet has still killed Polonius and Laertes, and Laertes has killed Hamlet. And if we look on the world prosaically, without the sheen of subjectivity, as Hamlet does when he traces "the dust of Alexander till 'a find[s] it stopping a bunghole," we will be unable to make sense of the claim that anything has changed through forgiveness. On the logic of empiricism, the statement is sheer nonsense and noise. And yet if we believe (in part) in the possibility of forgiveness, this act of forgiveness changes everything in the moral world, as did the ghost's story at the beginning of the play. Forgiveness takes place in the unverifiable realm of subjectivity.[55] The way in which it is done, the sense or meaning or intention with which it is done, makes all the difference to how the deed is understood. If we grant forgiveness, then the unnecessary deaths of Polonius, Laertes, and Hamlet can be laid to rest, without calling out for further action. The play can come to an end, freeing up a space for something new to happen. But more than this, forgiveness, while acknowledging that the subject performed the deed and is bound to it, also disjoins the subject from its deed ("Heaven make thee free of it"). Forgiveness brings to light the possibility that a subject can be out of joint with the world and its deeds, free in a word, not only when its plans and intentions fail ("When our deep plots do pall"), but even when they succeed. And that should teach us that there's a judgment that must shape our ends, rough-hewn though they will be. Unhinged, homeless like a ghost wandering the night, the subject can only make a home for itself in the world by accepting the burden and responsibility of judgment, through which it ventures out into the world and shapes it while still keeping itself apart from it.

Notes

1. The critique is deeply ingrained within structuralism and post-structuralism, but it can be traced back to Paul Ricoeur's triad of the "hermeneutics of suspicion": Marx, Nietzsche, and Freud. For a more recent example, see Fredric Jameson's injunction in *A Singular Modernity: Essay on the Ontology of the Present* (London: Verso, 2002) that "the one way not to narrate [modernity] is via subjectivity" (94).
2. Ibid., 42–57.
3. For an argument in favor of judgment and autonomy that argues against this misconception, see Hina Nazar, *Enlightened Sentiments: Judgment and Autonomy in the Age of Sensibility* (New York: Fordham University Press, 2012).
4. For a remarkable attempt to retrieve the concepts of will and personhood from their impoverishment in modernity, see Thomas Pfau, *Minding the Modern: Human Agency, Intellectual Traditions, and Responsible Knowledge* (Notre Dame: University of Notre Dame Press, 2013).
5. See Margreta de Grazia, *"Hamlet" without Hamlet* (Cambridge: Cambridge University Press, 2007), 7–22; Stephen Greenblatt, *Hamlet in Purgatory* (Princeton: Princeton University Press, 2001), 5.
6. See Walter Benjamin, *The Origin of German Tragic Drama*, trans. John Osborne (London: Verso, 1977); de Grazia, *"Hamlet" without Hamlet*. For a broader argument that goes beyond *Hamlet*, see Jonathan Dollimore, *Radical Tragedy: Religion, Ideology and Power in the Drama of Shakespeare and his Contemporaries*, 3rd ed. (Durham, NC: Duke University Press, 2004), 153–81. On the more widespread efforts in recent criticism to erase the sense of self and interiority in *Hamlet*, see John Lee, *Shakespeare's "Hamlet" and the Controversies of the Self* (Oxford: Oxford University Press, 2000). He argues that such readings threaten to undermine the possibility of agency (150). It is precisely the possibilities of agency I hope to recover through my attention to judgment in the play.
7. Readings of *Hamlet* in terms of subjectivity have persisted. See A. C. Bradley, *Shakespearean Tragedy: Lectures on "Hamlet," "Othello," "King Lear," "Macbeth"* (Harmondsworth: Penguin, 1991), 86, 106; Harold Bloom, *"Hamlet": Poem Unlimited* (New York: Riverhead, 2003), 7, 96–7, 134, 143–7; A. D. Nuttall, *Shakespeare the Thinker* (New Haven: Yale University Press, 2007), 192–205; Lee, *Shakespeare's "Hamlet."*
8. Especially relevant here is Sarah Beckwith's account of the genesis of this split, which she traces back to the emergence of a modern inward grammar of forgiveness from the Catholic sacrament of penance, a shift Beckwith describes as a move away from ritual action toward *metanoia* (2), or from "performative to passionate utterance" (5). For her, *Hamlet* is emblematic of "the mind's retreat from the face" (15–20). See

Shakespeare and the Grammar of Forgiveness (Ithaca: Cornell University Press, 2011), 20–33.

9. All quotations and line references are from *Hamlet*, ed. Robert S. Miola (New York: Norton, 2011).

10. For other examples where the play reflects on this problem, see 1.2.76–86; 3.1.149–60; 3.4.140–2; 4.2.25–26; 4.4.33–40; 3.2.339–46.

11. Johann Wolfgang von Goethe, *Wilhelm Meister's Apprenticeship*, ed. and trans. Eric A Blackall, in *Goethe's Collected Works*, 11 vols. (Princeton: Princeton University Press, 1989), 9:146.

12. Samuel Taylor Coleridge, "Lecture on *Hamlet*," in Shakespeare, *Hamlet*, ed. Miola, 246.

13. This claim, and my arguments about the importance of fiction in the play, should be seen in proximity to Stanley Cavell's observation about the lesson of assent or affirmation, both to one's own existence and to the "fantasy structure of human culture" in *Hamlet*: "To exist is to take your existence upon you, to enact it, as if the basis of human existence is theater, even melodrama. To refuse this burden is to condemn yourself to skepticism – to a denial of the existence, hence the value, of the world." See *Disowning Knowledge in Seven Plays of Shakespeare*, updated edition (Cambridge: Cambridge University Press, 2003), 189, 187. Judgment rewrites this assent as a more complex and fraught structure, one that is ethical rather than epistemological in its orientation. See also Beckwith's Cavellian claim that "acknowledgment is the ground of our relation to other minds" (*Shakespeare*, 6), and that "Shakespeare lends his art to restoring the mind and the soul to the face" (33), though she finds this restoration in the later, post-tragic plays, not *Hamlet*.

14. It also seems to me that, unlike the ways in which *Antigone* and Austen's *Pride and Prejudice* implicate their readers in a practice of judgment, *Hamlet* does not place the burden of judgment on its audience to nearly the same extent. See Julen Etxabe, *The Experience of Tragic Judgment* (London: Routledge, 2013); and Vivasvan Soni, "Committing Freedom: The Cultivation of Judgment in Rousseau's *Emile* and Austen's *Pride and Prejudice*," *The Eighteenth Century: Theory and Interpretation* 51 (2010): 363–87.

15. On the opposition of wit and judgment, see John Locke, *An Essay Concerning Human Understanding*, ed. Roger Woolhouse (Harmondsworth: Penguin, 2004), 153.

16. See Bloom, *Hamlet*, 3, 70; Nuttall, *Shakespeare the Thinker*, 197, 202–4; R. Clifton Spargo, *The Ethics of Mourning: Grief and Responsibility in Elegiac Literature* (Baltimore: Johns Hopkins University Press, 2004), 40, 66, 73, 75; Greenblatt, *Hamlet in Purgatory*, 229; de Grazia, *"Hamlet" without Hamlet*, 174. However, de Grazia's de-subjectivizing reading risks downplaying the importance of judgment and forgiveness (196). See also Etxabe, *Experience of Tragic Judgment*, 190.

17. I have only noted the moments in the play that have the greatest interpretive significance for understanding judgment. There are, in addition to these, a number of passing references to judgment throughout the play. See, for example, 1.3.68; 2.1.108–15; 2.2.152–4; 2.2.330–9; 2.2.362–4; 2.2.452–5; 3.2.15–25; 3.2.62; 4.5.151; 4.5.197–8.

18. See, for example, Goethe, *Wilhelm Meister's Apprenticeship*. See also de Grazia, *"Hamlet" without Hamlet*, 8, 40.

19. See Jacques Derrida, *Specters of Marx: The State of the Debt, the Work of Mourning, and the New International*, trans. Peggy Kamuf (London: Routledge, 1994); Greenblatt, *Hamlet in Purgatory*.

20. In this context, see Spargo's argument about how the intransigence of ordinary mourning, a protest against dying itself, leads to an investigation of actual injustice in *Hamlet* (*Ethics of Mourning*, 5, 45).

21. Greenblatt finds four different perspectives on ghosts in Shakespeare: "as a figure of false surmise, . . . as a figure of history's nightmare, . . . as a figure of deep psychic disturbance, . . . as a figure of theater" (*Hamlet in Purgatory*, 157).

22. See Derrida, *Specters of Marx*, 6. On the supernatural in Shakespeare, see also Bradley, *Shakespearean Tragedy*, 30–1.

23. Greenblatt argues that Shakespeare is already translating his ghosts in this way (*Hamlet in Purgatory*, 195–6).

24. See Lee, *Shakespeare's "Hamlet,"* 179; Greenblatt, *Hamlet in Purgatory*, 206.

25. Lee argues that Hamlet is more concerned with abstract questions like "what is a man?" than the particularizing question of "who am I?" (*Shakespeare's "Hamlet,"* 156, 187).

26. This does not mean that one cannot ask empirical questions about the veracity of the ghost's narrative.

27. For a description of this practice, see Soni, "Committing Freedom."

28. For a reconstruction of the complex temporal structure of tragic judgment, see Etxabe, *Experience of Tragic Judgment*, 2, 176–84, 191. On the question of tragic finitude, see Etxabe, *Experience of Tragic Judgment*, 122.

29. Georg Wilhelm Friedrich Hegel, *Phenomenology of Spirit*, trans. A. V. Miller (Oxford: Oxford University Press, 1977), 270–1.

30. See Spargo, *Ethics of Mourning*, 51, 56.

31. This is not to say that cultures do not set out appropriate times and rituals for mourning, to ease the burden of judgment. They do, and in many cases it makes sense to follow these prescriptions. But it must always be open to us to judge that the prescriptions are inadequate for a particular situation. See Spargo, *Ethics of Mourning*, 5–6, 39–40. But Spargo tends to make the resistance to cultural codes a duty, erasing the work of judgment (76). In the case of *Hamlet*, because we do not within the play have access to the cultural codes of the play's "Denmark" – unless we want to take Claudius as the representative of those codes, a tendentious

proposition – the work of judgment is brought more fully into view. See also Greenblatt, *Hamlet in Purgatory*, 247.

32. See Etxabe, *Experience of Tragic Judgment*, 111.

33. That Hamlet is not reluctant to kill Claudius is evident when he stabs Polonius, thinking it is Claudius behind the arras. And that his reasons for delaying the murder of Claudius are not simply an excuse may be surmised from the fact that he uses a similar logic when giving the king of England instructions to kill Rosencrantz and Guildenstern. De Grazia argues that the interpretation of Hamlet as delaying and indecisive arose in the eighteenth century as a way of mitigating or explaining away Hamlet's horrific claim that he wants to send Claudius to hell (*Hamlet*, 3.3.73–96). See de Grazia, *"Hamlet" without Hamlet*, 158–61, 191. On Hamlet's delay more generally, see Bradley, *Shakespearean Tragedy*, 97–132; de Grazia, *"Hamlet" without Hamlet*, 158–204.

34. I mean, of course, to allude to the debate Walter Benjamin and Carl Schmitt had by way of *Hamlet* concerning Baroque theories of sovereignty. Giorgio Agamben sketches the contours of this argument in *State of Exception*, trans. Kevin Attell (Chicago: University of Chicago Press, 2005). Schmitt, as is well known, outlined a theory of sovereignty as it emerged in the early modern period, in which sovereignty is defined by the ability to decide on the exception or state of emergency, the ability to suspend all laws and assume all power of decision. See, for example, Carl Schmitt, *Political Theology: Four Chapters on the Concept of Sovereignty*, trans. George Schwab (Cambridge, MA: MIT Press, 1985). For Schmitt, it is imperative that the sovereign decision be arbitrary and unaccountable, because any attempt to give it a reasoned and normative legitimacy would remove the power of decision from the person and authority of the sovereign and place it in a discursive realm which is shared and intersubjectively accessible. In the *Origin of German Tragic Drama*, Benjamin responds to Schmitt's theory of sovereignty by offering an interpretation of the Baroque *Trauerspiel* that accepts the terms of Schmitt's theory even as it unworks it. Benjamin insists that the indecision of the Baroque tyrant on the stage (and I take him to be including Hamlet here) is not to be understood in conventionally psychologizing terms. It is, rather, an effect of the Baroque theory of the sovereign decision that Schmitt describes: "The prince, who is responsible for making the decision to proclaim the state of emergency, reveals, at the first opportunity, that he is almost incapable of making a decision" (71). After Benjamin's untimely death, Schmitt insisted on having the last word in this exchange in his *Hamlet or Hecuba: The Intrusion of Time into the Play*, trans. David Pan and Jennifer R. Rust (New York: Telos, 2009), though he refuses to engage with Benjamin's larger theoretical claim that the Baroque theory of sovereignty is haunted by indecision and the imminence of catastrophe. However, as my argument about *Hamlet* has made clear, the play's conception of judgment is not

comprehended by this argument about decision and indecision. Judgment differs in at least two crucial ways from Schmitt's theory of the sovereign decision, and Benjamin's radically de-subjectivized account of Hamlet's indecision. First, judgment requires the inward deliberative space of subjectivity, the space of soliloquy, precluded by both Schmitt and Benjamin. Second, judgment is inextricably temporal, whereas neither decision nor indecision take any account of time. A decision is an immediate cut or separation that occurs in the blink of an eye. And indecision is an infinite temporizing or deferral. Although Julia Reinhard Lupton takes up Schmittian questions of political theology in *Citizen-Saints: Shakespeare and Political Theology* (Chicago: University of Chicago Press, 2005), she is not directly concerned with the problem of (in)decision in *Hamlet*, focusing rather on the tension between religious and secular modes of community formation and the unstable way these map onto the dyad of universal and particular.

35. See Beckwith, *Shakespeare*, 9, 33. De Grazia argues that the modern Hamlet is produced by abstracting him from the play, and specifically from the plot's interest in land (*"Hamlet" without Hamlet*, 4). For her perceptive reading of the importance of figures of earth, dust, and land in the play, see de Grazia, *"Hamlet" without Hamlet*, 23–44. Though she claims that "it is not clear that personal identity can survive deracination and disentitlement" (43), I argue below that this capacity for disjunction is essential to subjectivity.

36. Lee correctly sees the soliloquies as generalizing in their tenor, rather than focused on the particularities of an individual self (*Shakespeare's "Hamlet,"* 154). But this does not undermine their relationship to the inner conversation of subjectivity. Lee argues that the sense of self in *Hamlet* is not essentialist but constructed and rhetorical (159, 172–84, 209–27). He views the soliloquies as acts of self-creation (200–3).

37. In his essay "Soliloquy" in the *Characteristics*, Shaftesbury develops an account of judgment and conscience through inner conversation and self-division. Although *Hamlet* is mentioned only once in a passing footnote, it is hard to believe that these scenes from the play are not crucial for understanding Shaftesbury's conception of the practice of judgment, given that *Hamlet* is a play justly renowned for its soliloquies. The account of judgment through self-division and soliloquy that Shaftesbury develops is a neo-Stoic one, which if it is derived from *Hamlet* as I am suggesting, helps confirm Nuttall's argument that Hamlet represents a subjectivization of Stoicism (*Shakespeare the Thinker*, 192–205). Nuttall believes this leads to Hamlet's increasing isolation (194), but as I argue below, *Hamlet*'s and Shaftesbury's conceptions of judgment are predicated on engagement with others. However, the play also alerts us that self-division is not a guarantor of good judgment. Indeed, it will always involve a brush with madness ("poor Ophelia, / Divided from herself and her fair judgment" [*Hamlet*, 4.5.83–5]).

38. In *Joseph Andrews*, Henry Fielding will make this gesture central to his theory of the novel. Indeed, *Hamlet* casts a long shadow over the eighteenth-century novel and its struggles with the problem of judgment. Goethe's *Wilhelm Meister's Apprenticeship* proposes the argument that *Hamlet* resembles a novel more than a play in certain ways (185–6).

39. However, *Antigone* shows that such wildness is sometimes inevitable.

40. In her keynote lecture "Hamlet's Kindness" at the Globe Theater (April 17, 2015), Laurie Shannon offered a rich meditation on the unusual model of friendship and community in *Hamlet*, one that goes beyond a Ciceronian or Stoic ideal and "highlights our embodied vulnerability": "Hamlet departs from Montaigne's more exclusive script to envision an additive friendship, a friendship with room for more." See also Beckwith, *Shakespeare*, 1, 5, 12.

41. On the way the play implicates its audience within it, see Bloom, *Hamlet*, 13–16.

42. On the "tragic necessity" of judgment, see Etxabe, *Experience of Tragic Judgment*, 82.

43. See Lee, *Shakespeare's "Hamlet,"* 205.

44. Bradley sees this recognition as characteristic of Shakespearean tragedy more generally (*Shakespearean Tragedy*, 42).

45. However, Christian Thorne has alerted me to the revolutionary and republican overtones of this soliloquy. On the possibly covert republican and anti-imperial politics of the play, see de Grazia, *"Hamlet" without Hamlet*, 45–80, 181.

46. See Bloom, *Hamlet*, 118–19, 147.

47. Ibid., 36.

48. See Greenblatt, *Hamlet in Purgatory*, 252–3, for the link between this moment and the ghost's story.

49. On the importance of fictioning norms in tragic judgment, see Etxabe, *Experience of Tragic Judgment*, 89, 163–7.

50. He is similarly angered when he thinks Rosencrantz and Guildenstern play him like an instrument (3.2.339–46).

51. On the rhetorical character of the self implied by these images, see Lee, *Shakespeare's "Hamlet,"* 226.

52. Lee argues that the Hamlet of the second Quarto is more of a materialist, while that of the Folio has a more developed sense of an inward self (*Shakespeare's "Hamlet,"* 228–39).

53. See also de Grazia, *"Hamlet" without Hamlet*, 8.

54. See Bradley, *Shakespearean Tragedy*, 108.

55. Beckwith sees the split between inner and outer and the subjectivization and interiorization of forgiveness as a problem (*Shakespeare*, 27–33), indeed as "false pictures" (33) that she seeks to remedy through a notion of performative language derived from Wittgenstein and Austin. But she recognizes that this split is precisely what opens

the difficult and treacherous space of judgment: "When authority is no longer assumed in the speech acts of a sacramental priesthood, it must be found, and refound, in the claims, calls, judgments of every person who must single themselves and others out in these calls, grant them the authority in each particular instance" (4–5).

Chapter 3

Shakespeare's Law and Plowden's Authority

Constance Jordan

The challenge of interpreting the words of a statute so that they address the nature of the case to be decided has elicited abundant commentary from Aristotle in *Nichomachean Ethics* to members of the judiciary in countries that have relied on the English common law. Edmund Plowden's part in shaping this discourse has been decisive, in large part because he understood that the meaning of the words of a statute could only be discovered by considering the moral function of *equitas*, that is, of equity or what we might think of as a fairness reflecting both the "mischief" the statute under review was designed to cure and that which the case to be adjudicated could be seen to illustrate. This chapter will address Plowden's understanding of such equitable interpretation in one of the best known of his reports in his *Commentaries*, *Eysten vs. Studd*, 1574, with a preliminary account of his first report, *Reniger vs. Fogossa*, 1551.[1] Further than the penetrating analyses of law represented in the *Commentaries*, however, Plowden contributed to the language of the law in another way. Entering the Middle Temple as student of the common law in 1538, Plowden was exposed to (and may well have joined) perhaps the most notable activity undertaken at the Inns of Court in general: the "readings" or what were in effect mock trials of imaginary cases in which students argued for particular decisions. The "facts" of these "cases" were of course fictional; nevertheless they required effective interpretation. The trans-disciplinary character of these "readings" was also registered in contemporary theater that embraced legalistic intrigue. Demonstrated acutely in the unraveling of plot in George Gascoigne's *Supposes*, a source for Shakespeare's *The Taming of the Shrew*, such plays demonstrate the resources of a critical ambiguity available to authors who want to introduce audiences to a "reality" that is no more than fiction and that can in fact only be supposed.

Plowden's description of his own situation as a recusant law-yer after the accession of Elizabeth I and the consequent passage of the Act of Supremacy and the Act of Uniformity, 1559, shows how carefully he approached the use of words and language as they communicated political, ethical, or religious beliefs and positions. The Act of Supremacy required that "'all and every temporal officer and minister' and certain other persons should take an oath . . . that acknowledged the queen's ecclesiastical supremacy and renounced all foreign jurisdiction and authority including that of the pope." Plowden took that oath and attended church, although he did not take the sacrament.[2] In 1659, the privy council upped the ante: it insisted that Plowden and other Justices of the Peace for Berkshire not only attend church but also receive the sacrament as required by the Act of Uniformity. In his response Plowden defended his actions:

> that as towchyng cummyng to churche and hearing divine service according to the saide boke and statute he had ever sithens this service used cummen to the churche and hearde the same service and prayers according to the same boke. And saide that as he thought no man in his realme of his profession in the comen lawe . . . had oftener or dulier come to the churche and heard divine service . . . then he hath done as they of bothe the Temples and many others have seen and can testifie.

But Plowden also observes that the privy council now requires not only that he attend church but that he also subscribe to doctrine about which he has "some scruple in conscience," and he adds that because "great impiety should be in him if he should subscribe in full affirmance or belief of those things in which he is scrupulous in belief, he could not subscribe, butt [because] belief must precede his subscripcion . . ."[3] His refusal resulted in his signing a bond assuring his good behavior; after a year the privy council voided that bond.[4] Years later, it is possible that he refused the queen's invitation to be Lord Chancellor, and a letter on this occasion, if his, testifies to an extraordinary propriety:

> Hold me, dread sovereign, excused. Your Majesty well knows I find no reason to swerve from the Catholic faith in which you and I were brought up. I can never countenance the persecution of its professors. I should not have in charge your Majesty's conscience one week before I should incur your displeasure, if it be your Majesty's royal intent to continue the system of persecuting the retainers of the Catholic faith.

Here the writer demonstrates an unwillingness to pander to political expediency despite the distinct advantages that such expediency would bring.[5] Words – insofar as they conveyed the speaker's convictions – clearly mattered to Plowden; we can guess that if he detected that they did not matter to a particular speaker, he might have assumed that the speaker intended to deceive his listeners and perhaps also himself.

The education in law and pleading offered to students at the Inns suggests that in practice Plowden's concern for words and meaning was shared and indeed promoted by their Fellows. It is not a mistake to say that the language of the Inns was effective precisely because its interpretation was challenging. Accounts of their most publicized exercises, the "readings" devoted to the interpretation of the language of particular cases and required annually of members of an Inn, stress their verbal feistiness. To get a "reading" underway the benchers of the Inn in which it was to take place chose a "Reader" from the Inn's more advanced students or "utter-barristers." This Reader was then expected to present and analyze a particular statute, to illustrate its relevance by invoking imaginary cases, and finally to show how the law in question might apply to them.[6] The Reader began with an apology "usually decrying his own ability for the place, acknowledging his debt to the Inn and the present company, and explaining his choice of statute." His presentation consisted of a "number of 'cases,' a series of imaginary factual instances, with the Reader's legal conclusions upon them, intended to show how the law applied to a range of particular facts."[7] He was then subjected to questions from the utter-barristers that were designed to provoke further controversy:

> whereas they rehearse some one opinion or saying of him that readeth, and by all ways of learning and reason that can be invented do impugn his opinion: and sometimes some of them do impugn it and other do approve it, and all the rest of the house give ear unto their disputations; and at last the reader doth confute all their sayings and confirmeth his opinion.[8]

This "reading" was, of course, both an exercise in interpretation and itself a performance. Particular positions appear within contexts that celebrate the wit as well as the legal learning of their expositors, the Reader and the utter-barristers, who are essential to the success of this show. It is at least arguable that the outcome was in a sense pre-arranged. The Reader's confutation of the arguments advanced against him appears more ceremonial than justified.[9]

Not surprisingly, there were criticisms of such readings and their time-consuming investment in entertainment. In 1628, looking back to the previous century, Chief Justice Coke praised the "ancient lectures or readings upon statutes" as exemplified in Littleton's *Tenures*. By contrast, he claimed,

> now readings have lost . . . their former authorities, for now the cases are long, obscure, and intricate, full of new conceits, liker rather to riddles than lectures, which when they are opened they vanish away like smoke, and the readers are like lapwings, who seem to be nearest their nests when they are furthest from them, and all their study is find nice evasions out of the statute.[10]

Here Coke decries as theatrical readings that in another mood he might have recognized as designed to educate their participants in argument. As J. H. Baker observes, the readings held at the Inns were never regarded as "a common core of inherited wisdom"; they were practically superseded by "judge-made law."[11] Their purpose was not to establish what the law was but rather how it could be fashioned by language and thus made susceptible to interpretation, however extravagant. The "conceits," "riddles," and "evasions" these readings exploited were the very engines that moved them to realize their didactic purpose. Their effort was as much dramatic as jurisprudential. It was not enough that a reading be logically coherent and linguistically competent. The Reader would discover that his interpretation of a statute was convincing if it moved its listeners by its language, no matter how riddling or smoky. Its memorability was yoked to its value as entertainment.

In a more general sense, the Inns provided their Fellows with an education that suited the character of the work they would be called on to do. The language of the law was spoken not only in the courts of the land but also well outside the institutions that gave it formal hearings. As G. M. Young suggests, its purview was extra-local; it traveled from region to region and addressed all social classes: "We must remember that Star Chamber and Chancery, the Courts and the Inns, the stories that came back from assizes, and the evidence of rustics taken on commission, furnished a mirror in which the whole of English life from high to low could be observed."[12] That "mirror" was, of course, a constructed reflection of the myriad aspects of daily life, made up of the interpretation of the words in statutes, judicial decisions, and yes, perhaps even accounts of the ordinary business of the kingdom that never made its way into formal legal settings. In a diminutive form, its confrontational rhetoric of hypothesis, contradiction, and the exposition of the counterfactual were represented in the comedies performed at the Inns of Court.

Staged by the readers of Gray's Inn in 1566, George Gascoigne's translation of Ariosto's *I Soppositi* (1551) exemplifies the kind of wordplay heard at the "readings" performed at the Inns.[13] It represents the careers of characters who have supposed, assumed, or presumed knowledge of a condition or situation, characters who are often in error as well as in doubt. Do their suppositions prove true or do they await embarrassing falsification? And if what they have supposed to be true proves false, is the result detrimental to them as persons or merely disconcerting? Are they witless dupes of deception or deluded exponents of folly?

The action of the play is intricately complex. It features the kind of disputative questioning that characterized the "readings" at the Inns.[14] Two important "supposes" create the pretext for its action, each noted in an aside in the printed body of the text. First, Pasyphilo, identified as a "Parasite," overhears what he takes to be the servant Dulipo's seduction of Polynesta, the young mistress of the house, and exclaims: "O God, how men may be deceived in a woman! Who wold have believed the contrary but that she had bin a virgin?"[15] This "servant," whom Pasyphilo has called "Dulipo," is actually Erostrato, a rich gentleman who intends to marry Polynesta and therefore behaves creditably. And later, Philogano, the actual Dulipo's actual master and Erostrato's father, cannot believe his "servant Dulipo" (the actual Erostrato) will not recognize him: "Alas, who shall relieve my miserable estate? to whome shall I complaine, since he whom I brought up of a childe, yea, and cherished him as if he had bene mine owne, doth nowe utterly denie to knowe me?"[16] Philogano is therefore disappointed not by the behavior of a man he takes to be his former servant but by his son, whom (supposing him to have been murdered) he now seeks (although he does not recognize him when he confronts him). In a further complication of the plot, Erostrato, because he wishes to marry without his father's consent, will later create a false father, who will be impersonated by Scenaese, a stranger, and will consent to his "son's", that is, Erostrato's, marriage to Polynesta. In a series of similarly frustrated "supposes," the play dramatizes how the assumptions characters make about what they see and hear have allowed them to take unsuitable, inappropriate, and even dangerous actions. Some such "supposes" are merely accidental; others are contrived as deliberately fraudulent. Here the question becomes one of intention: is the fraud a benign deception, designed to benefit a person or company, or is it invested with a criminal intent?

Supposes concludes without demonstrating how to find answers to such questions. Its multiple instances of essentially benign fraud – the play lacks a villain and correspondingly a hero – are clarified by a simple confrontation between Philogano and his feigned counterpart that then leads to a general unmasking. Identities are established without violence; those who have been guilty of trickery are revealed as harmless clowns. Its discoveries reveal intentions to be someone, to do something. Dramatizing a state of being as a form of potency, its characters hover on the brink of being, living in a pseudo-reality that is always just beyond realization. Why might *Supposes* have appealed to the members of the Inns? Lawyers cannot expect that their investigation of "supposes," that is, hypotheticals, will always resolve the truth or falsehood displayed in a case or conflict. The play's "supposes" are appealing because the mischiefs they address are resolved without harming the reputations of any of its characters.

A generation after Gascoigne staged *Supposes*, Shakespeare's early comedies exploited similar strategies.[17] Suppositions that both delude and inform their characters drive their action. *The Taming of the Shrew* (1590–92), whose subplot describing Lucentio's courtship of Bianca follows the plot of *Supposes*, vividly illustrates the critical function of interpretation. Its characters are required to investigate a case or situation they have no reason to believe is suspect, and finally to acknowledge that its "reality" can be no more than "supposed." The disguises of its principal characters that sustain such misinterpretation prevail effectively to the end of the play. Bianca's suitor Lucentio gains access to Bianca by disguising himself as her tutor, "Cambio"; her second suitor, Hortensio, impersonates a music teacher, "Litio". Bianca supposes they are what they claim to be; her father Baptista is doubtful. Tranio, however, Lucentio's servant who appears as "Lucentio," convinces Baptista that "Cambio's father" has money. Baptista, thus favoring Bianca's marriage to "Cambio," insists on meeting this "father."

What is supposed throughout this subplot is complex: Bianca's courtship is predicated on an assumed identity: her "tutor" "Cambio" is actually Lucentio. More important, the only condition that their courtship demands – that her suitor Lucentio's father be rich – may be doubtful. The stranger who impersonates Lucentio's father is described as a "merchant" or a "pedant"; even so, Bianca's father, Baptista, accepts him as creditworthy. More telling: as Baptista negotiates Bianca's financial status, Bianca and Lucentio elope. The action of the subplot ends by benefitting its actors – its moments of farce end with the conclusion of the principal plot, Petruchio's "education" of his wife, the shrew Katherine, who is actually moved to accept her uxorial persona, that of the obedient wife.[18] What is gained by these successive tropes of supposition? More acutely than *Supposes*, *The Taming of the Shrew* dramatizes a human intelligence willing to forgo (or unable to realize) an interpretation of the evidence, "legalistic" if you will, that could have identified as suspect the identities it confronts. Conspicuously, indeed strategically, absent from the exchanges between its characters is any evidence that they have considered the status of language as trope: as figured and thus requiring interpretation. They are fundamentally literalists.

How to interpret the words of the law and chiefly of statutes was a question whose answers were evolving throughout the fifteenth and sixteenth centuries. As Theodore F. T. Plucknett notes, late medieval statutes were often treated summarily: "courts undoubtedly did disregard statutes when they thought fit, and secondly they expressed no principle of jurisprudence or political theory which would serve as an explanation – still less as a reason – for their attitude."[19] By the middle of the fourteenth century, however, judges began to regard statutes as "texts" that had to be interpreted in order that they address the particularities of the case to be decided. In effect, this gave the law courts and judges a power they had not previously enjoyed. Plowden's contribution to the evolving authority of the courts is evident when we consider his many explanations of the function of equity in the interpretation of statute: "words," it turns out, could be taken "quite contrary to the Letter,"[20] that is, their meaning could be construed and understood as "supposed." Plucknett states that with this power, "lawyers, notably Plowden, gloried in the liberty which the courts enjoyed in playing fast and loose with statutes."[21] By contrast, Baker notes the discipline that Plowden brought to the task of compiling the *Commentaries*:

> he deliberately refrained from reporting inconclusive or extempore discussions, and published only the set-piece debates resulting from formal demurrers, special verdicts, writs of error and motions in banc after trial: cases where a point of law had been settled by a final judgment of record. His method, he announced, led to 'most firmeness and suretie of law.'"[22]

Each of these observations is valid; as a whole, the reports vary in their conclusiveness.

To begin I would like to comment on Plowden's representation of the arguments in the first report in his *Commentaries*, *Reniger vs. Fogossa*, 1551. It indicates the kinds of fluid controversy that were characteristic of the readings at Inns of Court and by extension the theater of supposition associated with their rhetoric. In *Reniger*, the king, represented by his "informer" Robert Reniger, a customs officer and the plaintiff in the case, seeks assurance of a subsidy due him on imports that he claims have been improperly declared by Anthony Fogossa, the defendant, a Spanish merchant shipping woad, a flowering plant that is the source of a blue dye, into the port of Southampton. Fogossa, however, is cleared of default because the reason for his failure to declare is deemed to have been the result of an unintentional and unavoidable accident. The case raises the question of intention as critical to the determination of a crime. In *Reniger*, the question of *mens rea* is set aside because the defendant was helpless before an external reality, a storm at sea, to which reason and prudence forced him to respond in order to save his life, the lives of his sailors, and his ship. He had no intention to defraud the king; he acted prudently, given the conditions. Beyond questions of intention, arguments defending Fogossa allude to a special kind of equity that was due to foreigners. Because many persons were called on to testify, the case acquired a multifaceted character, much like that we gather was typical of readings at the Inns of Court.

Upon leaving Portugal, Fogossa's ship contained 4,500 "kintals" or about 450 kilograms of woad. Just short of Southampton, a storm forced him to toss overboard some of this cargo. Having secured permission to dock at Southampton, he unloaded his remaining cargo at customs. It was then seized by Reniger's servant, Roger Porter, who assumed that it was to be marketed absent any payment of customs and thus was no longer Fogossa property. Fogossa then complained that his goods had been seized unjustly.[23] Having asked Thomas Wells, the customs collector at Southampton, if he could "enter" 2,000 kintals in Wells's book of customs, Fogossa stated that he would pay the "subsidy," that is, custom duty, on that 2,000 kintals and whatever remained (if anything) then in Reniger's custody that must await weighing. Having received "surety" (bond, guarantee) from John Ellen that Fogossa would pay the subsidy that was owed, Wells accepted this "surety" and Fogossa then asked that his woad be weighed and released from the control of customs.

Bradshaw, the Attorney General, states that Fogossa's plea is unbelievable; he dismisses the reason for the customs on the woad in custody not having been paid, namely that Porter has seized it;

he observes that it is up to Wells to weigh the woad and that he has not done so.[24] Sergeant Pollard testifies that the woad in custody can and must be weighed in order to determine what custom is owed on it. But Bradshaw, in conclusion, says none of the evidence that is available is sufficient for the purpose of determining customs, and he asks that Fogossa's woad in customs simply be forfeit. Furthermore, he states that the "Agreement" Fogossa made with Wells to pay subsidy on the woad in custody is insufficient.[25] He is seconded by Griffith, the king's solicitor, who declares that the agreement between Fogossa and Wells is not, in fact, a "perfect" agreement but only a "conversation," a "nude communication," and asks who can say when the woad will be weighed?[26]

Atkins, an attorney for Fogossa, bases his opinion on "Reason":

> For in our Law and in all other Laws there are some things that happen which may not be prevented by foresight nor by any Diligence or possible means be eschewed or avoided and when any such thing happens to a man the law will not punish him for it, for the Law will not punish any man but for his own Default . . . for if the Law should punish a man for an Accident, it would be utterly against Reason.

Therefore Fogossa should be excused from any penalty.[27] Sergeant Saunders, however, dismisses Atkins's understanding of "Reason" and "Accident," and, focusing on the intention of the statute, gives judgment for the king for reasons like those offered by Bradshaw. He insists "although the Statute is general . . . by the Intent of the Legislature it ought to be taken that Way which is most beneficial for the King, inasmuch as it was made for his Benefit and Advancement." The king's interest requires that the agreement in question be "certain"; Fogossa's "Ignorance of the Certainty is an affected Ignorance" because he should have had his cargo weighed; therefore he has not done his duty and is negligent.[28]

Countering further arguments for the king, Robert Brook, a Recorder from London, introduces the concept of a "beneficial" interpretation of statute and advances a subtler claim. He takes the concept of equitable interpretation beyond questions of the letter and to matters of setting and circumstance:

> And as to the construction of the Statute, it seems to me that it shall be taken and construed beneficially for Fogossa being a Stranger, for in the same Statute there is a Request, that all Merchants, as well Denizens as Strangers, coming into this Realm, be well and honestly treated and

demeaned, as they were in the Times of the Kings Progenitors, without Oppression, &c. which Words prove that it was the Intent of the Makers of the Statute that it should be construed favourably for Strangers.

He introduces the possibility of a futurity of outcome: he states that the "Agreement" in question is "good enough and is within the Intent of the Statute; for in many Cases Gifts and Grants shall not be certain at the beginning, and yet shall be good, if there is a Mean to reduce them afterwards to a Certainty."[29] And he continues: it is agreed that the subsidy shall be paid, even though its amount is not specified; also, it is not "material" when the woad shall be weighed because it may be "weighed upon Request."[30] Finally, he asks:

> notwithstanding that the Words of the Statute had been against us (as *in rei veritate* they are not) – for Fogossa being ignorant [of the exact amount of woad cast overboard] could not by any Possibility have compounded or agree more certainly for the Subsidy and therefore Reason will say that we have accomplished the Intent of the Statute . . . [I]t seems to me that Judgment is to be given against the King.[31]

The matter is finally settled by the ingenious argument of Sergeant Pollard, who manages to split the difference between the king's case and that of Fogossa. First, Pollard declares that the king is to be "satisfied": "the Collector on behalf of the King shall have the Subsidy, and this is the principal Thing"; moreover the woad must be weighed (by the collector, Wells) "for without the Certainty be known the King cannot be satisfied," and Fogossa cannot bring an action of trespass against the collector for meddling with the woad because its weighing is justified. Thus there is a "Means" to come to "Certainty," and after that "the King may have his Remedy . . . so that none can deny the Agreement to be good."[32] Second, Pollard maintains that although the statute in question is "penal" and addresses a case of default, Fogossa is to be judged "strictly," that is, narrowly; in this case equity is not to imply or mandate a harsh or extensive penalty. In explaining his position, Pollard plays with a kind of ambivalence: there is a

> Principle in the Common Law that penal Statutes shall be taken strictly, and not extended by Equity to the Penalty is inflicted . . . we see many Cases where the general Words of Statutes shall be restrained and abridged for the Benefit of him upon whom the Penalty is inflicted.[33]

In other words, a strict interpretation of statute does not mean that it will be punitive; it may apply in so limited (or strict) a manner that it will affect few or none of the persons who are at risk. Pollard summarizes his opinion by considering in a more general way how equitable interpretation of the law actually works:

> for in every Law there are some things which when they happen a Man may break the Words of the Law, and yet not break the Law itself; and such Things are exempted out of the Penalty of the Law, and the Law privileges them although they are done against the Letter of it, for breaking the Words of the Law is not breaking the Law, so as the Intent of the Law is not broken.[34]

As I have suggested, Pollard's conclusion is ambivalent, and I would say equitably so. On the one hand, the king has "Assurance of a Subsidy." On the other hand, Fogossa, because of the conditions in which he was forced to take action, is not guilty of "Default" and therefore "judgment is to be given against the King." His portion of his cargo of woad was thrown overboard "in order to avoid the greater Mischief of the Loss of Life" and his agreement with the collector "ought to be adjudged a sufficient Agreement and warranted by the Statute." He is to be discharged and may "go at present without Day."[35] In simple terms, therefore, the plaintiff's right to a subsidy is protected by law and thus the defendant's goods must be weighed and valued accordingly. But at the same time, the defendant is not guilty of default: because of the circumstances leading up to his failure to pay customs on the goods he unloaded at the port, he can be judged to have broken no law. True, he broke "the Words of the Law," but "he shall not be said to have broken the Law." For "where the Words of a Law are broken to avoid a greater Inconvenience; or by Necessity, or Compulsion or involuntary Ignorance, in all these Cases the Law itself is not broken."[36] There is, of course, the larger question of when to go through the literal meaning of a statute to get to a meaning suited to the case in question. Experience is varied; prescription is by definition limited. Law must cover experience even though its words cannot; their significance must be capable of embracing the otherness that virtually every case in which a law is invoked will display. Here *Reniger* submits to a double analysis that yields a kind of conundrum: yes, the merchant obeyed the rules – eventually he paid customs after a considerable delay; and no, the merchant evaded the rules – he did not pay up front. But his delay, occasioned by a rationally encountered ignorance, did not constitute default. Both plaintiff and defendant are satisfied.

Despite or perhaps because of its even-handed conclusion, *Reniger* may be thought to represent an unsatisfactory jurisprudence, at least if considered in the terms we are accustomed to today. But our terms are not those that organized the business in Plowden's courts. Their function yielded to a purely professional sociability that allowed for the kind of decision we find in *Reniger*. As Baker notes:

> Every opportunity for exploring doubts was therefore given [the judges] before judgment was entered. If the judges of one bench had doubts, they could consult the other bench across the hall. If the doubts persisted, they might adjourn for a confabulation in Serjeants' Inn or a full-scale public moot in the Exchequer Chamber. If after all that they still had qualms – they did nothing. Judicial inaction was not seen as a dereliction of duty, as it would be today, because it encouraged and helped parties to settle their differences when the merits were balanced. That is by no means less or more fair than our system, under which – even if the law is doubtful at the outset – the winner takes all.[37]

Far from strange in its historical setting, *Reniger* can be understood to convey the fluid and dynamic character and quality of English law in this, perhaps its most formative, period. The dynamic and conflicted arguments of its lawyers have a performative quality like that characterizing the readings at the Inns. In *Eysten vs. Studd*, 1574,[38] however, Plowden, rejecting the theatricality evident in *Reniger*, demonstrates the cogency and usefulness of interpretive principles that transcend the limits of particular cases and relate to an understanding of law in general.

Eysten provides a much-quoted account of how to interpret the words of a statute so that they fairly convey how they should apply to a particular case. In a rhetorical sense, it counters the ambivalence in *Reniger*. The Court of Common Pleas had ruled that the plaintiff, Thomas Eysten, had no rights to a property occupied by the defendant, Richard Studd, and to justify its decision it invoked 11 H 7, cap. 20, a statute that was intended to protect a child from disinheritance of his or her *father's* property by actions of his or her *mother*: "CAP. XX: Certain Alienations made by the Wife, of the Lands of her deceased Husband, shall be void."[39] That is, the heir to his or her father's property cannot be disinherited by actions of his or her mother.

The case opens with an action of *Ejectione firmae*: Thomas Eyston, plaintiff, sues Richard Studd, defendant. The reasons for the action are as follows: William Latton and his wife Margaret are seized of a "Moiety [i.e. a portion of a real property held by Richard Alexander] . . . in right of said Margaret." (Whether that "right" is hers by join-ture or inheritance is not clear. This will prove critical to the decision in the case.) The Lattons acknowledge the moiety to be Alexander's, with "Warranty of them and the Heirs of the said Margaret against all men." Alexander then renders that moiety back to William and Margaret Latton, and to the heirs of their bodies. This transfer is described as the Lattons' "Purchase" of Alexander's moiety.

The Lattons have a son, John Latton. William Latton dies; his widow Margaret marries Richard Alexander, "whereby they [i.e. the newly wed couple] were seized [of the moiety] . . . in right of the said Margaret in form aforesaid." Then, through a fine imposed on Alexander by John Kettle, Kettle acquires rights to the Lattons' moiety, which he deeds to the use of Alexander, who in turn leases it to Richard Studd. However, John Latton – "supposing that the said Richard Alexander and Margaret by the said fine [imposed on Alexander by Kettle] . . . had forfeited their Estate in the said Moi-ety" – takes possession of it "by Force of the Statute made in the 11th Year of the Reign of King Henry 7" (i.e. 11 H 7, cap. 20); that is, he assumes it is the property of a married couple by virtue of jointure – it is their estate – and he leases it to Thomas Eysten, who evicts Studd. Justifying his claim, Eysten asserts that Alexander, after being fined by Kettle and then deeded the use of the moiety by Kettle, was possessed of the moiety to the exclusion of Margaret: the "land was out of the wife and became the Land of the Conusee," that is, of Alexander, "and it was his own to all Intents . . . and the Estate which the Wife had before was gone out of her" and became her husband's. Its legal character was altered.

Puzzled, the jurors cannot resolve the case: should the fine on Alexander "be a Cause of Forfeiture of the Estate of the said Richard Alexander and Margaret"? If so, then John Latton is in possession and Richard Studd is rightly evicted. But the court finally decides the case in favor of Studd; the reasons are those Plowden outlines in his account of the case: Margaret's moiety is hers not by virtue of jointure but rather of inheritance: "to bar her, after the Death of her Husband, from disposing of her Inheritance, would be contrary too all Reason, and it has no Affinity or Connection with the Matter or Intent of the Statute of II H 7." Studd correspondingly declares that the moiety Alexander and his wife Margaret leased to him was not that of the couple but entirely Margaret's. It was not subject to the condition of a "Purchase." In other words, from the very inception of the exchanges of the moiety, the moiety itself was always Margaret's; it was hers by "right." Had the moiety been Margaret's by jointure, 11 H 7 would have obtained as Eysten had claimed; as it was hers by inheritance, it was less irrelevant than in need of further interpretation.[40]

Looking at this decision that awards the property to Studd, Plowden sees its enigmatic conformity to the original intent of 11 H 7, a statute that protected children from being disinherited of a father's property by the actions of a mother. Plowden insists that the statute is to be understood in the entirety of its intention. It requires what he later refers to as an "extensive" or "enlarged" reading: it was created to prevent a child from being disinherited not only of a father's but also of a mother's property. *Eysten* respects the words of the statute, interpreted, as they should be, in light of their comprehensive intention of protect the property of children.[41]

Here Plowden addresses the issue of interpretation per se; abstracted from the particularities of *Eysten*, he discovers how the words of a statute may acquire meaning in light of the particular mischief they address.

> From this Judgment and the Cause of it the Reader may observe that it is not the Words of the Law but the internal Sense of it that makes the Law, and our Law (like all others) consists of two parts, viz. of Body and Soul, the Letter of the Law is the Body of the Law, and the sense or Reason of the Law is the Soul of the Law: *quia ratio legis est anima legis* . . . And it often happens that when you know the Letter, you know not the Sense, for sometimes the Sense is more confined and contracted than the Letter and sometimes it is more large and extensive. And Equity, which in Latin is called *Equitas*, enlarges or diminishes the Letter according to its Discretion, which Equity is in two ways.[42]

Plowden distinguishes the "internal sense" or "Reason" of the letter of the law as effectively constituting the law; empty of this sense or reason the letter itself is no more than a pretext for construing the law in whatever way the interpreter wishes.

The sense the interpreter seeks to find is a creation of "*Equitas*," the moral agency that can discover what the letter means in light of the case to be decided. An equitable interpretation may reduce the scope of a literal meaning; correspondingly, it may enlarge it. In *Eysten*, the law that applies to a paternal inheritance is to be enlarged so that it applies to a maternal inheritance even though the latter is not mentioned in the words of the statute. Equitable interpretation solicits the interpreter's "Discretion," that is, his or her attention, wit, wisdom, and knowledge of history and the present social order.[43]

Plowden's own appeal to history is remarkable both for what he says and does not say. He refers first to Aristotle, who he notes has observed that "Experience shews us that no Law-makers can foresee all things which may happen and therefore it is fit that if there is any Defect in the Law it should be reformed by Equity which is no part of the Law but a moral Virtue which corrects the Law."[44] From his own experience but also following Aristotle, Plowden then instructs the interpreter of a law how to proceed:

> And in order to form a right Judgment when the Letter of a Statute is restrained, and when enlarged by Equity it is a good Way, when you peruse a Statute, to suppose that the Law-maker is present, and that you have asked him the Question you want to know touching the Equity, then you must give yourself such an Answer as you imagine he would have done, if he had been present.[45]

And although Fortescue also relied on the imagination as a heuristic tool – "we need in this case to vse coniecture and ymaginacion"[46] – his reference is limited to a single case, that is, "in this case." Plowden establishes it as a working principle that contributes to a virtual methodology of mind:

> [T]herefore when such Cases happen which are within the Letter, or out of the Letter, of a Statute, and yet don't directly fall within the plain and natural Purport of the Letter, but are in some Measure to be conceived in a different Idea from that which the Text seems to express, it is a good Way to put Questions and give Answers to yourself thereupon, in the same Manner as if you were actually conversing with the Maker of such Laws, and by this Means you will easily find out what is the Equity of those Cases.[47]

Plowden's advice looks not only to a present but also indicates a future yet to be inscribed in memory; it is the interpreter's part also to look forward, to fashion in his mind what the lawgiver would make of a present he could not yet know.

Plowden's reference to the "Idea" inhering in a statute that the letter of its "Text" may not fully express invites expansive interpretation. It recalls the efforts of an audience to piece together the disparate parts of a play, and more vividly the system of interrogation at readings at the Inns. These processes are concluded when the audience is satisfied that the drama it has witnessed is both plausible and memorable, and more decisively when the Reader makes up his mind that he has discovered the correct reading of the statute under review. Summarizing the significance of *Eysten*, Plowden describes a kind of reliance on a concept of equity "notwithstanding the Words of the Law" that stretches the authority of the words of the statute to virtual breaking point: he seems to be saying that the act of discovering an "answer" to the question of how a statute is to be interpreted may require, if not an actual rewriting of that statute, at least a modification of the literal meaning of its words, and he assures his reader that such a procedure conforms to what is equitable: "for while you do no more than the Law-maker would have done, you do not act contrary to the Law, but in Conformity to it."[48] Here, in effect, Plowden makes the interpreter of a statute its quasi-author.[49]

Notes

1. Edmund Plowden, *The Commentaries or Reports* [1578] (London: Edward Brooke, 1779).
2. Geoffrey Parmiter, *Edmund Plowden, an Elizabethan Recusant lawyer* (Catholic Record Society, 1987), 55–6.
3. Geoffrey Parmiter, *Elizabethan Popish Recusancy in the Inns of Court* (London: University of London, Institute of Historical Research, 1976), 6–7.
4. Parmiter, *Edmund Plowden*, 106–8.
5. The document does not exist; this extract is from a copy. See Parmiter, *Edmund Plowden*, 137.
6. Ibid., 13–14.
7. J. H. Baker, *Readers and Readings in the Inns of Court* (London: Seldon Society, 2000), 229–30.
8. *State of the Fellowship of the Middle Temple*, BL Cotton Ms., 1539; printed in W. Dugdale, *Origines Juridiciales* (1680), quoted in Baker, *Readers*, 232.
9. For an account of these "readings," see Karen Cunningham, *Imaginary Betrayals: Subjectivity and the Discourse of Treason in Early Modern England* (Philadelphia: University of Pennsylvania Press, 2002), 23–39. See also W. R. Prest, *The Inns of Court 1590–1640* (London: Longmans, 1972).
10. Sir Edward Coke, *The first part of the Institutes* (1628), cited in Baker, *Readers*, 237, who refers to Coke on *Lyttilton Tenures truely translated into Englysshe* (1538). Coke edited Littleton's *Tenures* in *The first part of the Institutes of the laws of England. Or a commentarie on Littleton*, first published in 1481 in law French.

11. Baker, *Readers*, 237.

12. G. M. Young, *Shakespeare and the Termers* (London: G. Cumberlege, 1947), 15.

13. See Lorna Hutson, "The Evidential Plot: Shakespeare and Gascoigne at Gray's Inn," in *The Intellectual and Cultural World of the Early Modern Inns of Court*, ed. Jayne Elisabeth Archer, Elizabeth Goldring, and Sarah Knight (Manchester: Manchester University Press, 2011), 245–63.

14. Charles Gayley cogently observes that Ariosto's play was "done into English, not for the vulgar, but for the more advanced taste of the translator's own Inn of Court; it has, therefore, qualities to captivate those who are capable of appreciating high comedy . . . Both whimsical and grave, its ironies are pro bono publico; it is constructive as well as critical, imaginative as well as actual." *Representative English Comedies*, vol. 1 (New York: Macmillan, 1903), lxxxiv–v.

15. George Gascoigne, *Supposes and Jocasta*, ed. John W. Cunliffe (Boston: D.C. Heath, 1906), 57.

16. Ibid., 76.

17. For Shakespeare's connection with activities at the Inns of Court, see O. Hood Phillips, *Shakespeare and the Lawyers* (London: Routledge, 1972), 23–36.

18. Shakespeare's late comedies also reflect the rhetoric of supposition. *The Merchant of Venice* exemplifies the fluid quality of justice illustrated in the *Commentaries*. The most telling of the play's departures from established legal practice is figured in the vexed though unremarked status of Portia, the "judge", who is neither qualified for the task of judging and thus fraudulent in assuming the role of judge in Shylock's case, nor disinterested in the actual outcome of the trial over which she presides; she is actually a party to the case. See Thomas Bilello, "Accomplished with what she lacks: Law, Equity, and Portia's Con," in *The Law in Shakespeare*, ed. Constance Jordan and Karen Cunningham (Basingstoke: Palgrave Macmillan, 2007), 109–26.

19. Theodore F. T. Plucknett, *A Concise History of the Common Law* (Boston: Little, Brown, 1956), 323.

20. Plowden, *Commentaries*, 205.

21. Plucknett, *Concise History*, 332–4. See J. H. Baker on the early understanding of a statutory text: "texts had no special authority in themselves. In the early days when judges helped to draw statutes in parliament, and were therefore closely acquainted with underlying policy, it is not surprising to find them applying that policy rather than the letter of the text." *An Introduction to English Legal History* (London: Butterworths, 1979), 239.

22. Plowden, *Commentaries*, prologue, quoted in J. H. Baker, "English Law and the Renaissance," *The Cambridge Law Journal* 44 (1985): 60.

23. Plowden, *Commentaries*, 1.

24. Ibid., 2.
25. Ibid., 4.
26. Ibid., 5.
27. Ibid., 8.
28. Ibid., 11.
29. Ibid., 12.
30. Ibid., 13.
31. Ibid., 14.
32. Ibid., 15–17.
33. Ibid., 17.
34. Ibid., 18.
35. Ibid., 20.
36. Ibid., 19, 20.
37. Baker, "English Law and the Renaissance," 58.
38. Plowden, *Commentaries*, 459–64.
39. John Cay, *The statutes at large from Magna Carta to the thirtieth year of King George the second*, 6 vols. (London: Thomas Baskett, 1758), 1:723–4.
40. Plowden, *Commentaries*, 463, 464. Further analyzing the decision, Carolyn Sale observes: "to reach this judgment the justices in *Eyston v. Studd* had to resist the assumptions about patriarchy, property, and coverture that Dyer promulgated in his report of *Hales v. Petit*. . . [T]hey granted her holding an integrity unaffected by coverture." "The Amending Hand," in *The Law in Shakespeare*, ed. Karen Cunningham and Constance Jordan (Basingstoke: Palgrave Macmillan, 2007), 195–7.
41. For an analysis of *Eyston vs. Studd* and cases relating to the legal status of women, see Sale, "The Amending Hand," 189–207.
42. Plowden, *Commentaries*, 465.
43. For an account of the development of equitable jurisdiction in the sixteenth century, see Stuart E. Prall, "The Development of Equity in Tudor England," *The American Journal of Legal History* 8 (1964): 1–19. For the interpretation of statute before Plowden's *Commentaries*, see S. E. Thorne, "The Equity of Statute and Heydon's Case," *Illinois Law Review* 31 (1936–37): 202–17.
44. Plowden, *Commentaries*, 466.
45. Ibid., 467.
46. John Fortescue sees that equity is essential to the king's exercise of power because "oftentimes the written law lies as it were dead under a covering of words"; in such instances, equity will rouse the law's "vital spirit as if from sleep" and "fulfill a law by reason of the law of nature." *De Natura Legis Naturae*, chap. 24, quoted in J. W. Tubbs, *The Common Law Mind: Medieval and Early Modern Conceptions* (Baltimore: Johns Hopkins University Press, 2000), 94–5.
47. Plowden, *Commentaries*, 467 (my italics).

48. Ibid., 467.
49. For the above and other cases in Plowden's *Commentaries*, see Tubbs, *The Common Law Mind*, 110–28; for an analysis of Plowden's concept of a "consideration" as a feature of contract law, see Baker, *English Legal History*, 386–8.

Part II

Audience Judgment: Deliberation in the Theater

"Gently to hear, kindly to judge": Minds at Work in *Henry V*

Katherine B. Attié

In the tavern scene of *1 Henry IV*, Falstaff and Prince Harry enact a "play extempore" as a rehearsal for Hal's royal beratement the following day.[1] Falstaff prompts the prince, "thou wilt be horribly chid tomorrow when thou comest to thy father. If thou love me, practise an answer" (2.5.340–1). Harry is perfectly happy to play along: "Do thou stand for my father, and examine me upon the particulars of my life" (2.5.342–3). The critical attention is supposed to be on Harry, but true to form, Falstaff steals the show – the scene's ebullient humor depends on the fat knight's self-inflation and subsequent rebuke. Playing the king, Falstaff sings the praises of that "goodly, portly man" (2.5.384) with whom the prince spends so much time, then Harry, playing the king, lays into "that bolting-hutch of beastliness, that swollen parcel of dropsies, that huge bombard of sack" (2.5.410–11) and so on, forging a brilliant chain of metonymns with which to adorn the lord of misrule. While the rhetorical elaboration of Falstaff's character makes for delightful theater, it is something of a red herring, because the real point is to practice judging Harry. When the sparring partners switch roles, Falstaff is forced into a different rhetorical position, exchanging a braggart's pride for a supplicant's plea. But even after the switch, Harry's position remains constant: standing before his father's throne of judgment, he is everywhere pointed at and complained of as an "ungracious boy" (2.5.406).

Framing this metatheatrical scene are Mistress Quickly and the tavern patrons, the members of the onstage audience, who are not openly judging the prince but the performance and judging it favorably. Even as Falstaff assumes the part of a king/father judging his wayward prince/son for his bad behavior, he simultaneously anticipates his own acting being judged. And he knows exactly what prop he needs to help him play the part convincingly: "Give me a cup of sack to make my eyes look red, that it may be thought I have wept; for I must speak in passion, and I will do it in King Cambyses' vein" (2.5.350–2). As Falstaff gets into character, Mistress Quickly does indeed judge his performance kindly: "O Jesu, this is excellent sport, i'faith . . . O the Father, how he holds his countenance! . . . he doth it as like one of these harlotry players as ever I see!" (2.5.356, 358, 361–2). These aesthetic judgments may not be sophisticated, but they are aesthetic judgments nonetheless: the spectator is affirming that the performance pleases her, which is of course what Shakespeare and his "harlotry players" wanted to hear from groundlings and gentles alike.

I begin with the tavern scene's playlet because, with respect to how it represents moral and aesthetic judgment as simultaneous but separable activities, it is the Henriad in microcosm. Across the two parts of *Henry IV* and *Henry V*, Shakespeare developed a narrative pattern in which other characters judge Harry on moral grounds. Implicitly, Shakespeare expected his audience to do the same. But while he expected and even encouraged audiences to differ in their moral judgments, he cultivated "the unifying effect of publicly exercised critical judgment."[2] Irrespective of whether or not audiences were wild about Harry, Shakespeare wanted them all to take pleasure in the play – to agree wholeheartedly with Mistress Quickly, "this is excellent sport, i'faith." In what follows, I consider how the Chorus directs aesthetic judgment of the play before turning to how Shakespeare dramatizes ethical judgment in the play. I concentrate on *Henry V* because it is the play in which, due to the king's instigation of war with France, the moral stakes of judging Harry are the highest. At the same time, I show that the Henriad as a whole establishes a pattern of judging Harry's character and fitness for rule, a pattern that starts "high," with the judgment of his father Henry IV, and ends "low," with the judgment of the enlisted man Williams – a commoner who thinks critically about and speaks truth to power. I conclude that while aesthetic and ethical judgments can and do diverge, they are alike in their requirement of mental labor, which produces something meaningful and which ennobles the common spectator in Shakespeare's audience even as it ennobles the common soldier in Harry's army.

The problem *qua* problem of the protagonist's ethics points back to Norman Rabkin and his familiar picture of *Henry V* as a "rabbit/duck" whose "rival gestalts" present irreconcilable alternatives: either we see "an exemplary Christian monarch" who is the last of England's chivalrous warrior-kings, or we see "a Machiavellian militarist who professes Christianity but whose deeds reveal both hypocrisy and ruthlessness."[3] For Rabkin, this moral ambiguity "is the heart of the matter," perhaps even suggesting "a crisis in Shakespeare's spiritual life" as the playwright found himself hopelessly deadlocked.[4] Unable to choose between opposite views, Shakespeare forces his audience "to share his conflict" and to reach our own "point of crisis" as we confront in frustration the main character's inscrutability.[5] I see two main problems with Rabkin's argument. First, he makes Shakespeare sound far less in control of his dramatic material than he actually was. Second, and most important for my purposes, his analysis effectively removes the moral "heart of the matter" from its aesthetic body. Shakespeare purposefully and dispassionately designed this play to be an exercise in judgment, an opportunity for his audience to work their thoughts upon Henry's motives, methods, and morals. But for the playwright, audience judgment of a particular character is always set within and subordinate to their judgment of the play as a whole. Ultimately, *pace* Rabkin, it was of little consequence to Shakespeare whether his audience approved of Henry V. It was of great consequence to him whether they approved of *Henry V*. Not in a moral but in a critical sense, the Chorus promotes "an overall homogeneity of response . . . the single audience member is encouraged . . . to surrender his individual function in favour of the larger unit of which he is a part."[6] This is not to suggest that moral and aesthetic judgments have nothing to do with one another. On the contrary, Shakespeare aestheticizes the process of moral judgment on two levels: first, he thematizes it in the play whenever other characters judge Harry and whenever Harry responds to their judgments; and second, he encourages his audience to draw their own conclusions about the morals of the prince. Thus for the spectator, moral judgment, and the work of thinking required by it, become a part of the pleasure of playgoing, a part of the aesthetic experience of theater.

Drama, like all narrative arts, is inherently incomplete; "every narrative makes an indeterminate number of presuppositions and it is the task of readers, viewers and listeners to fill these in."[7] Using this incompleteness to his advantage, Shakespeare wooed his audience by addressing them as partners in the collaborative work of playmaking. Here too, the Chorus is key to bridging the distance between actors and audience, between creative invention and critical judgment, as he turns theatrical inadequacy to rhetorical enticement. When he bids the audience to "Still be kind, / And eke out our performance with your mind" (*Henry V*, 3.0.34–5), the Chorus calls attention both to the limitations of the playing space and to the incompleteness of the play's historical narrative. As Jeremy Lopez has argued, dramatists and audiences alike "were very much aware of the limitations of the early modern stage . . . the potential for dramatic representation to be ridiculous or inefficient or incompetent was a constant and vital part of audiences' experience of the plays."[8] No play articulates these limitations more explicitly than *Henry V*, and no play uses them more strategically in winning over an audience. If the spectators help imaginatively to build or "make" the play, as it were, they become invested in it as co-creators, hence they are more likely to judge it favorably. Shakespeare's Chorus is a Brechtian figure in that he calls attention to theatrical artifice as such, while the play as a whole is Brechtian in that the audience is kept at an emotional distance from the characters. This distance empowers the audience to judge King Harry's behavior on ethical grounds. At the same time, the Chorus presents himself as the audience's "colleague in a necessary creative endeavour."[9] The creative endeavor by which actors and audience forge an aesthetic whole, or "force – perforce – a play" (2.0.32), must also be a collective endeavor. Addressing the playgoers as a community of thinkers, the Chorus compels them all to identify, empathize, and cooperate with the professional players by "completing" the play, as it were. This is not a theater of alienation but a theater of collaboration, one ingeniously designed to make it possible for all spectators to like the play even while some spectators may dislike the main character or censure his behavior.

The question of whether and how aesthetic judgment and ethical judgment interconnect has preoccupied a number of contemporary philosophers, including Noël Carroll, whose theory of "moderate moralism" is especially germane to my reading.[10] I accept (and I think Shakespeare would accept) moderate moralism's basic tenet that for some works of art, moral evaluation is appropriate, and a work's moral implications contribute to its aesthetic effect. When a play "[activates] moral judgements from audiences,"[11] as *Henry V* is designed to do, the audience helps complete the play in part by supplying its moral meaning. A problem arises, however, in how Carroll judges an audience's judgment: "Securing the right moral response of the audience is as much a part of the design of a narrative artwork as structural components like plot complications. Failure to elicit the right moral response, then, is a failure in the design of the work, and, therefore, is an aesthetic failure."[12] But what is, or what is intended to be, the "right" moral response to *Henry V*? And thus we come back to rabbits and ducks, about which the moderate moralist presumably would say the following: the play's ethical ambivalence is an aesthetic flaw insofar as it impedes audience comprehension and narrative intelligibility. For this position to be tenable, one must pre-suppose that there is a "right" moral response to be expected from those who truly understand the play.

In a subsequent essay, Carroll more prudently steers clear of mor-alizing the outcome of judgment and focuses instead on judging as a cognitive process: "[narratives] provide us with opportunities to . . . exercise our moral powers," and our aesthetic assessment of the narra-tive may rest in part "upon the quality of that moral activity or experi-ence" of moral judging.[13] Carroll describes how a morally absorbing story affects an audience: "In the course of engaging a given narrative we may need to reorganize the hierarchical orderings of our moral cat-egories and premises, or to reinterpret those categories and premises in the light of new paradigm instances and hard cases."[14] Seen in this light, the "hard case" of King Henry's ethics is a pleasurable challenge, a nar-rative complexity, and an aesthetic virtue. Even more fundamentally, moral alternativity is an aesthetic tool by which Shakespeare formally structures and balances the play, as he systematically subverts, depre-cates, or parodies – but stops short of invalidating – his own represen-tations of Harry's heroism, England's greatness, and war's justness.

Like Hamlet's "to be or not to be" speech, the moral ambiguity of *Henry V* owes something to Shakespeare's grammar school educa-tion and the rhetorical training he received there. As Joel Altman has explained, schoolboys in the early modern period learned "to argue *in utramque partem* – on both sides of the question."[15] For dramatists, this training manifested itself in their plays as "frequently disconcert-ing shifts of viewpoint" such as we encounter in *Henry V*, which is especially illustrative of the dialectical structure found in early mod-ern drama: "The plays are essentially questions, not statements at all . . . [they] functioned as media of intellectual and emotional explora-tion for minds that were accustomed to examine the many sides of a given theme, to entertain opposing ideals . . . Thus the *experience* of the play was the thing."[16] Altman's generalization helpfully eluci-dates *Henry V*, but only up to a point. His claim that the theatrical experience was "set apart from that of ordinary life, so as to provide a leisured *otium*" does not square with Shakespeare's representation of spectatorship as intellectual labor.[17] "Work, work your thoughts" (*Henry V*, 3.0.25), urges the Chorus, invoking an Aristotelian under-standing of thought as a kind of *technê* – craft or skill. And skill, as Evelyn Tribble has shown, "is profoundly social . . . the development of expertise builds upon internal mechanisms of perception and atten-tion, situated within an embodied and socially rich environment" like that of the public theater.[18]

To return to the tavern playlet for a moment, Falstaff grandiosely invites the crowd to decide which player-king they prefer: "Judge, my masters," says the knight to the commoners, whom he jokingly calls "nobility" at the start of the scene (*1 Henry IV*, 2.5.355). To be sure, Falstaff is speaking ironically. At the same time, when he imagines the tavern audience as upper class, Falstaff holds a flattering mirror up to Shakespeare's audience. His socially inflating mode of address anticipates the rhetorical strategy of the Chorus, who similarly addresses the socially diverse audience in the Globe as "gentles all" (*Henry V*, 1.0.8), thereby making their mental participation not only ordinary and productive but also dignified and respectable. Granted, class difference remains sharply defined within the narrative frame of the choric speeches: the king visits both "mean and gentle" (4.0.45) on the eve of Agincourt; upon his victorious return to London he is welcomed by "The Mayor and all his brethren, in best sort, / Like to the senators of th'antique Rome / With the plebeians swarming at their heels" (5.0.25–7). But when the Chorus steps outside the historical frame and into the metatheatrical moment, he ennobles every tailor, tinker, and tapster in Shakespeare's audience when he beseeches them "Gently to hear, kindly to judge, our play" (1.0.33–4). Although this plea has been described as merely conventional, "like any number of Elizabethan prologues,"[19] it is transformed by the public theater into something more significant. As Ann Jennalie Cook contends, "[a]t the public places, playgoers were customers; in the private places, they were guests."[20] At the Globe, customers were addressed like guests. They were invited to imagine themselves in a higher social rank as freely as they imagined the onstage action moving from England to France or from court to battlefield. As a metadramatic figure, the Chorus seems especially designed to cultivate what Paul Yachnin calls the "populuxe theatre," which "afforded the cultural consumers of Shakespeare's time an opportunity to play at being their social 'betters' and a limited mastery of the system of social rank itself."[21] The public theater was selling among other things a social fantasy; "[a]t commercial locations, where placement depended on payment, money could overturn rank."[22] Even so, whether standing anonymously among the groundlings or seated conspicuously in the stalls, "every person with the price of admission could recapitulate what kings, peers, gentlemen, and scholars did simply by watching the performance of many of the same works shown in more exclusive settings."[23] Shakespeare played to and played up the "gentling" of the general audience because he knew it was one of the pleasures that kept ordinary people coming back to the theater.

Shakespeare's need for the enthusiasm of his audience corresponded to Harry's need for the enthusiasm of his troops. The Chorus prefigures the king's rhetorical strategy before the Battle of Agincourt, when he famously inspires his common soldiers by ennobling them: "For he today that sheds his blood with me / Shall be my brother; be he ne'er so vile, / This day shall gentle his condition" (4.3.61–3). Of course, the "gentling" of these soldiers is temporary;[24] after the battle, when the king reads the English death roll, he identifies only four titled gentlemen before dismissing the fallen commoners as "None else of name, and of all other men / But five-and-twenty" (4.8.99–100). His erstwhile "band of brothers" (4.3.60) end up as numbers of nameless men. The gentling of Shakespeare's audience is also temporary, lasting only so long as the play itself. And yet there is a sense in which the audience does carry some power – the power of critical judgment – out into the community. Just as Harry could not conquer France without the efforts of common soldiers, Shakespeare could not conquer the London theater scene without the charitable judgments of groundlings who tell their friends his plays are worth a penny. He wooed the public by taking the indispensible rhetorical convention of courtly authorship – self-deprecation in the interest of flattering a powerful patron – and democratizing it by tailoring it to the playhouse. Where *Venus and Adonis* and *The Rape of Lucrece* have their dedications to the Earl of Southampton, *Henry V* has its Chorus. In private poem and public playhouse alike, "our bending author" (Epilogue, 2) stoops to conquer.

Even though Shakespeare had compelling economic reasons to flatter his paying audience, it would be a mistake to dismiss the Chorus's respectful mode of address as mere flattery. His rhetorical preferment reflects the inherent dignity of the mental labor he asks the audience to perform. As Aristotle asserted, judging something well "is the same as judging it nobly."[25] Implicitly affirming the nobility of good judgment, Shakespeare creates a platform where every auditor, regardless of his social status, is asked to think and to judge for himself. The important point is that regular folk who congregate in the Globe are not only capable of critical judgment but also dignified by it. They are dignified by moral judgment too, which Shakespeare makes a function of reason. I think he would have warmed to Hannah Arendt's democratization of moral thought: "If the ability to tell right from wrong should have anything to do with the ability to think, then we must be able to 'demand' its exercise in every sane person no matter how erudite or ignorant . . . the faculty of thinking . . . must be ascribed to everybody; it cannot be a privilege of the few."[26] Shakespeare implied as much through the Chorus's democratic calls to contemplation, in which the faculty of thinking is ascribed to everybody.

Of course, well-educated early moderns routinely denied that uneducated people could judge anything intelligently. Supposedly weak in the noble faculty of reason, the masses were thought to crave only the baser pleasures of the senses. Interestingly, Shakespeare gives this opinion to one of his best villains, Claudius, who complains to Laertes that Hamlet is "loved of the distracted multitude, / Who like not in their judgement but their eyes" (*Hamlet*, 4.3.4–5). Hamlet clearly does not love them back. Privileging his own educated judgment over that of "unskillful" (3.2.23) and "barren spectators" (3.2.37), the prince recalls his favorite speech from a play that "pleased not the million. 'Twas caviar to the general. But it was – as I received it, and others whose judgements in such matters cried in the top of mine – an excellent play, well digested in the scenes, set down with as much modesty as cunning" (2.2.418–22). According to Hamlet, a discerning critic found "no matter in the phrase that might indict the author of affectation" (2.2.423–4). Yet the speech Hamlet loves so much, Aeneas's account of Priam's slaughter by Pyrrhus (2.2.430–98), turns out to be a veritable showcase of affectation. Shakespeare deliberately (and I think gleefully) lays it on thick; it is hard to imagine him keeping a straight face while writing the line, "But who, O who had seen the mobbled queen" (2.2.482). By composing a speech that is stilted and swollen with rhetorical pretense, the playwright undercuts his main character's judgment and implicitly affirms the wisdom of the crowd. Granted, Shakespeare's usual adjectives for the general public are rarely complimentary: "the multitude" is consistently described across a range of plays as "wav'ring" (*2 Henry VI*, 1.0.19), "giddy" (*2 Henry VI*, 2.4.22), "rude" (*2 Henry VI*, 3.2.135), "ragged" (*2 Henry VI*, 4.4.31), "fool" (*Merchant of Venice*, 2.9.25), "barbarous" (*Merchant of Venice*, 2.9.32), and "many-headed" (*Coriolanus*, 2.3.15). Nevertheless, I am suggesting that Shakespeare thought of the theatergoing public as transformed, if only temporarily, by the work of judgment: once the "fool multitude" becomes a judging audience, charged with evaluating both the aesthetic value and the moral meaning of what they see, they are empowered and ennobled by their intellectual labor.

By implying that the common theatergoer was capable of judging good from bad and right from wrong, Shakespeare opposes the standard argument of sixteenth-century antitheatrical tracts. Even though it had been seventeen years since the publication of Stephen Gosson's

Playes Confuted in Fiue Actions (1582), the critical debate still had momentum at the turn of the century; Sir Philip Sidney's own rebuttal of Gosson, *The Defence of Poesie*, would have re-energized the debate when it was published in 1595. Gosson's attack on the public theater was in large part an attack on the playhouse audience, an "assemblie of Tailers, Tinkers, Cordwayners, Saylers, olde Men, yong Men, Women, Boyes, Girles, and such like."[27] In his contempt for the multitude, Gosson took for granted the intellectual and moral weakness of "the meaner sorte," whom he considered utterly incapable of distinguishing good from evil when they are mixed together in a play:

> At Stage Plaies . . . no indifferency of iudgement can be had, beecause the worste sorte of people haue the hearing of it, which in respecte of there ignorance, of there fickleness, and of there furie, are not to bee admitted in place of iudgement. A Iudge must be graue, sober, discreete, wise, well exercised in cases of gouernement, which qualities are neuer founde in the baser sort.[28]

Yet the contrary notion, that good judgment is not an outcome of education or social privilege but is a natural ability, has a long philosophical heritage. In the *Nichomachean Ethics*, Aristotle attributes the power of judgment to the common man: "no one is held to be wise by nature, though he may by nature have discernment, judgment and intellect."[29] Cicero understood aesthetic judgment (unlike aesthetic making) to be innate: "Considering the great difference between the expert and the unschooled in terms of performance, it is remarkable how little they differ when it comes to making a judgment."[30] In late sixteenth-century England, Cambridge rhetorician Richard Rainolde asserted that "Nature hath indued every man, with a certain eloquence, and also subtilitee to reason and discusse of any question or proposicion propounded," while his fellow Cambridgian Abraham Fraunce asked pointedly, "Coblers bee men, why therefore not Logicians? And Carters haue reason, why therefore not Logike?"[31] For his part, Shakespeare would not have *Henry V*'s Chorus say to the mass of spectators, "Work, work your thoughts" (3.0.25) if he believed them incapable of serious thought in the first place. Moreover, the valorization of intellectual labor in *Henry V* served to refute the standard antitheatrical equation of playgoing with idleness. As Andrew Gurr has established,

> Playgoing in London was viewed even by the playgoers as an idle occupation. The largest numbers who went to the Globe were apprentices

and artisans taking time off from work, often surreptitiously . . . These
fugitives were linked with the wealthier kind of idler, "gallants" or rich
gentlemen and other men of property, along with soldiers and sailors on
leave from the wars.[32]

However, by keeping the audience busy working their thoughts, the
Chorus turns the playgoers' idle hours into a period of productive
mental exertion, and as he does so, Shakespeare turns a major antitheatrical assumption on its head.

From the moment the play opens, the Chorus privileges not
theatrical spectacle but the labor that goes into making theatrical
spectacle. Exposing the structure of the humble but solid frame
on which this entertainment is built, he invokes and immediately
deflates the very idea of "the swelling scene" in which a mythol-
ogized Harry "Assume[s] the port of Mars" (*Henry V*, 1.0.6).
Instead, he grounds us in the reality of the players' workspace "On
this unworthy scaffold . . . Within this wooden O" (1.0.10, 13). In
the absence of "a muse of fire, to ascend / The brightest heaven of
invention" (1.0.1–2), the players will need to enlist the concerted
effort of the audience; only their active imaginations can "bring
forth / So great an object" (1.0.10–11) as this epic history. The Chorus humbly asks for permission to use the audience in this way, to
"let us . . . On your imaginary forces work" (1.0.17–18). Coming
precisely at the midpoint of the passage, the full stop puts metri-
cal, rhetorical, and thematic weight on the word "work." This is
also the point at which the passage pivots from the inadequacy of
the stage to the agility of the mind. Instead of casting the audience
members as passive beholders of the action unfolding before them,
the actors work at playing in order to help the audience work at
thinking. Belying Claudius's opinion that the multitude "like not
in their judgement but their eyes," the Chorus asks the audience to
compensate for the play's visual shortcomings and to judge it kindly
despite the lack of spectacle. Instructing them to "make imaginary
puissance" (1.0.25), he refers to both the product of the audience's
fancy – the legions of military forces that they will pretend to see –
and the process of invention itself, the "imaginary forces" (1.0.18)
of their minds at work, as they share in the prerogative of the poet
as maker. For his part, George Puttenham liked the English term
"maker" for poet: "it giveth to the name and profession no small
dignity and preeminence above all other artificers, scientific or
mechanical."[33] While ennobling the poet, particularly the poet writing in the vernacular, to the level of godlike craftsman, Puttenham's

gloss on "maker" also places the poet in the social class of "arti-ficers" or artisans, albeit at the top of that class. His rhetorical strategy, like Shakespeare's dramatic one, encourages admiration and respect for the ordinary English craftsman along with the English poet who proves the literary worth of the vulgar tongue. More industrious artisan than idle aristocrat, the English "maker" takes a common, humble language and turns it into something beautiful.

In a seeming departure from the flattering conceit of an entirely "gentle" audience, Shakespeare figures them as artisans in order to figure their mental efforts as materially productive. Addressing the audience members not merely as creative collaborators but as creative superiors, the Chorus respectfully requests that they con-descend to "Piece out our imperfections with your thoughts . . . For 'tis your thoughts that now must deck our kings" (1.0.23, 28). Even though the audience is "gentle," they are busy and productive, using their minds to "deck" the royals as carefully as court tailors use their hands. At the start of Act 5, the Chorus aligns the audience with blacksmiths when he prompts them to make something "In the quick forge and working-house of thought" (5.0.23). Strikingly unlike Arendt's characterization of thinking as a "soundless solitary dialogue" and an interruption of "all doing, all ordinary activities no matter what they happen to be,"[34] Shakespeare's artisanal metaphor transforms thinking into a noisy, cooperative, and above all ordinary activity, which in turn transforms the theater into a site of "[h]abitu-ation, routine, and domestication."[35] For a company playwright who needed to bring the same audience back repeatedly, the figurative association of audience cognition with artisanal routine had positive commercial implications: "it was, perversely, the theater industry's operative strategy to convert sport into work, to rebrand theatrical attendance from 'playing holidays' into the tediousness, or at least regularity, of a workaday enterprise."[36]

In its industrial, material thrust, Shakespeare's smithy of thought resists Arendt's claim that thinking "leaves nothing . . . tangible behind" and is "resultless by nature."[37] The playwright calls atten-tion to the everyday mental work of bringing art into being, as does Heidegger: "Works are shipped like coal from the Ruhr or logs from the Black Forest . . . Every work has this thingly character . . . even this much-vaunted 'aesthetic experience' cannot evade the thingliness of the artwork."[38] The play's the thing, as Hamlet says, and it becomes a thing when the audience by thinking makes it so. In figuring the playhouse as working-house, Shakespeare counters the early modern antitheatrical polemicists who complained that the playwright does not actually make anything, at least not anything useful. Gosson contrasts the folly of poetic invention with

> those things that are inuented for necessarie vses, as, Shippes, clothing wollen or linnen, Manuary craftes, [which] may be accepted of Christians without error, for they are the blessings of God bestowed on vs; but those things which are neither necessary nor beneficiall vnto man . . . as Maygames, Stageplaies, & such like, can not be suffred among Christians.[39]

To the contrary, Shakespeare metaphorically turned the theater into an artisanal space where players and audience together produce a theatrical experience whose "market value" cannot be separated from its aesthetic value, its power to give pleasure, which can only be determined by the audience.

I turn now from judgment of the play to judgment in the play. As I have already suggested, *Henry V* arouses moral judgment by establishing a pattern of undermining its own previous manifestations of Henry's heroism and unflagging leadership. By approving the hanging of his old friend Bardolph for stealing a "pax of little price" (3.6.40) and by ordering the hasty throat-cutting of all the French prisoners (4.6.37–8), Harry compels the audience to question his benevolence – and to wonder whether he is, after all, "the mirror of all Christian kings" (2.0.6). Both episodes are recounted in the chronicle histories of Edward Hall and Raphael Holinshed, but that does not mean Shakespeare was obliged to include them. In the case of the English thief, Shakespeare arguably makes Harry look more cruel than he does in the source materials, where the condemned is a nameless soldier. By making him Bardolph, Shakespeare makes it personal, so that when Gower claims, "Our King . . . never killed any of his friends" (4.7.34), the audience thinks of not one but two examples to the contrary: Falstaff and Bardolph.[40] We might also think back to Falstaff's playful injunction to Prince Hal, which now takes on a much darker resonance: "Do not thou when thou art king hang a thief" (*1 Henry IV*, 1.2.54). He does; he will.

The punishment of Bardolph provides Shakespeare with another opportunity to make Henry seem hypocritical; the king's harsh sentence, "We would have all such offenders so cut off" (3.6.98), clashes conspicuously with the policy of leniency he proclaims four lines later: "For when lenity and cruelty play for a kingdom, the gentler gamester is the soonest winner" (3.6.102–3). One also wonders whatever happened to the "gentler gamester" when the king issues the following perfunctory order: "The French have reinforced their scattered men. / Then every soldier kill his prisoners" (4.6.36–7). Seconds later, Gower announces a contradictory and militarily weaker explanation for Henry's order: "[the French] have burned and carried away all that was in the King's tent; wherefore the King most worthily hath caused every soldier to cut his prisoner's throat. O 'tis a gallant king" (4.7.6–8). Even though Shakespeare does not linger on the cruelty of Henry's decision the way the chroniclers do, the playwright still makes his audience question the "worthiness" of this summary execution and wonder at the appropriateness of Gower's praise along with the accuracy of his account. In Gower's judgment, Henry can do no wrong, which is also true for Fluellen, who unhesitatingly affirms the king's gallantry along with his likeness to "Alexander the Pig" (4.7.10). Fluellen's mistake, ironically insulting the king he means to praise, forces the audience not only to question Harry's status as hero-in-chief but also to question the credibility of the characters who judge him. We are expected to think before jumping on Gower and Fluellen's bandwagon.

However, there are three pivotal instances across the Second Tetralogy where the character judging Harry commands his and our respect. Interestingly, this pattern moves across – or rather down – the social spectrum, from King Henry IV to the Lord Chief Justice to the commoner Williams. In all three cases, I argue, moral judgment is work that authorizes and empowers the judge. As soon as the pragmatic, no-nonsense Bolingbroke gets down to business as King Henry IV, the first thing he does is judge Harry, "my unthrifty son . . . young wanton and effeminate boy" (*Richard II*, 5.3.1, 10), for his dissolute behavior. In *1 Henry IV*, the king is never stronger than in Act 3 scene 2, when he berates the hell out of the shame-faced prince. This scene is the king's finest rhetorical moment; his poignant, powerful speeches carry him to heights of eloquence he has not reached before and will not reach again. He may be shaken and "wan with care" (*1 Henry IV*, 1.1.1) as erstwhile supporters fall away and the rebels gain ground, but when he is judging Harry, Henry IV seems every inch a king.

In response to this chastisement, the prince promises to collect the debt he owes his father by demonstrating valor on the battlefield, represented as a marketplace where honor is a material commodity in limited supply and high demand. He anticipates the day of reckoning when he will settle the score with his Northumberland rival:

> I shall make this northern youth exchange
> His glorious deeds for my indignities.
> Percy is but my factor, good my lord,

To engross up glorious deeds on my behalf;
And I will call him to so strict account
That he shall render every glory up. (3.2.145–50)

It is when Hotspur transfers his hoard of honor to Hal that the latter can pay the debt he never promised and satisfy his father, who is pleased at last that "this business so fair is done" (5.3.44).

In *2 Henry IV*, the "seat of judgement" itself seems a throne. When the prince expresses his indignation over having been imprisoned for giving the Lord Chief Justice of England a box to the ear, the Justice flawlessly defends his decision by invoking the royalist view of legal authority, one that remains, in this instance at least, strikingly impervious to Shakespeare's ubiquitous irony:

Whiles I was busy for the commonwealth,
Your highness pleasèd to forget my place,
The majesty and power of law and justice,
The image of the King whom I presented,
And struck me in my very seat of judgement;
Whereon, as an offender to your father,
I gave bold way to my authority
And did commit you. (*2 Henry IV*, 5.2.75–82)

In this passage, "the majesty and power of law and justice" becomes less – and more – than a Neoplatonic abstraction. The ideology of royal reflection is grounded and reified by an ethos of labor; the Chief Justice was "busy for the commonwealth" and did nothing "that misbecame [his] place" (5.2.99). Moreover, the use of the word "commonwealth" does not mean that "the king has disappeared,"[41] since "commonwealth" in early modern usage signified a polity in general, not necessarily or exclusively a republic. The mystical portrait of kingly authority, if it is to have any value or efficacy whatsoever, requires "th'administration of his law" (5.2.74) in an everyday framework, or frame of work, such as Shakespeare gives it here. In standing for the king and condemning Harry's offensive behavior, the Justice was simply doing his job. Won over by this argument, Harry proceeds to judge the judge in the most favorable terms: "You are right Justice, and you weigh this well" (5.2.101). The work of judging Harry fairly and honestly has vindicated the Chief Justice, whom Harry promises to honor "as a father to my youth; / My voice shall sound as you do prompt mine ear, / And I will stoop and humble my intents / To your well-practised wise directions" (5.2.117–20).

Harry further promises that he "shall have foremost hand" (5.2.139) among the "princes all" (5.2.121) who have been busy for the commonwealth.

Also judging Harry are the soldiers on the eve of Agincourt, who "by their watchful fires / Sit patiently and inly ruminate / The morning's danger" (*Henry V*, 4.0.23–5), as the Chorus puts it. The scene may be still and quiet, but the men's minds are not; their campfire lights up the quick forge and working-house of thought. In the heated exchange between the king disguised as "a gentlemen of a company" (4.1.40) and the commoners Bates, Court, and Williams, the verb "think" (including the variant "methinks") is used seven times. This is a scene whose action is precisely the unspectacular work of thinking and judging, and it is through Williams that "Shakespeare provides access for the common man to enter the debate and confront the king."[42] The commoner dares the king to distance himself from the lives – and possibly the damnation – of those who die in his service:

> if the cause be not good, the King himself hath a heavy reckoning to make . . . I am afeard there are few die well that die in a battle, for how can they charitably dispose of anything, when blood is their argument? Now, if these men do not die well, it will be a black matter for the King that led them to it – who to disobey were against all proportion of subjection. (4.1.128–38)

Here, ethical judgment proceeds by deductive reasoning from premise to conclusion ("if–then"), and as Williams's rational exercise progresses, the king's moral culpability increases. Initially, the king faces a "heavy reckoning" if and only if he sends men to their death in battle for an unjust cause. But then Williams questions the justice of dying in battle for any cause at all, which leads him to the following moral hypothesis: if "blood is their argument" – that is, if men die while killing or trying to kill – then in most cases they cannot "die well." Now, their deaths are a "black matter for the King" no matter the cause for which they fought.

In his response, Harry attempts to evade personal blame by making a distinction between, on one hand, the cause of the war, which is subject to the king's will, and, on the other hand, the soldiers' physical deaths and spiritual fate, which are subject to God's will. But this distinction, on which Harry's self-exoneration depends, collapses when he equates crime with sin and royal justice with divine justice, as sovereigns who claimed to rule by divine right routinely did. If some of the fallen soldiers happened to be outlaws, he argues, then they are finally getting what they deserve: "though they can outstrip men, they have no wings to fly from God. War is his beadle. War is his vengeance. So that here men are punished for before-breach of the King's laws, in now the King's quarrel" (4.1.156–60). Although Harry intended to distance himself from "the particular endings of his soldiers" (4.1.146–7), his argument winds up doing the opposite, embroiling him even more in their deaths as God's vengeance and the king's quarrel become one and the same. Moreover, the alignment between divine and royal justice does nothing to prove Harry's innocence whenever "unspotted soldiers" (4.1.151) die in combat. Under such circumstances, the king has no excuse but to suggest lamely that he "purpose[s] not their deaths when [he proposes] their services" (4.1.148). In any event, Harry's argument is beside the point if the audience accepts the principle that underpins Williams's argument, which is that wars are waged not by God but by men; "blood is *their* argument," not God's, so men bear the burden of proving that a "just war" is possible. Not only does Harry fail in this scene to establish that "his cause [is] just and his quarrel honourable" (4.1.121–2), he also fails to answer Williams's most damning objection: the blood of the soldiers is on the king's hands regardless of the cause.

The common soldier's judgment is not easily discounted. While his social rank is low, his perspicacity is high. Unlike Pistol, Williams is not a rogue. When he asks the disguised Harry in whose company he serves, the king names Sir Thomas Erpingham, whom Williams judges to be "A good old commander and a most kind gentleman" (4.1.93–4). As the audience is given no reason to doubt Williams's credibility in judging Erpingham, neither are they given any reason to doubt his credibility in judging Harry. When Williams hits Harry with a sarcastic remark about the utter inconsequence of a commoner's distrust of the king – "That's a perilous shot out of an elder-gun, that a poor and a private displeasure can do against a monarch" (4.1.183–5) – the "commoner" Harry *le roi* may be offended, but Williams is absolutely right. The subsequent exchange of gloves gives a certain structural symmetry to the pattern of judging Harry; the moment is subtly and ironically foreshadowed in *Richard II*, when Prince Hal, eager to piss on the chivalric code, tells Harry Percy that "he would unto the stews, / And from the common'st creature pluck a glove, / And wear it as a favour, and with that / He would unhorse the lustiest challenger" (*Richard II*, 5.3.16–19). Yet when Prince Hal finally does pluck a glove from "the common'st creature," he does so as King Harry, and the "creature" is not a whore in a brothel but a soldier in his own army: "Give me any gage of thine, and I will wear it in my bonnet. Then if ever thou darest acknowledge it, I will make it my quarrel" (*Henry V*, 4.1.193–5), he challenges Williams, who asks in turn for a glove of Harry's that he might wear in his cap. Williams's threat is tellingly specific: "If ever thou come to me and say, after tomorrow, 'This is my glove', by this hand I will take thee a box on the ear" (4.1.198–200).

The line may well remind the audience of Harry's infamous box on the ear of the Chief Justice. By having Williams threaten to return the blow that Harry gave the Justice, Shakespeare subtly signals a connection between these two characters insofar as their respective judgments of Harry form a pattern, which is as follows: both the Chief Justice and Williams judge Harry harshly, are made to defend themselves for doing so, and are subsequently not just forgiven but rewarded. I have already discussed from a different angle Harry's exchange with the Justice, but a brief recap of that exchange here will help to illustrate the parallel with the Williams episode. Shortly before his offstage coronation in *2 Henry IV*, Harry challenges the Justice to exonerate himself for the offenses done to his royal person: "How might a prince of my great hopes forget / So great indignities you laid upon me? / What – rate, rebuke, and roughly send to prison / Th'immediate heir of England?" (*2 Henry IV*, 5.2.67–70). After the Justice successfully persuades the prince, "if I be measured rightly, / Your majesty hath no just cause to hate me" (5.2.65–6), Harry offers his hand as a gesture of reconciliation and respect (5.2.116). He then grants the Justice "foremost hand" (5.2.139) among the "limbs of noble counsel" (5.2.134) chosen to serve as Harry's advisors.

Similarly, once Williams realizes that he had actually exchanged gloves with the king, Harry commands him to justify himself: "'Twas I indeed thou promisèd'st to strike, / And thou hast given me most bitter terms . . . How canst thou make me satisfaction?" (*Henry V*, 4.8.38–42). Williams's defense, like that of the Chief Justice, is respectable, dignified, and fair-minded: "All offences, my lord, come from the heart. Never came any from mine that might offend your majesty" (4.8.43–4). Like the Chief Justice, Williams did nothing that misbecame his place, and as a soldier in the king's army, he too was busy for the commonwealth. Both characters rightly apologize for their boldness without admitting fault, for in both cases the fault was Harry's own. Williams makes this especially clear: "You appeared to me but as a common man. Witness the night, your garments, your lowliness. And what your highness suffered under that shape, I beseech you take it for your own fault, and not mine, for had you been as I took you for, I made no offence" (4.8.46–50). Harry evidently finds Williams's response to be honorable, for he rewards him by filling his glove with coins. Like the blessing he bestows on the Chief Justice while giving him the scale and sword – "I do wish your honours may increase / Till you do live to see a son of mine / Offend you and obey you as I did" (2 *Henry IV*, 5.2.103–5) – the blessing he bestows on Williams while giving him the crown-filled glove includes a reference to the pattern continuing: "Keep it, fellow, / And wear it for an honour in thy cap / Till I do challenge it" (*Henry V*, 4.8.53–5). In both cases, Harry rewards a servant of the crown for having judged him fairly. Williams's rebuff, "I will none of your money" (4.8.62), is directed at Fluellen, not the king, who has condescended to show Williams a modicum of respect. The soldier deserves it; after striking the man wearing his glove, he can rightly say, "I have been as good as my word" (4.8.30). This is more than the king can say. Harry admits, "I by bargain should / Wear it myself" (4.7.159–60), but he tricks Fluellen into wearing the glove instead. Once again, the king's substitute takes a box to the ear. For his part, Williams can hold his head up high: he has demonstrated that the work of judging Harry, while difficult and dangerous, can also be rewarding. In this respect, he shadows another Englishman – William S. – who also took risks and reaped rewards by working at thinking.[43]

And thus we come back to the Chorus, who leaves us with the dual task of judging both Harry's political work and Shakespeare's aesthetic work. Still enabling the audience to judge Harry harshly while judging Shakespeare gently, the Epilogue further complicates and perhaps undermines Harry's imperial achievements by putting them into historical context. By reminding us how short-lived the English rule of France actually was, the Epilogue forces us to think about the "Small time" (5) of Henry's domination and how its transience matters. To admire "This star of England" (5) is to gasp at his meteoric brilliance in the brief moment before it passes out of sight – and then to decide that Henry's glory endures even if his conquest did not. But if we do not admire him, we may find it appropriate that his legacy turns out to be one of an empire lost and a kingdom torn by civil war. His heirs did not deserve to keep what he did not deserve to have, and when we inventory his unlawful possessions – his stolen property – we find not only the French crown but also the English crown, which his father had usurped. The Chorus is often viewed over-simply as Harry's cheerleader, "a response-regulator whose function is to magnify and glamorise Henry and all he stands for,"[44] but he too equivocates and sparks thought by doing so. Poised on the caesura after "this star of England," the Chorus pivots to "Fortune made his sword" (6), which implicitly withdraws heroic agency and effort from Harry, making him instead a beneficiary of auspicious stars and serendipitous circumstances.

Although the play in performance is an ephemeral product, the audience activity of thinking together (even when thinking differently) has a community-building effect that potentially outlasts the performance itself. While the Chorus does not entreat the audience to "like" Harry, he certainly does try to sway them toward liking the play with one final stroke of flattery: "In your fair minds let this acceptance take" (14). The closing line represents aesthetic judgment as intellectual work, but it does more than that: it aestheticizes the intellectual process of judgment itself. An etymological nexus of the aesthetic and political domains, the adjective "fair" in early modern usage could mean either "beautiful" or "equitable"; in this instance, Shakespeare invokes both senses. An audience of judicious minds could only be expected to favor *Henry V*, and to favor it unanimously; "spectators exist only in the plural . . . the faculty that they have in common is the faculty of judgment."[45] For Arendt as for Kant, a synonym for judgment is "common sense," with "common" primarily signifying not "vulgar" but "social" – *sensus communis* or "community sense."[46] Elaborating on the Kantian distinction between unproductive thinking and productive knowing, Arendt argues that "the activity of knowing is no less a world-building activity than the building of houses."[47] For Shakespeare, however, thinking was constructive in its own right, and bringing people into the theater to be entertained meant bringing people together to work at thinking. In the imaginative conceit of a socially elevated audience, Shakespeare projected an element of himself: an artisan-maker who labored productively in the quick forge and working-house of thought, and who earned, "non sanz droict,"[48] the status of gentleman not in spite of but because of that work. Paraphrasing Plato's *Seventh Letter*, Arendt represents thought as insubstantial "wind," but then – in spite of herself – she moves to a more material metaphor: "if the wind of thinking, which I shall now arouse in you, has roused you from your sleep and made you fully awake and alive, then you will see that you have nothing in your hand but perplexities, and the most we can do with them is share them with each other."[49] But perplexities are something, and to share them with each other is to connect with each other, to build the foundation of a thinking community. Shakespeare never tells us what to think, but he does tell us to think, and to think together.

Notes

1. *1 Henry IV*, in *The Norton Shakespeare*, 2nd ed., ed. Stephen Green-blatt, Walter Cohen, Jean E. Howard, and Katharine Eisaman Maus (New York: W.W. Norton, 2009), 2.5.257. All Shakespeare quotations are from this edition and will be cited parenthetically by Act, scene, and line number.
2. Paul Menzer, "Crowd Control," in *Imagining the Audience in Early Modern Drama, 1558–1642*, ed. Jennifer A. Low and Nova Myhill (Basingstoke: Palgrave Macmillan, 2011), 19–36 (p. 26).
3. Norman Rabkin, *Shakespeare and the Problem of Meaning* (Chicago: University of Chicago Press, 1981), 62, 58, 34.
4. Ibid., 62.
5. Ibid., 61.
6. Keir Elam, *The Semiotics of Theatre and Drama*, 2nd ed. (London: Routledge, 2002), 87.
7. Noël Carroll, "Moderate Moralism," *British Journal of Aesthetics* 36.3 (1996): 223–38 (p. 227).
8. Jeremy Lopez, *Theatrical Convention and Audience Response in Early Modern Drama* (Cambridge: Cambridge University Press, 2003), 2.
9. Sharon Tyler, "Minding True Things: the Chorus, the Audience, and *Henry V*," in *The Theatrical Space*, ed. James Redmond (Cambridge: Cambridge University Press, 1987), 69–79 (p. 71). See also Pamela Mason, "Henry V: 'the quick forge and working house of thought,'" in *The Cambridge Companion to Shakespeare's History Plays*, ed. Michael Hattaway (Cambridge: Cambridge University Press, 2002), 177–92.
10. Carroll's work was brought to my attention by Heather Dubrow, "The Politics of Aesthetics: Recuperating Formalism and the Country House Poem," in *Renaissance Literature and its Formal Engagements*, ed. Mark David Rasmussen (Basingstoke: Palgrave Macmillan, 2002), 67–88, esp. 69–70.
11. Carroll, "Moderate Moralism," 228.
12. Ibid., 232–3.
13. Carroll, "Art, Narrative, and Moral Understanding," in *Aesthetics and Ethics: Essays at the Intersection*, ed. Jerrold Levinson (Cambridge: Cambridge University Press, 1998), 126–60 (pp. 141, 145).
14. Ibid., 142.
15. Joel Altman, *The Tudor Play of Mind: Rhetorical Inquiry and the Development of Elizabethan Drama* (Berkeley: University of California Press, 1978), 3.
16. Ibid., 3, 6; emphasis original.
17. Ibid., 6.
18. Evelyn B. Tribble, *Cognition in the Globe: Attention and Memory in Shakespeare's Theatre* (Basingstoke: Palgrave Macmillan, 2011), 117.
19. Tyler, "Minding True Things," 72.

20. Ann Jennalie Cook, "Audiences: Investigation, Interpretation, Invention," in *A New History of Early English Drama*, ed. John D. Cox and David Scott Kastan (New York: Columbia University Press, 1997), 305–20 (p. 308).
21. Paul Yachnin, "The Populuxe Theatre," in Anthony B. Dawson and Paul Yachnin, *The Culture of Playgoing in Shakespeare's England: A Collaborative Debate* (Cambridge: Cambridge University Press, 2001), 41.
22. Cook, "Audiences," 309.
23. Ibid., 310.
24. Anthony Dawson argues that the "gentility" of the common soldiers at Agincourt will be fixed through narrative remembrance (Dawson and Yachnin, *The Culture of Playgoing*, 164). However, for the gentility of any given soldier to endure, his name must be known and repeated by successive generations of storytellers. In this case, the names that will live on, freshly remembered and familiar as household words, are royal and noble: "Harry the King, Bedford and Exeter, / Warwick and Talbot, Salisbury and Gloucester" (*Henry V*, 4.3.53–4).
25. *Nichomachean Ethics*, ed. and trans. Roger Crisp (Cambridge: Cambridge University Press, 2000), VI.10.1143a.
26. Hannah Arendt, "Thinking and Moral Considerations: A Lecture," *Social Research* 38 (1971): 417–46 (pp. 422, 425).
27. Stephen Gosson, *Playes Confuted in Fiue Actions* (1582), in *Markets of Bawdrie: the Dramatic Criticism of Stephen Gosson*, ed. Arthur Kinney (Salzburg: University of Salzburg Press, 1974), 164.
28. Ibid.
29. *Nichomachean Ethics*, ed. Crisp, VI.12.1143b.
30. Cicero, *On the Ideal Orator (De Oratore)*, trans. and ed. James M. May and Jacob Wisse (Oxford: Oxford University Press, 2001), 3.197.
31. Richard Rainolde, *A booke called the Foundacion of rhetorike* (1563), quoted in Sister Miriam Joseph, *Shakespeare's Use of the Arts of Language* (New York: Columbia University Press, 1947; reprint Mansfield Centre, CT: Martino Publishing, 2013), 6; Abraham Fraunce, *The Lawyers Logike* (London, 1588), unpaginated.
32. Andrew Gurr, "The Shakespearean Stage," in *Norton Shakespeare*, ed. Greenblatt et al., 82.
33. George Puttenham, *The Art of English Poesy* (1589), ed. Frank Whigham and Wayne Rebhorn (Ithaca: Cornell University Press, 2007), 93.
34. Arendt, "Thinking and Moral Considerations," 444, 423.
35. Menzer, "Crowd Control," 28.
36. Ibid., 29.
37. Arendt, "Thinking and Moral Considerations," 421, 426.
38. Martin Heidegger, "The Origin of the Work of Art," in *Off the Beaten Track*, ed. Julian Young and Kenneth Haynes (Cambridge: Cambridge University Press, 2002), 3.
39. Gosson, *Playes Confuted*, ed. Kinney, 155.

40. On this point see also Mason, "Henry V," 186.
41. Richard Strier, "Shakespeare and Legal Systems: The Better the Worse (but Not Vice Versa)," in *Shakespeare and the Law: A Conversation Among Disciplines and Professions*, ed. Bradin Cormack, Martha C. Nussbaum, and Richard Strier (Chicago: University of Chicago Press, 2013), 174–200, (p. 175).
42. Mason, "Henry V," 184.
43. On Shakespeare's implicit association of himself with this and other commoners named William in the plays, see Phyllis Rackin, *Stages of History: Shakespeare's English Chronicles* (Ithaca: Cornell University Press, 1990), 243–7.
44. E. A. J. Honigmann, *Shakespeare: Seven Tragedies Revisited*, 2nd ed. (Basingstoke: Palgrave Macmillan, 2002), 204.
45. Hannah Arendt, *The Life of the Mind* (San Diego: Harcourt Brace, 1978), 262–3.
46. Ibid., 270.
47. Arendt, "Thinking and Moral Considerations," 421.
48. "Not without right," the motto of the Shakespeare coat of arms, granted in 1596.
49. Arendt, "Thinking and Moral Considerations," 434.

Chapter 5

"Practis[ing] judgment with the disposition of natures": *Measure for Measure*, the "Discoursive" Common Law, and the "Open Court" of the Theater

Carolyn Sale

Measure for Measure is not the only Shakespeare play to end with a crowd within the fiction gathered for a final scene of judgment. It is, however, the only play that ends such a scene with such uncertainty for the audience as to how it is to judge what it has witnessed that the play itself appears vitally to concern itself with the audience's capacity to judge. This chapter tackles that theatrical situation from two perspectives: the political implications, in 1604, of the play's appeal to its audience's capacity for judgment and the resonances of the historical concerns for contemporary politics in the twenty-first century. The chapter aims to recognize the historical specificity of the play's interest in jurisprudence, particularly in who has the means and authority to judge in early modern common law, in order to open these concerns out onto the present. The play may be set in a civil law jurisdiction, but at stake in its representation of judgment in the theater is the question of where the authority of the common law resides, who executes it, and what forms of judgment align with it, questions that are just as pressing in 2016 as they were in 1604.

The Common Law's "Reason"

Measure for Measure occupies an important moment in the history of the English common law. It was written and performed in the first few years of the century in which, as the legal philosopher Gerald Postema notes, "modern notions of law took shape."[1] Central to modern conceptions of the common law is the idea that the common law is "judge-made law," a conception seen as arising from the work of Edward Coke (Attorney General 1594–1606, Chief Justice of the Common Pleas 1606–13, and Chief Justice of the King's Bench 1613–16). Most famously, in contradiction of James I's claim that he could "take what causes he shall please to determine, from the determination of the Judges, [to] determine them himselfe," Coke argued for the common law's "artificiall" reasoning or the practice of analogical thinking through which lawyers and justices set the "facts" of a case before them in relation to previous cases like it.[2] The practice, one that depended in Coke's view on "long study and experience," excluded the king from directly rendering judgment in any case.[3] Under the English common law, Coke insisted, "Judgements are given, *Ideo consideratum est per Curiam*," or by a court.[4] At the same time, more than one lawyer, Coke among them, went so far as to claim that the common law was nothing more than "common reason."[5] From this perspective, the common law was not a "set of norms, prescriptions, or propositions of law," but rather a "discoursive" "practice of common practical reasoning" which proceeds as "a matter of deliberative reasoning and argument in an interlocutory, indeed forensic, context" oriented to the "lay sense of reasonableness" and pursuing a "convergence" of "contextually situated reflective judgment."[6] In its strongest formulation, even the most "artificiall" processes of the common law were understood to be oriented to the law's "common reason" as a *sensus communis* that common law jurisprudence both drew upon and shaped in its "enterprise of judging particular cases through grasp of concrete relations and arrangements woven into the fabric of common life."[7] The common law's "artificiall" reason and its common reason existed, in short, in mutually constitutive relation. In formal practice, of course, in "open court" no one other than someone charged with judicial authority had any formal opportunity to judge.[8] A stronger conception of the "common" character of the common law, one consistent with John Davies's contention in the preface to his 1615 volume of Irish *Reports* that the English "haue made theire owne lawes out of their wisdome & experience (like a silke worme that formeth all her webb out of her selfe onely)," would require that the "artificiall" reasoning of the common law's lawyers and justices was not only always oriented to and in dialectical exchange with "common reason" but also engaging all those for whom the law obtains as comprehensively as possible in the law's processes.[9]

This is precisely what James I, the king whom *Measure for Measure* is often construed as flattering, positioned himself against. From his 1598 *True Lawe of Free Monarchies* forward, James was on record as construing his own authority in relation to the law as absolute. "The King is above the Law," he wrote, and "the power flowes all-wayes from himselfe."[10] Not only did the king himself have the right to judge, he had the right, James believed, to restrain the "discoursive" character of the common law. He did not "dislike" the common law, he asserted, and did not wish "to preferre the Ciuill Law before" it.[11] He did, however, wish to see the common law "bounded."[12] To this end, he declared his desire for a "cleare Law" expressing itself in "solide reason" and a "setled Text" that "needed no Iudges" but only its own "bare letter."[13] This chapter considers the play's engagement with the king's antagonism to the discursive character of the common law, or what James derides as its "Sophistrie or straines of wit," by focusing on the play's representations of the kind of activity associated with English common law juries in the early seventeenth century, "fact"-finding, and its converse, the "fault"-finding that James I favored.[14] The chapter asserts that the experience of taking in a performance of *Measure for Measure* in the first two decades of the seventeenth century was the occasion for audiences to experience their own "discoursive" potential not simply to participate in practices of judgment at the common law, but to comprehend themselves in their aggregate as the common law's makers. It is from this that the play derives its continuing political force for contemporary audiences.

"Tryers of the fact"

Coke does not have much to say about juries, but Davies does, and his remarks suggest why, for a king preferring the practices of the civil law to the common law, the English jury system at the turn of the seventeenth century was a problem. Contending that the English would never have agreed to have been "ruled and gouerned by the Ciuill law," Davies argues that the English have shaped a law, "the *peculiar inuention* of this Nation," that is "framed and fitted" to the "nature and disposition of the people."[15] For Davies, all of the common law's practices, including the justices' riding-out on their Assize circuits, furnished the means by which the "streames of Iustice," for which the people were the first source, were brought "by conduit pipes or quills euen home, as it were, to their owne doors."[16] Participation in juries was, however, a specific means by which the "people" had the opportunity discursively to demonstrate their "strength of wit and reason" at the common law.[17] As Lorna Hutson has argued in her seminal book *The Invention of Suspicion*, the early modern

English common law depended upon the discursive process of forensic reasoning as manifest in the participatory fact-finding of juries. We see Davies establishing the importance of this as he defends the common law against charges of its "incerteinty," which rarely turns, he argues, on questions of law. It turns, rather, on "*questio facti*." For every cause "wherein a *question of lawe* doth arise," there are in his view "a thousand causes at least wherein the *fact* is onely in question, & wherein if the truth of the *fact* were knowne, the *lawe* were cleer & without question."[18] These "thousand causes" more strenuously engaged the common law's thinking than any cause involving merely a "point in *lawe*": "And in the Courts of lawe where the trial is by Jurors, are there not a thousand issues ioyned vpt on matters of *fact*, for one demurrer that is ioyned vppon a point in *lawe*?"[19] The challenge for jurors was to harness their "forensic" abilities in relation to the complexities of life, something that no judge merely seeking application of a "cleare" rule could do. By having the law that originates in the people negotiated in relation to their construal of the "infinite diuersitie of mens *actions*, & of other *accidents*" in the production of the "fact" to be judged, the common law puts the forensic and "discoursive" capacities of "the people" at the heart of its jurisprudence.[20]

The role of jurors in the production of "fact" was of sufficient concern to James that a 1607 proclamation aimed to limit who might participate in juries. In *The Invention of Suspicion*, Hutson cites a detail from the proclamation to suggest James's desire to "dignify the jury's role by aligning it with the most famous judgement in all Scripture, the judgement of Solomon."[21] The explicit intention of the proclamation, however, was to dust off an old law and renovate it to guarantee that the "wise sifting and examination of the fact" could be performed only by "the ablest and fittest persons," with ability and fitness defined as a matter of property holding.[22] The sixteenth century witnessed more than one formal relaxation of the rule that all jurors must "possess land worth at least 40s a year" – as in the play, laws were "let slip" (1.3.20) as "sheriffs continued to return unqualified men"[23] – but the 1607 proclamation opposed the "embasing" of the old rule with the introduction of a stronger one: only those who possessed freehold property might be "tryers of the fact." James's proclamation thus worked against precisely the power that Hutson argues the drama of early modern England cultivates, the "power of fact finding" through acts of "probable forensic reasoning" as practiced by the "ordinary people, the 'commons'."[24] But if we follow Hutson, as I think we must, in "tak[ing] seriously the idea that a participatory justice system might have had an impact on dramatic epistemology, and vice versa,"[25] we should look to *Measure for Measure*, written a decade after the Shakespeare play about which Hutson writes as she discusses forensic reasoning on the public stage, *2 Henry VI*, as offering us a more complex instance of how the "commons" might participate in or reshape the common law's forms of judgment to strengthen its "common reason."

Pompey's Dish

Consider, for example, the only scene in the 1604 comedy that benefits from clear comic exuberance, that in which Pompey, the tapster at the Bunch of Grapes, a "house" threatened with closure under Angelo's application of laws out of use, accompanies a patron of the establishment, Master Froth, when he is hauled before Angelo and Escalus by Elbow, in his role of constable of the peace, to answer for his conduct in some encounter with Mistress Elbow. It is not clear what this encounter involved (though Mistress Elbow may have spat in Froth's face) as Elbow makes no specific accusation, Master Froth would, if he could, say nothing, and Pompey is brought up short in his attempt to narrate the circumstances when his details about a dish on the Bunch of Grapes' counter prompt Escalus's declaration "No matter for the dish, sir!" (2.1.92). We cannot know why Pompey thinks it is important to note that the dish, which was holding some stewed prunes that Mistress Elbow wished to eat, was "a fruit dish, a dish of some three pence" (2.1.89–90); why, though not china, the dish should still be regarded as "very good" (2.1.91); or why it matters that there were only two prunes in it at the time. The presumption is that these facts tell us something about the material life of the inn that is important to the circumstances of whatever it is Master Elbow wishes to complain about. Pompey's attempted narrative also presumes that no case at law can be properly decided unless an account of the circumstances that gave rise to the purported action to be judged is sufficiently exhaustive that its "fact" can be properly set in relation to the "fact" of other cases and the judgments therein. We have little concrete historical evidence of the fact-finding procedures of early modern juries, or "the ways in which facts were usually proved,"[26] but the scene suggests not only the desirability of expansive narrative to it, but also the importance of the community's involvement: without that, the judgment cannot be oriented to "common life," here represented by the practice of furnishing prunes to customers in a humble yet "very good" fruit dish. In the mundane resides evidence of the community's ethos and its common sense, those phenomena in relation to which the common law must orient itself.

Pompey's presumptions are, in short, the presumptions of common law jurisprudence, and his attempted narrative prospectively engages the audience's sensibility of the importance of its own relation to the production and adjudication of judicial "facts." Escalus would hasten past crucial details in search of a simple fact, "what was done to her" (2.1.108), despite the fact that the implicit refusal of a chain of causality, in altering the common sense of the "thing" "done," might undermine the process of judgment. (The "judicial pedagogy of narrative," Hutson suggests, "fostered an awareness of the 'facts' as being generated by the order and coherence of their telling.")[27] Pompey, on the other hand, would build up detail, and let it accrete, in the hope, as he declares more than once, that the scene at which he finds himself is one for the production of judicial "truths" (2.1.121, 127). As he does so, the scene makes comic hay out of the presumption that the "infinite diuersitie of mens *actions*, & of other *accidents*" cannot and should not be reduced to a "fact" involving a single action. "Truths" at the common law must, as Hutson has argued, be "boulted out" in a discursive practice of forensic reasoning. In *Measure for Measure*, Shakespeare comically makes this "boulting" a process that resists narrative simplification with Pompey's retort to Escalus's demand "Now, sir, come on! What was done to Elbow's wife, once more?": "Once, sir? There was nothing done to her once" (2.1.133–4). When Escalus, frustrated that he cannot secure any such narrow "fact" from Pompey, informs Froth that the community at the Bunch of Grapes must be left free to "continue" in their "courses" until such time as Froth can properly "discover" them (2.1.178–9), the scene comically renders the defeat of a "science" of law unable to draw upon the community's narrative powers to develop and construe the "fact" to be judged. Inasmuch as there is any judgment here, it is judgment of a very poor kind, judgment that believes in the right of a singular authority figure to override narrative production of the "fact." Angelo's remark when he departs – he hopes Escalus will "find good cause to whip them all" (2.1.116) – suggests a mutually reinforcing dynamic between this kind of judgment and a punitive law. This law has no interest in creating the means whereby a given community, through processes of deliberative reasoning, evaluates the acts of individuals to judge what the community values in human conduct and what it does not;

it seeks, rather, unilaterally to impose a "cause" according to which one form or another of retribution may be wreaked.

In Pompey's view, this is a killing law through which Angelo and Escalus, as they apply particular rules for the regulation of sexual activity, would destroy the community for which the law supposedly acts even as they produce economic benefits for those who survive: "If this law hold in Vienna ten year, I'll rent the fairest house in it after three pence a bay" (2.1.229–31). As the play's rhetoric and tropes of generativity, pregnancy, and prosperity suggest, Pompey would produce a form of life other than that approved or "allowed" by the law, not merely as "bawd" facilitating sexual conjunctions, but as someone committed to discursive procedures at law. There is thus an inherent and important tension between the kind of judgment that prevails in the fictional world of the play and the kind of narrative that Pompey would produce, with Angelo's analogue taking us directly to the point: Pompey will produce narrative talk that might "last out a night in Russia / When nights are longest there" (2.1.128–9), and all of this discourse is, for Angelo, beside the point, not simply because Pompey has no office from which he can formally argue on Master Froth's behalf or judge whatever Master Elbow attempts to offer by way of accusation, but because he wishes to offer a kind of matter that is irrelevant to the forms of judgment that Angelo and Escalus practice and endorse, forms of judgment that make no recourse to what is so central to judgment at the English common law, the discursive reasoning-in-common that produces the "fact." The mediating figure of Pompey facilitating the conjunctions of others must be transformed from tapster to executioner to guarantee that the existing apparatus of law can regulate all forms of life, including the discursive forms that might shape another kind of law.

Barnardine's "Fact"

Presenting audiences early on with comic material about a failed attempt to produce a "fact" for judgment, the play directs audiences to the importance of fact-making as the core activity of the jurisprudence of the common law as a law understood to arise from the "people" and orienting itself to their common reason and "common life." It thus directs them to their own discursive capacity and power in relation to law. The play then goes on to ask audiences to apprehend the active suppression of a complex "fact" in representations that cultivate in its members the desire and capacity for heightened participation in the making and adjudication of law.

The scene at which the audience most extensively witnesses the suppression of the community's capacity to participate in "fact-finding" and judgment is the long final scene in which Duke Vincentio publicly "manifests" the various goings-on in Vienna in such a way that he may unilaterally render judgment on various persons in series. In the extended theatrical spectacle for the "generous and gravest citizens" who "have hent" the city gates to witness the Duke's return to Vienna (4.6.13–14), Vincentio presents himself as the intermediary who guarantees the system of retribution in which "measure" is secured for "measure" in a process that positions him to pass judgment with no need of assistance from any "brother-justice" (3.1.507) or substitute. By bringing the exercise of judgment into his hands alone, Vincentio renovates not a specific law, but a jurisprudential scheme of retribution that is much closer to the idea of law James I urged than to any semblance of the common law. In Vincentio's case, this involves reversing the situation that had prevailed, in which the community was determining its law for itself by ignoring his decrees and refusing to prosecute his laws, in order to suppress the possibility of the law being spun out of the people.

Vincentio achieves this most obviously in his handling of Barnardine who is hustled on stage in Act 5 to have judgment rendered on his case in a mere six lines:

> Sirrah, thou art said to have a stubborn soul
> That apprehends no further than this world,
> And squar'st thy life according. Thou'rt condemned;
> But, for those earthly faults, I quit them all,
> And pray thee take this mercy to provide
> For better times to come. Friar, advise him. (5.1.483–8)

The rapidity with which the Duke acts here involves no reference whatsoever to what ought to concern the common law, the "fact" of what Barnardine has allegedly done. That "fact" is first of interest to the play in Act 4.2 when the Duke is in need of a head to substitute for Claudio's in order to satisfy Angelo that Claudio has been executed at his command, the central action of the play turning on his need to prevent, for Isabella's sake, Angelo's execution of Claudio. The Duke needs a substitute for Claudio; who substitutes for Claudio, or why, is of no interest whatsoever. He thus responds to the Provost's declaration that Barnardine's "fact" had not until now, "in the government of Lord Angelo," come to "an undoubtful proof" (4.2.136–7) with only one question, "It is now apparent?" (4.2.138). We, as the audience, might think we know a little more, for earlier in the scene the Provost, briefly alone when Abhorson the executioner and his newly minted assistant Pompey exit to summon Barnardine and Claudio, declares "The one has my pity, not a jot the other, / Being a murderer though he were my brother" (4.2.58–9). But as we have already been entertained with a scene mocking the production of fact-finding in the play's Vienna, we cannot with confidence claim to know anything at all. What is Barnardine's "fault," really? That his "stubborn soul" makes him irreligious and impervious to either divine or temporal authority? Who can properly say, or say in a way that meets the common law's standards for public forensic reasoning? If Barnardine were to let himself be executed, which, in one of the play's funniest exchanges, he expressly refuses to do – "I will not consent to die this day, that's certain" (4.3.52–3) – his death would affirm for an English audience the injustice of judicial proceedings in the play's Vienna: Barnardine has not been brought to public trial or his "fact" adjudicated according to the standards of the English common law.[28] It is not a common law process that the Duke enacts, but the kind of process that James would approve, that in which a sovereign figure, free to judge as he will, may choose to "forgiue faults . . . as [he] thinke[s] conuenient."[29] The Duke not only finds a "fault" without specifying where it lies, he keeps that "fault" from coming to any "court" except one that the common law would not recognize. What is being staged, then, in Act 5 is not simply the judicial operations or acts of judgment that allow (*contra* the common law) for the exercise of a singular authority without any reference to "fact" or past judgments, but rather a performance of a particular kind of sovereign exception in which the law is not merely suspended, but is never properly known.[30] Vincentio thus stands not for law, but, from the common law's perspective, lawlessness, the lawlessness of the singular judicial authority who presents himself either as the most immediate and uncontestable source of law or as "above" it, and who acts as if his judgments need not be justified.

Much of this is achieved, through the greater part of the play, covertly, as the Duke, disguised as the Friar, does what he claims to Claudio Angelo is doing with his bribe to Isabella that she sleep with him to save her brother's life, "practis[ing] his judgment with the disposition of natures" (3.1.166–7). The Duke's plot is one that would fashion the "dispositions" of others to make them freshly compliant to singular judicial authority, applying "cleare" Law without recourse to "discoursive" processes, though in his figure rather than Angelo's. As Friar, he marshals others to use within the hierarchical structure of the legal apparatus, with all others (Barnardine aside) agreeing either implicitly or explicitly to subordinate themselves to the authority of the Duke even in his absence and even in the face of talk that he may be "mad." Much depends on the Duke keeping everyone's participation in his "remedy" "several": no one else has an understanding of how others' actions are being coordinated by him, or to what ends; whatever their knowledge, it is always partial; and in Isabella's case, knowledge is actively withheld from her so that the Duke can reap benefits in his own time as he chooses. The partialness of the other characters' knowledge ensures that no other person can successfully exercise their judgment in any way that might threaten Vincentio, who is, as his name implies, conquering the citizens of Vienna through his machinations. Asked to witness the managing of "several" capacities for judgment by a singular figure who retains full control over these capacities, the audience has a choice: to accept the kind of authority that the Duke secures through these actions, and celebrate the play as a conventional comedy, or to understand that the truly comic resolution is to be produced by itself, in a celebration of its members' individual and collective capacities for judgment felt and exercised by them as the body in whom Shakespeare's plot, with the Duke's embedded, coheres.

In its construal of the play's "fact" the audience negotiates its own potential to judge. Its experience of the plot as singular entity bounded in the time and space of performance is important to this, as is our attention to the integrity of the play as a unit. The bounded nature of the plot means that the audience has a closed set of "actions" and "accidents" from which to construe the play's "fact." Its experience, in other words, is of a circumscribed set of the "infinite diuersitie of mens *actions*, & of other *accidents*" that allows the exercise of judgment within controlled parameters. As it addresses concrete questions in relation to the bounded plot – what is the representation of life that it has just witnessed, what does it entail, what must not be left out of any account of it for there to be adequate consensus on what has been seen? – the play exercises precisely what the common law's forms of reasoning demand of its participants, a production of the narrative of the "fact" developed in relation to what the assembled members of the community regard as the characteristics of their "common life." This activity is not itself bounded within what enables it, the time and space of playgoing. The point, rather, is that the play makes the audience feel the necessity of such activity and comprehend what it entails, for this is how comedy properly fulfills its social function: in affirming to the community where the power to constitute itself as community resides. The plot denaturalizes the workings of sovereign and judicial authority to create the opportunity for audience members, whatever their existing predilections, to dispose themselves differently both to the law and judgment at it as a consequence of their experience of the plot.

"Measure for Measure"

The kind of judgment for which the Duke stands is presented most bluntly by the Duke himself, in the passage from which the play takes its title:

> The very mercy of the law cries out
> Most audible, even from his proper tongue,
> "An Angelo for Claudio, death for death,
> Haste still pays haste, and leisure answers leisure;
> Like doth quit like, and Measure still for Measure."
> Then, Angelo, thy fault's thus manifested,
> Which, though thou wouldst deny, denies thee vantage.
> We do condemn thee to the very block
> Where Claudio stooped to death, and with like haste.
> Away with him. (5.1.408–17)

The judgment on display here is precisely the kind that James I espoused, for it works with a law or rule that expresses itself in a "bare" or self-evident letter that needs no interpreter and no exercise of reason. This kind of judgment needs only the authorizing figure of force who can ensure its execution. The production of judgment according to this ethos is inherently retributive, and the idea of law to which it is tied fundamentally anti-life, for what it refuses is the forms of life that flourish – to use contemporary language now – as the "intersubjective" "communicative power" through which a community makes its own laws.[31] This kind of law does not permit the community to judge. Instead, the sovereign figure substitutes so wholly and irreversibly for the members of the polity that they are left without any communicative power whatsoever, an operation succinctly captured in the language by which the Duke arrogates to himself the law's "voice" (2.4.61) which speaks "from his proper tongue" to assert a different kind of equivalency from that by which the common law proceeds. The "likeness" here pursued is merely between an action to be designated a "fault" and the compensatory retributive "measure," which does not involve construction either of the "fact" of any case or the analogical thinking that would seek to set similar cases in relation to pursue in the present instance a judgment that in its congruence with past judgment expresses a trans-historical rationality to the law, or where it breaks with past judgment does so knowingly, according to a rationale that makes sense to the present community for which the law obtains. It matters that Isabella plays a covert role in producing the "fault" that the Duke subsequently makes "manifest" to his own ends, a matter to which I will return, for she is caught up in the process by which the Duke transforms "mercy" into "amercement" or the payment secured when "like quits like."[32] Shakespeare's syntactical game, in which the "mercy" of the law crying out for retributive judgment obscures the person calling in a debt and producing from it an interest for himself, designates the law over which the Duke presides as a system of accounts in which one figure has the right to determine where a fine or payment is due in a conception of law that is fundamentally economic.

As Jeffrey Reiman has argued, this is the logic that continues to inform – indeed, has been greatly deepened by – "modern capitalist law," which recognizes only one kind of disposition to law, "the fact of the economic relations in which exchangers stand to one another," and produces its yields for the holders of capital.[33] In this sense, the play is generally far more modern that we tend to allow. Its legal critique involves an exposure of the dynamics by which modern Western law was emerging in the early seventeenth century as a law privileging economic relations through the strategic reiteration of a long-standing retributive logic derived from scripture. In the play's representation, this law is crucially tied to the singular sovereign figure breeding interest for himself from the retributive jurisprudential scheme that necessitates the suppression of any idea of the "people" as the source of the law, along with any sense of the importance of their "discoursive" capacity. The characters in the play, especially the voiceless cohort of "citizens" that watches the spectacle of the play's final act, are asked, in effect, to grant another economic logic in the eradication of their discursive capacity in relation to law, which is not necessary to the processes of judgment that seek nothing more than to tie a plain "fault" to its retributive "measure." Their discursive capacity is directly displaced by the kind of sovereignty the Duke would embody, which depends upon the reminder, through the exercise of mercy, of his authority to take life. The Duke's revolution can only be bloodless if everyone is aware anew of the potential for blood to be shed according to the sovereign power over life and death as a power that may, if the sovereign desires, be executed outside the processes of any court.

In a 1616 speech, James I invited his auditors to imagine that such exercises of mercy are exercises of equity, but this is a conflation that would itself displace the "discursive" character of the common law.[34] Although James does not define it this way, equity is oriented toward the perceived intention of the lawgiver(s), which the adjudicator imagines in order to ensure that a sense of the spirit of the law may be taken into account in all interpretations of its letter, usually to devise a "remedy" for a legal predicament that the law might not otherwise, on the face of the law, allow. "Mercy," on the other hand, involves an excepting or setting aside of the law, and thus has no need of the law's "discursive" forms, and certainly no need of the "central and distinctive technique" of the common law, analogical thinking. The point is that "like" must not "quit" "like" as we see in the scene – that is, in a neat conflation secured through sovereign declarations – for the pursuit of the "like" is the means by which, at the common law, the "wit," "reason," "self-sufficiencie," and "discursive" capacity of the community grows. The play's correlation of retributive justice and singular judicial authority operating as "the top of judgment" suggests a relation that the community must question, to bracket "mercy" as a practice not consistent with the common law's theoretical source of legal authority in communal forms of reasoning. Where any one person has the authority to "enforce or qualify the laws / As to [his] soul seems good" (1.1.66–7), the "discursive" character of the common law is effectively displaced.[35]

In its very staging of the Duke's acts of "mercy," however, the play works to paradoxical effect to highlight the capacity of all always to set aside what prevails as law in order to inaugurate another legal order. As Jacques Rancière has argued, the theater is a place of "constitution – sensible constitution – of the community."[36] Occupying together "a place and a time, as the body in action as opposed to a mere apparatus of laws," a theatrical audience experiences, both individually and collectively, its law-making capacity.[37] It does so in the first instance by "inhabit[ing] a set of perceptions, gestures and attitudes that precede and pre-form laws and political institutions" from which they shape between them a "third thing owned by no one" that is the aggregate of their powers of apprehension and comprehension.[38] The audience is not outside law or legality when taking in the play; rather, the experience of the play is the occasion for collectively comprehending how its members are constituted by or disposed to law so that they might reconstitute these relations or orchestrate different dispositions *to* law, and, indeed, different dispositions *of* law. This experience is the experience of the very constitutional power that James sought to deny, especially in *True Lawe*; as he would have it, both the English and Scottish polities had no choice but to concede to his absolute sovereign authority, the power to constitute the political arrangements and the law under which they live having been long ago decisively surrendered to conqueror-kings.[39] The plot shows clearly, in Vincentio's attempt to renovate his legal authority, that any such argument is always nonsense. The unfolding of the means by which Vincentio would reconstitute his authority is the orienting "fact" around which the audience's capacity for judgment and legal invention organizes itself. That judgment is to be exercised in part in relation to their own metonymic stand-in within the fiction, the citizens at the constitutional threshold of the city gates in Act 5 who are given no formal opportunity by the Duke to say anything at all.

The audience of *Measure for Measure* has the opportunity, in short, to experience in a performance of this play precisely what is suppressed in the dramatic fiction, the communicative power of citizens as a group, especially communicative power as the means by which to determine the legal order in which they live. As Jurgen Habermas argued in his 1995 book *Between Facts and Norms*, any law that claims to be legitimate must be founded upon and support the "communicative power" of all those for whom it obtains and to whom legal authority must be equally distributed: citizens, as "self-directing rational agents," must "give themselves" laws "in a discursively structured opinion- and will-formation" in which everyone has "equal opportunities for making effective use of equally distributed legal powers."[40] In 1604, the English had not yet achieved a political situation that permitted the members of the realm to act as "legal consociates . . . exercis[ing] their autonomy in a system of rights in need of interpretation and elaboration."[41] Their orientation to what kind of law they might create would, then, necessarily differ from our sense in relation to the situations that confront us in the early twenty-first century. But what remains the same in trans-historical experiences of the play is the sense of the potential of an aggregated communicative power to create new legal forms.

This communicative power, which in the existing common law forms of the early seventeenth century involved the narrative power of "fact"-making, can only be realized, however, to the extent that the audience engages in another order of forensic "suspicion" from that Hutson has discussed. The "fact" to be established by the audience via its experience of the play together in performance is how the given order of law has come to prevail, and how it sustains itself, a "fact" whose "discovery" and narration would itself be, for the audience, an inaugural instance of the process of making a new legality, one achieved through its forensic analysis of how its members are disposed to law, and why. Without this forensic enquiry, audience members are themselves prey to precisely the kind of singular judicial authority on display in the play, one that organizes the capacities of others so that they cannot cohere except in the forms that he has predicted and desires. With it, they are engaged in activities that predispose them to greater or more rigorous exercises of their communicative power or "discursive" capacity, in the interests of a legality that does not allow for retributive judgment, for retributive judgment is the means by which one person consolidates law-making authority in his own hands over and against the reasoning powers of the community or the intersubjective discursive forms by which the community, rather than any singular figure, might shape and adjudicate law. Pompey may let himself be incorporated into the apparatus of the kind of law that prevails in Vienna, but the audience's response is far more likely to be the opposite: to wish to align itself with a different kind of law than that which seeks the means to kill, even if this is subsequently avoided by an act of "mercy," and to find the source of this other law, and perhaps other forms of judgment, in itself.

When, for example, the audience witnesses, at play's end, the capriciousness of the Duke's judgments – a supposed murderer is pardoned, but a "slanderer" is not – its understanding that it knows more than the audience within the fiction involves the challenge of doing what the audience in the fiction cannot directly or explicitly do – exercising its own powers of judgment. The audience members' experience of their own powers to apprehend, think, act, and judge in concert in the time and space of playgoing in relation to the "fact" of the play is the experience of their constitutional potential or their capacity to inaugurate a new legality, or what Habermas, following Hannah Arendt, calls "juris-genesis."[42] In this experience, whether in 1604 or 2016, singular apprehension of the "fact" of the play is not enough. The individual's experience of the play as one member of the cohort who finds a group of "most generous and gravest" citizens as its stand-in within the fiction is the experience of the need for an aggregation of apprehensions. Without that, there can be no *convergence* of judgment. Only the coordinated sense of what has occurred in the fact of performance can manifest the forms of reasoning required of the common law, and that is precisely what the playgoing experience affords: the time and occasion for feeling the necessity of exercising together the capacity for reasoning-in-common required of judgment at the common law.

A "prosperous art" for "reason and discourse" in the "Open Court" of the Theater

As I have been arguing, audiences of *Measure for Measure* experience their constitutional power in regard to law or their powers of juris-genesis paradoxically – by watching, in Shakespeare's play, the dispersal or fragmentation of such capacities in the Duke's plot. One way to think of this, as Hutson has argued, is that the dramatic fiction, by affording the audience the opportunity of functioning like a jury in relation to the theatrical representation, exercises the audience's capacity for "forensic" reasoning or the production of "suspicion." I am arguing, however, that the audience experiences not simply its capacity to judge, but its capacity to make the legal order in which it lives, and not just by spinning pretty tropes, but as a matter of concrete practice. Within the fiction, one man alone takes judgments in a time and place in which he has the exclusive authority to determine what constitutes judgment, and whether or not judgment will be enforced, in an extended theatrical spectacle of his authority that displaces the fact-making power of all others; but the representation of the power unilaterally to create a court wherever he chooses serves as the specific means to engender in the audience questions about where law-founding and court-shaping power lies, and why. What is a court, after all, but a formal place in which the law is brought into being through an assembly that the community grants has the authority to constitute the law through its actions? The law must not be treated as a hypostasized entity of uncertain provenance that makes use of persons who can be shifted in and out of offices by a singular figure arrogating all constitutional power to himself or herself, and to whose decrees others are subjected when and where he alone determines. As Habermas has argued, "legitimate law" must involve no coercion.[43] Habermas's "legitimate law" and its necessary corollary, just judgment, require that the law's creative authority be assumed and exercised in public by those for whom the law obtains, and exercised in processes of deliberative reasoning.

What Habermas was seeking to articulate in the 1990s was, I suggest, a renovated and strengthened conception of the ideals of early modern common law jurisprudence.[44] We might think that democratic jurisprudence in the early twenty-first century has achieved what common law jurisprudence in the early seventeenth century could not, inclusive forms of adjudication at law; but this is, I think, not true. Democratic jurisprudence still depends on the functions of a specialized cohort doing the work of law, and judging on behalf of the community, and these cohorts do this work in forms that involve a genealogy that needs to be examined. As Ernst Kantorowicz argued in *The King's Two Bodies*, the early modern state emerged from medieval political theology by transferring the sacrality for which the king was formally the locus to the state and its apparatus. James's techniques may have differed from the process that Kantorowicz describes when he writes that "the ancient idea of liturgical kinship gradually dissolved [to give] way to a new pattern of kingship centered on the sphere of Law" through a "hallowing of the *status regis et regni*, of state institutions and utilities, necessities and emergencies,"[45] but they nevertheless crucially depended on the conflation of sovereign and divine authority that Shakespeare neatly reduplicates in his Friar-Duke, who looks "like power divine" on others' "passes" (5.1.370–1). This conflation continues silently to inform the figure of the sovereign from the early modern period forward, even as sovereignty itself takes new, seemingly more democratic forms in secular cultures. A kind of authority has transferred, and it still most commonly takes singular form in the figure of presidents, prime ministers, and chancellors. By presenting us with an antecedent form of sovereignty that continues to inform contemporary forms, Shakespeare's play makes possible another kind of forensic analysis for contemporary audiences. To what extent are our contemporary forms of judgment limited by their derivation from these historical forms? What more just forms of law do not yet exist because the derivation of our contemporary forms from the historical forms continues not only to prevent an equal distribution of legal authority, but also to hamper a legal creativity that might require new forms of "suspicion" or even a participatory system of justice expressing itself in forms other than "suspicion"? What intersubjective forms of life might decisively break with retributive judgment and the strictly circumscribed discursivity of the law that it depends upon and supports to inaugurate another legality? A judgment that is comprehensive in its inclusion of all in its processes as fully rational agents will necessarily differ from retributive judgment secured in relation to a "cleare" rule or a purportedly self-evident "fault."

For audiences in 1604, there would have been some urgency to treat Isabella, the character identified as the possessor of a "prosperous art" of "reason and discourse" (1.2.182–3), as a figure in relation to whom to test its own dispositions to law and judgment, and it is in relation to her predicament that it is most urgent that we think analogically. When Isabella argues, in exoneration of Angelo, that Claudio "did the thing for which he died" (5.1.450), she shows herself disposed to the kind of rule that defines itself in relation to narrow "things" and has no need of construction of a complex "fact" before it proceeds to judgment. This disposition carries through to her argument on Angelo's behalf, that in that other matter for which he stands accused, his attempt to sleep with her, his failure to succeed at what he intended exempts him from condemnation: "His act did not o'ertake his bad intent / And must be buried as an intent / That perished by the way" (5.1.451–3). This argument would obscure her own role in depriving him of intention behind closed doors with her participation in the bed-trick, in which Mariana took her place in the bed in which Isabella has agreed to sleep with Angelo. The two aspects of her argument in fact contradict one another: Isabella cannot justly argue for the protection of a private domain in which "thoughts are no subjects" (5.1.454) when she herself has acted, from a private domain, against the autonomy of another, to get him to translate "thoughts" into actions for which he can be subsequently condemned. Isabella is nevertheless a figure for the imposition of discursive restraint from without when she and the audience find her argument, whatever its merits or difficulties, dismissed by the Duke, and the audience must feel how compromised she is, or the extent to which she is unable to exercise freely her powers of consent in relation to the man now asking her to be his wife.

In 1604, the predicament of the character would have had some urgency for the audience, for her situation was tropically their own as the "wife" to a sovereign figure antagonistic to its members' powers of "reason and discourse."[46] As Postema notes, the common law "is rooted in consent";[47] indeed, it is its own (unwritten) "record" of the consent of the English to a "political constitution" that is the product of their customary practices. Isabella's "consent" may be, as James argued the consent of the English was to his rule, already surrendered. As such, her predicament is the predicament of the English people in relation to a sovereign antagonistic to their common law. But even the most minor of characters, those who function as nothing more than a name in a roster of those imprisoned for debt such as Master Rash or Master Caper, matter to the play's depiction of a community that is compromised in its ability to find the means by which its members may function as the source of law. In both 1604 and 2016, the play fulfills its function as comedy most powerfully where the experience of the forms of judgment on display in the play becomes the occasion for feeling the necessity of stronger forms of reasoning-in-common that would begin to approximate the "shared power of the equality of intelligence" that Rancière argues is felt in the course of the theatergoing experience, and the equal distribution of legal authority that is for Habermas essential to democratic jurisprudence.[48]

It is precisely this that makes Isabella such a resonant figure for contemporary audiences, despite everything else about the character that marks her as so thoroughly a figure for the predicaments of English culture in 1604. She is a figure for our own potential collusion in operations that, by depriving individuals of their autonomy, deprive us collectively of the capacity to make law together as equals. Contemporary democratic legal cultures tend to take us away from rather than toward a renovated ideal of common law jurisprudence that would not merely meet its responsibilities to the contemporary "commons" by being public and forensic, but by heightening the legal order's capacity to include all comprehensively within its rationality so that any judgment at law might justly be construed as the judgment of "the people." As Wendy Brown has recently argued, the "dedemocratization" of "neoliberalized law," which promotes the "conversion of political processes, subjects, categories, and principles to economic ones," aims to eliminate "popular power" from the "democratic political imaginary."[49] In this attempt it allows for:

> anything but collaborative and contestatory human decision making, control over the conditions of existence, planning for the future; anything but deliberate constructions of existence through democratic discussion, law, policy. Anything but the human knowledge, deliberation, judgment, and action classically associated with *homo politicus*.[50]

The compromising of Isabella, that compromising in which she colludes, finds a fitting corollary in all those subject to "neoliberalized law" whose legal judgments are increasingly rendered in one or another form of private adjudication, as states permit a privatization of law centered on promoting exchanges between private economic actors or states as actors whose interests are only economic. The "sovereign" in his different contemporary forms, whether individual or corporate, may know what the "people" may not, but often even sovereignty itself is compromised by the economic transactions that it agrees to allow in non-public spheres. Subject to a growing body of legal decisions for which rationales are never publicly declared, we have a greatly reduced opportunity to produce the "facts" of the economic transactions that aggregate to structure our "common life" in situations that reduplicate on a vast scale the dynamics with which Shakespeare's play confronts us: legal facts are not necessarily even publicly known, never mind publicly tried, thereby making it impossible for a given polity to exercise its capacities for judgment together in relation to legal matter; and even those who believe they know the facts of such arrangements are publicly positioned in such a way that their capacities to use their discursive powers for another kind of law are, like Isabella's, foreclosed.[51] In such a situation, the "people" cannot claim to be the source of law, and cannot begin to orient themselves to the "facts" that are killing off "common life" as a vastly more complex set of economic and legal actors than those with which the play confronts us works to suppress the possibility of a legality originating in and shaped by all. A world of private arbitrations and secret trade agreements between countries is one in which the distribution of legal authority notionally secured in democracies is thwarted in direct proportion to the law's increased privatization. Individuals find themselves disposed to law without knowing what forces are at work determining the possibilities and limits of their legal relations; and whatever arguments they may then seek to pose to law are necessarily narrowed and weakened not only by the partial nature of individual knowledge, but any mechanism that works to keep individuals' discursive capacities from cohering with the capacities of others. In the worst of situations, individuals actively collude to shape the law's force over others to secure the economic interests of a few. At the very least what is required by way of response is a heightened legal creativity that can generate not only new objects of "suspicion" or the ability of members of the polity in general to investigate not merely offenses against law but actions taken in law's name, in private transactions, but new legal forms that guarantee comprehensive public reasoning about the existing forms. The invention of new legal forms would simultaneously, as Habermas suggests, generate a new "code" while exemplifying the discursive capacity and authority from which that "code" springs.[52]

In the Globe in 1604, those subject to the law had the opportunity to assemble to be confronted with and apprehend fictional dynamics of judgment at law so that they might construe their congregation in the time and space of playgoing as the means whereby another legal order might take incipient form through the intellectual activities of those gathered there. As a public thing, open to the experience of everyone, the "common house" of the theater was, like Mistress Overdone's, a place of production that could never be fully regulated by any state, a place where audience members could experience (whatever else may have gone on there) the possibility of their intellectual conjunction as well as the possibility of their aesthetic judgments shaping the social relations from which the law springs and which it then sustains. Now, as a textual artifact of a cultural form that engaged historical audiences in noncoercive discursive relations through which players and audience might together shape relations to law, the play continues to be an aesthetic toy from which new ideas of law might be shaped, especially by engaging audiences in analysis of the forces militating not simply against exercises of their powers of "suspicion," but their powers of juris-genesis. An old form, one that involved a practice with the disposition of natures and capacities to judge, might also help us finally resolve the problem with which the play continues to leave us in its representation of a sovereignty that displaces law-making discursive power with an economics of judgment. Where its own discursive capacity is freshly harnessed to stimulate the desire for and commitment to a legality that effectively regulates the economic dynamics that interfere with and suppress not only an equal distribution of legal authority but discursive forms that would function free of economic exchange (whether in compensatory schemes of retributive judgment or the debt production of finance capital), *Measure for Measure* may help bring into being new legal forms that break with the antecedents with which it confronts us to shape a collective "nature" and a jurisprudence that refuses to allow any form of retributive judgment at all.

Notes

1. Gerald Postema, "Classical Common Law Jurisprudence (Part 1)," *Oxford University Commonwealth Law Journal* 2 (2002): 156. The phrase itself was not used until the eighteenth century, by Bentham.
2. Edward Coke, *The Twelfth Part of the Reports of Sir Edward Coke, Kt.* (London, 1658), 63, 65.
3. Ibid., 65.
4. Ibid., 64.
5. Postema, "Classical I," 176.

6. Gerald Postema, "Philosophy of the Common Law," in *The Oxford Handbook of Jurisprudence and Philosophy of Law*, ed. Jules L. Coleman, Kenneth Einar Himma, and Scott J. Shapiro (Oxford: Oxford University Press, 2004), 588–622 (pp. 602, 594, and 602); "Classical Common Law Jurisprudence (Part II)," *Oxford University Commonwealth Law Journal* 3 (2003): 1–28, 7; "Classical I," 164; "Philosophy," 595, 597.

7. Postema, "Philosophy," 595.

8. Edward Coke, *La Neuf^{me} Part des Reports de Sr. Edw. Coke* (London, 1613), c vi^v.

9. John Davies, *Le Primer Report des Cases & Matters en Ley resolues et adiudges en les Courts del Roy en Ireland* (Dublin, 1615), *2v.

10. James VI, *The True Lawe of Free Monarchies: or The Reciprock and Mutuall Dutie Betwixt a Free King, and his Naturall Subiectes* (Edinburgh, 1598), D^r. As Constance Jordan notes in her recent account of the play, James's position that he was above the law contradicted English conceptions of the king's relation to law from the thirteenth-century legal writer Henri de Bracton forward. See Constance Jordan, "Interpreting Statute in *Measure for Measure*," in *Shakespeare and the Law: A Conversation Among Disciplines and Professions*, ed. Bradin Cormack, Martha C. Nussbaum, and Richard Strier (Chicago: University of Chicago Press, 2013), 101–20.

11. James I, *The Workes of the Most High and Mightie Prince, Iames by the grace of God, King of Great Britaine, France and Ireland, Defender of the Faith, &c.* (London, 1616), 532.

12. Ibid.

13. Ibid., 556, 533.

14. For a quite different approach to how the play engages questions about judgment at the common law, see Bernadette Meyler, "'Our Cities Institutions' and the Institution of the Common Law," *Yale Journal of Law and the Humanities* 22 (2010): 441–66. Meyler's exploration of the tension between Coke and James around the question of the king's right to judge involves consideration of the various kinds of "flawed" judgment that we witness in the play, especially in Angelo and Escalus. Meyler finds in the play "a nascent common law justification for prohibiting the King for judging in person" (461), a justification engaged with Coke's concept of the common law's "artificiall" reason, in Escalus's conception of Angelo as a "brother-justice" (455).

15. Davies, *Le Primer Report*, *2v, Davies's emphases.

16. Ibid., *6v.

17. Ibid., *2v.

18. Ibid., *4r, Davies's emphases.

19. Ibid.

20. Ibid., *4v, Davies's emphases.

21. Lorna Hutson, *The Invention of Suspicion: Law and Mimesis in Shakespeare and Renaissance Drama* (Oxford: Oxford University Press, 2007), 76.
22. "A Proclamation for Jurors," in *Stuart Royal Proclamations*, ed. James F. Larkin and Paul L. Hughes, 2 vols. (Oxford: Clarendon Press, 1973), 1:167–71. For a related account of James's relationship to Elizabethan laws, see Jacques Lezra, "Pirating Reading: The Appearance of History in *Measure for Measure*," *ELH* 56 (1989): 255–92, esp. 267–8.
23. J. H. Baker, *The Oxford History of the Laws of England, Volume VI: 1483–1558* (Oxford: Oxford University Press, 2003), 353.
24. Hutson, *Invention*, 251, Hutson's emphases.
25. Ibid., 68.
26. Baker, *Laws of England*, 362.
27. Hutson, *Invention*, 7.
28. On the "mystery" of Barnardine, see Lezra, "Pirating Reading," esp. 255–9, and Andrew Majeske, "Equity's Absence: The Extremity of Claudio's Prosecution and Barnardine's Pardon in Shakespeare's *Measure for Measure*," *Law and Literature* 21.2 (2009): 169–84, esp. 176–8.
29. James, *Workes*, 545.
30. On the state of exception, see Giorgio Agamben, *State of Exception*, trans. Kevin Attell (Chicago: University of Chicago Press, 2005), esp. 3 and 79.
31. Jürgen Habermas, *Between Facts and Norms: Contributions to a Discourse Theory of Law and Democracy* (Cambridge, MA: MIT Press, 1995), esp. 150–2.
32. As the Oxford English Dictionary notes, the old French "merci" is derived from the Latin *mercēd*, wages, fee, bribe, rent, price, commodity.
33. Jeffrey Reiman, "The Marxian Critique of Criminal Justice," in *Radical Philosphy of Law: Contemporary Challenges to Mainstream Legal Theory and Practice*, ed. David S. Caudill and Steven Jay Gold (Atlantic Highlands, NJ: Humanities International Press, 1995), 111–39 (p. 125).
34. See James, *Workes*, 558: "And where the rigour of the Law in many cases will vndoe a Subiect, there the Chancerie tempers the Law with equitie, and so mixeth Mercy with Iustice, as it preserues men from destruction."
35. On this topic, see David Bevington, "Equity in Measure for Measure," in *Shakespeare and the Law: A Conversation Among Disciplines and Professions*, ed. Bradin Cormack, Martha C. Nussbaum, and Richard Strier (Chicago: University of Chicago Press, 2013), 164–73; Majeske, "Equity's Absence"; and Eric V. Spencer, "Scaling the Deputy: Equity and Mercy in Measure for Measure," *Philosophy and Literature* 36 (2012): 166–82.
36. Jacques Rancière, *The Emancipated Spectator*, trans. Gregory Elliott (London: Verso, 2009), 6.
37. Ibid., 6.

38. Ibid., 6, 15.
39. See especially James's discussion of Scotland's first king, Fergus, and his construction of William of Normandy's conquering of England in *The True Lawe of Free Monarchies*: he "gaue the law," he writes, "& tooke none" (C8^r).
40. Habermas, *Between Facts and Norms*, 612 and 170, and "Introduction," *Ratio Juris* 12 (1999): 329–35, 333.
41. Habermas, *Between Facts and Norms*, 159.
42. Ibid., 148.
43. Ibid., 121.
44. There is an irony to this, as Habermas claimed that the legal propositions of *Between Facts and Norms* derived from his experience of German civil law jurisprudence. In a 1999 essay, however, he expanded upon the book's legal ideas in a statement that clearly shows their debt to the thinking of the English common law: "private legal subjects cannot enjoy equal liberties if they themselves do not in advance exercise their civic autonomy in common in order to specify which interests are at stake and which standards of evaluation are justified in the light of which cases should be treated alike." See Habermas, "Introduction," 334.
45. Ernst Kantorowicz, *The King's Two Bodies* (Princeton: Princeton University Press, 1957), 192.
46. For James's metaphor of the "whole isle" of England and Scotland as his "lawfull Wife," see *Workes*, 488.
47. Postema, "Classical II," 22.
48. Rancière, *Emancipated Spectator*, 17.
49. Wendy Brown, *Undoing the Demos: Neoliberalism's Stealth Revolution* (Cambridge, MA: MIT Press, 2015), 152, 158, and 153.
50. Ibid., 221–2.
51. For an important recent example of such issues being investigated by the mainstream press, see the *New York Times*' companion pieces on private arbitrations, Jessica Silver-Greenberg and Robert Gebeloff's "Arbitration Everywhere, Stacking the Deck of Justice," 31 October 2015, and Jessica Silver-Greenberg and Michael Crockery's "In Arbitration, a 'Privatization of the Justice System'," 1 November 2015.
52. Habermas, *Between Facts and Norms*, 122.

Chapter 6

The Laws of *Measure for Measure*
Paul Yachnin

Near the end of *Measure for Measure*, a woman kneels before a judge and pleads for the life of the man who has dishonored her and who (she believes) has had her brother beheaded. She performs this extraordinary action for a number of reasons – to give the condemned man another chance to be better than he has been, to assure that the condemned man's new wife will not be made a new widow, and, finally, to honor what she evidently believes is the cause of justice.

In the moments that follow and that close the play, the urgency, complexity, and gravity of the woman's plea are washed away by a flood of what are supposed to pass as acts of mercy, but which are so indiscriminate as to be empty of moral weight altogether. Then, without a scintilla of warning, the judge, who is scattering his acts of mercy wildly among almost everyone on the stage, turns and asks the woman to marry him. It is as if a severe stone statue facing us were suddenly revealed to be a helium-filled balloon. The action and meaning of the play float crazily away.

Why does the play swing from the seriousness of Isabella's plea to the weirdly profligate forgivings that Vincentio showers on all? To answer this question, we will have to consider how the play develops a critical representation of three kinds of law, each one having its own special relationship with the ideal of justice. At the end, we will come back to Isabella. To a considerable degree, Isabella is us – the figure of how the play summons its audiences and readers to the labor of judgment, situates our judging apart from the machinations of the powerful, characterizes theater-born judging as a form of serious play (after all, Isabella has not been raped by Angelo, her brother has not been killed), and reveals the stakes of judgment for the judges themselves. But first, let us look again at the play's ending.

* * *

When she elects to plead for Angelo's life, Isabella takes the play's thematic lines of law and justice and ties them in a knot. At the start, the play pits law against justice. Isabella herself is the lead witness against the law. When she first hears that her brother is in prison for getting his betrothed pregnant, she says, "Someone with child by him? My cousin Juliet? . . . O let him marry her!" (1.4.45–9).[1] To Isabella, imprisonment and death do not seem just treatment for someone who has made love to his betrothed in advance of the formalities of the wedding. It is hard to imagine very many spectators at the play, then or now, disagreeing with her.[2]

In the course of the action, the relationship between law and justice gets more complex. It is remarkable that by the time she comes to plead before Angelo for her brother's life, Isabella seems to have changed her mind about the law. She says to Angelo, "There is a vice that most I do abhor, / And most desire should meet the blow of justice; / For which I would not plead, but that I must" (2.2.29–31). And when he rebuffs her plea, she simply declares her support for the statute: "O just but severe law! / I had a brother then" (2.2.41–2). This sudden reversal might be sincere or strategic on her part. In any case, her support of the law is very brief: in what follows in the scene, she opens a yawning gulf between law and justice by insisting on the fallenness of all humankind, judges included; by placing true justice with God and not with human beings; and by characterizing as an act of tyranny the application of an out-of-use statute to punish a single person for something that everyone everywhere does almost all the time.

But here, at the end of the play, when Mariana enjoins her to support her (Mariana's) plea for the life of Angelo, Isabella mixes up law and justice thoroughly:

> Isabella (*kneeling*): Most bounteous sir,
> Look, if it please you, on this man condemned
> As if my brother lived. I partly think
> A due sincerity governed his deeds
> Till he did look on me; since it is so,
> Let him not die. My brother had but justice,
> In that he did the thing for which he died.
> For Angelo,
> His act did not o'ertake his bad intent,
> And must be buried but as an intent
> That perished by the way. Thoughts are no subjects,
> Intents but merely thoughts. (5.1.444–55)

She talks as if she thought that the law could readily produce a just outcome. She petitions for the life of the wicked judge even though he had ordered the execution of her brother – and ordered it a second time (by "private message" – 5.1.461) after he had promised to spare Claudio's life in exchange for her virginity. She says that her brother "had but justice, / In that he did the thing for which he died" (5.1.449–50). The thing he did, of course, was to have sex with Juliet before marriage. That means that she has to ignore the parallel act of the man for whose life she is pleading.

It makes sense to argue that you cannot punish someone for thinking he has committed a crime when in fact no crime has been committed. "Thoughts are no subjects," Isabella says, "Intents but merely thoughts" (5.1.454–5). It makes less sense to argue for a pardon for someone's (unrealized) evil intentions when that someone is a judge and his evil intentions have defamed the formal institution of justice. And if it is just to execute Claudio for breaking the law against extra-marital sex, which is what Isabella says, then it is hard indeed to credit her justification of the pardon of Angelo, who seems also to have committed the crime of extra-marital sex.

By the way, it doesn't help to argue for the coherence of Isabella's position by pointing out that Claudio and Juliet lacked "the denunciation . . . Of outward order" (1.2.146–7) while Angelo and Mariana had already made the arrangements for their wedding (see 3.1.215–16). Both couples were contracted to be married. Claudio's claim that "upon a true contract / [he] got possession of Julietta's bed" (1.2.143–4) is compelling.[3] The difference between the two couples is no better than legalistic hair-splitting with little bearing on the justice of Isabella's plea.[4] Indeed, the only bearing such a legalism might have would be to call further into question Isabella's simultaneous assertion of the justice of the execution of one man who had sex with his betrothed and the justice of a pardon of another man who did the same thing.

Isabella's petition is legalistic special pleading. Worse still, her excuse for Angelo, that he only had evil *thoughts*, brushes aside the weighty Christian argument that she had made against his legal formalism in her first meeting with him. "It is the law," Angelo said, "not I condemn your brother" (2.2.81). Her counter-argument was that punishment and mercy are exemplarily the means and the signs of God's judgment and love of humankind; human judges should seek that inward knowledge of others and certainly of themselves. "Go to your bosom," she said to him, "Knock there, and ask your heart what it doth know / That's like my brother's fault" (2.2.138–40). Here she brackets off thoughts and intents as if they were no part of the business of the law even as she is concocting a legalistic argument for the justice of a pardon for Angelo.

But, ironically enough, the contradictoriness of her argument makes it more rather than less compelling. She is speaking against her own interests and convictions – her love of her brother, her justifiable fury at Angelo, her belief in the importance of *mens rea*, and even her love of straight talking. Shakespeare is careful to remind us about what is at stake for her. Against Mariana's request that Isabel take her part, Vincentio says,

> Against all sense you do importune her.
> Should she kneel down in mercy of this fact,
> Her brother's ghost his pavèd bed would break
> And take her hence in horror. (5.1.434–7)

But Isabella brackets her love, her anger, and sense/reason itself in order to do the right thing, which is to begin the process of forgiveness of the wrongdoer, assure the life of the new marriage between Angelo and Mariana, and offer support to the woman who has become a kind of sister to her. Against Vincentio's formalist exegesis of the biblical verse that gives the play its name, she enacts the inward conscientiousness of judgment that is the true meaning of "measure for measure." He had said to her, "'An Angelo for Claudio, death for death; / Haste still pays haste, and leisure answers leisure; / Like doth quit like, and Measure still for Measure'" (5.1.410–12). In Matthew 7.2, the metaphor is not about the mechanistic operation of the *lex talionis*, but rather about the ethics of judging and the necessary implication of judges in their judgments: "For with what judgment ye judge, ye shall be judged, and with what measure ye mete, it shall be measured unto you again."[5]

What happens in the wake of Isabella's plea for Angelo's life is not an unknotting of the tangle of law and justice but something more like the transformation of that urgent, difficult interrelationship into a kind of pardon party. The actions that end the play simply dissolve the problems that the play has put before us from the start. Law and justice both seem to have gone on holiday. Mercy falls on everyone with no account given to what crimes they have or have not committed and no attention paid to the guilt or innocence of their state of mind. The remorseless murderer Barnardine is set free for no apparent reason. Angelo is pardoned. Lucio's only punishment is having to marry Kate Keepdown, a woman who had a child by him. (That, by the way, makes Lucio also guilty of the capital crime of having sex outside marriage, but that charge isn't mentioned.) Even the impeccable Provost is accused of wrongdoing, only, it seems, so that he can join the congregation of the freshly pardoned. The scandalous lightness of the final moments of the play is exemplified by the Duke's pardon of Claudio, which is given simply because he is Isabella's brother, because Isabella is lovely, and because the Duke wants to marry her (5.1.493–5).[6]

*   *   *

In a recent essay, Richard Strier has argued (mostly by way of *2 Henry IV* but also with an eye on *Measure for Measure*) that Shakespeare does not anywhere in his drama imagine "a well-functioning legal system": "in every instance in which Shakespeare seems to imagine such, and to give it the recognizable features of such, he also immediately raises issues that complicate, undermine, or call into question the possibility and even desirability of such a thing."[7] When he gets to *Measure for Measure*, Strier's argument anticipates mine in important respects. The rain of pardons that blankets everyone at the end of the play is alien to the character of any legal system – "or rather," he says, "the only one conceivable would postulate a judge (like Christ at the Last Judgment) who does not have to be forgiven for anything."[8] Justice itself is disabled since a legal process that cannot distinguish between Barnardine and Claudio can hardly be said to be functioning at all:

> If the legal system were working at all, and able to provide punishments as well as pardons, it would differentiate clearly between the legal situations of Claudio and Barnardine. Claudio's legal guilt as a "fornicator" is . . . questionable at best, and the "crime" at issue questionable (and questioned) as such. But Barnardine's crime is murder, a major offense in any imaginable legal system. The Provost, a model of integrity in the play, sharply distinguishes between the two prisoners condemned to execution.[9]

In what follows, I do not take issue with Strier's particular observations, with which indeed I agree, but I do undertake to shift the angle of view so that it becomes possible to see how Shakespeare is in fact imagining a system of judgment and law-making in *Measure for Measure*. To focus our attention on the play in the playhouse rather than on the world in the play is to begin to see how playing and playgoing might have enabled the creation of a system of popular, collective judgment and law-making – a new "common law" – emerging from the playhouse. The law, Shakespeare suggests, cannot be something that stands apart from us or is transcendent over us. It must be something that we own as the expression of our collective judgment over time and in public space. In the simplest way and in relation to one of the most usual features of Shakespeare's dramatic art, we can already discern how the play invites audience judgment by noting, as Strier has pointed out, that the play puts in question, by virtue of the Provost's view of the two criminals, the justice of Vincentio's indiscriminate pardoning of Barnardine and Claudio.

I want to make a case for the lawfulness of *Measure for Measure* and for the lawfulness of Shakespeare's drama in general and for theatrical performance and reception as law-making practices, not of course in the sense of establishing legal statutes, setting the terms of contractual agreements, or apportioning penalties for transgressors of the law. Rather, I want to consider the relationship between the space of the playhouse, the practices of performance, and the ways by which groupings of people undertake to regulate and legitimate (and delegitimate) actions, utterances, exchanges, and relationships, how they form themselves into lawful communities, and how they, by law-making, give meaning and value to the world. It makes sense to call these practices law-making because they organize and empower collective judgment by establishing model narratives, core texts (like the works of Shakespeare), understandings of the inner worlds of other people, world-shaping vocabularies, and informal procedures for discussing, debating, and judging.[10]

The social creativity of Shakespeare's theatrical art in plays like *Measure for Measure* was of a piece with a larger movement in early modernity toward the growth of a larger, more vital, and more inclusive public space, a space for speaking, judging, and acting for an increasingly diverse population, both in England and on the Continent. Research over approximately the past two decades has begun to demonstrate in considerable detail how the rapid expansion of the production, circulation, and uptake of works of art and intellect (much of that expansion enabled by a nascent entertainment industry that included controversialist publication as well as theatrical performance and much else) enabled new forms of public association and public debate among those who had formerly been merely "private" people.[11] For an overview of these massive socio-political changes, it is worth quoting historians Peter Lake and Steve Pincus on the normalization of relatively free political discussion by the end of the seventeenth century:

> while participants in the post-Reformation public spheres considered political communication to be a necessary evil, by the end of our period many (though by no means all) political actors understood relatively unfettered public discussion to be normatively desirable . . . In the post-Revolutionary period not only did actors perceive the existence of the public sphere as the normal state of affairs; some came to see that state of affairs as a positive good.[12]

* * *

My way into this account of the legal generativity of *Measure for Measure* is by sketching the three genres of law that are salient in the play as well as active in Shakespeare generally – I look especially at *Richard II* – and then by following them into the play. The three genres are the law of sovereign will, the law of kind, and the law of judgment.

Sovereign will is the law underpinning public and private life that is projected from the living world of the lawmakers and the subjects of the law into a timeless, transcendent, and authoritative realm. The law as sovereign will can be located in the monarch. King James, who well understood the complex overlapping legal systems of early seventeenth-century England, nevertheless claimed his supreme authority on the basis of his special relationship with the divine:

> The state of monarchy is the supremest thing upon earth. For kings are not only God's lieutenants upon earth and sit upon God's throne, but even by God himself they are called gods. . . . [kings] make and unmake their subjects: they have power of raising and casting down, of life and of death – judges over all their subjects and in all causes, and yet accomptable to none but God only.[13]

The law of sovereign will can be the written law as devised by figures such as Moses, Justinian, or the Founding Fathers. It can be authorized by reference to God, as in the case of James, or the "ancient constitution," as with James's opponents (such as Edward Coke), or to some other figure or force that stands apart from the world itself.[14]

The "sovereign," says Carl Schmitt, "is he who decides on the exception."[15] Schmitt does not mean merely that the sovereign can be brought in to adjudicate particularly tricky cases that cannot be decided straightforwardly according to codified legal norms. His claim is more radical than that. Since the ground of any logical structure is necessarily of a piece with and yet also must stand out-side that structure, it is precisely the decision that is not determined by anything codified that constitutes the founding act of the law. "After all," Schmitt says, "every legal order is based on a decision, and also the concept of the legal order, which is applied as some-thing self-evident, contains within it the contrast of the two distinct elements of the juristic – norm and decision. Like every other order, the legal order rests on a decision and not on a norm."[16]

For Schmitt, the sovereign is a person. With a few controversial exceptions (such as Henry V or Vincentio), Shakespeare is skeptical about any individual's fitness for rule. For Shakespeare, the law of sovereign will finds its home in the realm of ideas rather than in the hands of a human being. It includes both divine right theory and also the idea of the ancient constitution. A number of plays, includ-ing *Measure for Measure*, mine below the system of political hier-archy that is said usually to be based on sovereignty, based, that is, on an authority that stands apart from and is a priori to the politi-cal system and its political actors. The history play *Richard II* pits divine right theory against constitutionalism. The contest cannot be settled definitively, since both views of the foundation of power depend on principles external to the operations of power them-selves. When Richard decides to plunder the estate of the Duke of Herford (the Duke has just died), York makes a constitutionalist case against the king's assumption that monarchy is not bound by the established laws of inheritance:

> Take Herford's rights away, and take from Time
> His charters and his customary rights;
> Let not to-morrow then ensue to-day;
> Be not thyself; for how art thou a king
> But by fair sequence and succession? (*Richard II*, 2.1,189–99)[17]

York's point is not merely that monarchy is bound to the law, but rather that law is the ground of monarchy. It had been a familiar principle for centuries. "For there is no *rex*," said the medieval jurist Henry de Bracton, "where will rules rather than *lex*."[18] This is a strong argument, but it cannot be decisive, especially since the play maintains and develops the debate on both sides – the king retains a kind of sacredness even though his political and moral shortcomings as a ruler can justify his ouster; the king's opponents espouse vari-ously a constitutionalist view, sheer pragmatism, and even a divine right idea of monarchy even as they are deposing the king.[19]

More decisive than the constitutionalist vs. divine right debate (which unfolds within the jurisdiction, so to speak, of the law of sovereign will) is the king's encounter with his own mortality and humanity. As he passes into the jurisdiction of the law of kind, his monarchy is revealed to him as something merely artificial – constructed out of nothing more substantial than high-sounding language, ceremonial practices, habits of deference, and laws and customs, all of which turn out to be alarmingly malleable. This, according to Shakespeare, is the humbling fate of the divine right monarch of Jacobean ideology, Schmitt's "sovereign . . . he who decides on the exception," or any mortal creature that claims to be "the supremest thing upon earth."

At the start of his heartbreak, with enemies gathering against him, and no sign of the legions of angels he has said were at hand to come to his defense, King Richard says,

> Cover your heads, and mock not flesh and blood
> With solemn reverence, throw away respect,
> Tradition, form, and ceremonious duty,
> For you have but mistook me all this while.
> I live with bread like you, feel want,
> Taste grief, need friends: subjected thus,
> How can you say to me, I am a king? (3.2.171–7)

The law of kind overlaps with but is not the same as natural law. The latter is law predicated on natural reason. According to Coke, "[t]he law of nature is that which God at the time of creation of the nature of man infused into his heart, for his preservation and direction; and this is *lex aeterna*, the moral law, called also the law of nature."[20] In contrast, the law of kind is based on our recognition of our shared rootedness in nature, and it calls on a range of natural feelings (including feelings of pain and aloneness), appetites, capacities, needs, and frailties that we share with other humans as well as with non-human animals. When Prospero in *The Tempest* shifts from a conviction about his rightful sovereignty over others to a felt kinship with his former enemies, he credits his new-found embrace of the law of kind to his passion and capacity for suffering first of all. Although he avows the standard view of the superiority of reason over passion, it is in fact his kindly passion that gives birth to his "nobler reason":

> Hast thou, which art but air, a touch, a feeling
> Of their afflictions, and shall not myself,
> One of their kind, that relish all as sharply

Passion as they, be kindlier mov'd than thou art?
Though with their high wrongs I am strook to th' quick,
Yet, with my nobler reason 'gainst my fury
Do I take part. The rarer action is
In virtue than in vengeance. (5.1.21–8)

Here, by the way, Shakespeare seems to be in conversation with Michel de Montaigne. This scene owes something to Montaigne's essay, "Of Cruelty."[21] More generally, Shakespeare's law of kind is an elaboration of the French thinker's argument in *The Apologie for Raymond Sebonde*, where he says,

> I have said all this to maintain the coherency and resemblance that is in all humane things, and to bring us unto the general throng. We are neither above nor under the rest: what ever is under the coape of heaven (saith the wise man) runneth one law, and followeth one fortune.[22]

It is usually the case in Shakespeare that the law of kind trumps the law of will. It is a higher court, so to speak. We see this in the arc of action in *Richard II* and pre-eminently in *King Lear*, which moves from the rituals of power, royal determination of inheritance, strong bonds of fealty, and sacral kingship to Lear's recognition that humans, including the king himself, are animals too. The same movement from one court to another plays out also, in a different register, in a comedy like *Love's Labor's Lost* or in the romance *The Winter's Tale*, where political hierarchy and all the juridical accoutrements of rule turn to air before the rising power of natural desire and natural growth and reproduction – what the latter play calls "great creating Nature" (4.4.88).

The laws of sovereign will and of kind are related processually in Shakespeare, with the former typically giving way to the latter and the latter emerging as the ground of value and legitimacy. But they also share a key similarity. They both give us law as something that stands above time and change and that is independent of individual and collective agency. The third genre, the law of judgment, is, in contrast, of a piece with active, collective public life, action, and discourse. Being without any foundation outside the living social world, it is necessarily open to challenge, change, and revision. The law of judgment, we might say, belongs to the people whereas the people belong to the laws of sovereign will and kind.

The law of judgment is related to the English common law in as much as both are not a matter of statute but of case law and precedent, where each new judgment is based on previous judgments but where each new ruling also is capable of changing the legal force of precedent cases. In the common law, the sagacity and learning of the judges are always in play, at least ideally, since the law is subject to correction and dialogical rethinking in an open-ended way. The differences between the common law and Shakespeare's law of judgment, however, are more significant than the similarities. The common lawyers were a closed, credentialized group. Their professional language, as King James pointed out, was an artificial, incomprehensible "Law French." "I could wish," the King said, "that it were written in our vulgar language, for now it is an old, mixed, and corrupt language, only understood by lawyers, whereas every subject ought to understand the law under which he lives."[23] The "ancient constitution" was itself a fiction. According to Ian Ward, the "common law [was] an imaginary body of law, the origins of which were deliberately lost in the mists of time, and which provided an essentially fictional foundation upon which the liberties of the free Englishman were secured, and the powers of the sovereign supposedly defined."[24]

Ironically enough, one of the hallmark features of English legal judgment was, according to contemporary jurists, its open, public character. Sir Thomas Smith wrote in 1601,

> This is to be understood, although it will seem strange to all nations that do use the civil law of the Roman emperors, that for life and death there is nothing put in writing but the indictment only. All the rest is done openly in the presence of the judges, the justices, the inquest, the prisoner, and so many as will or can come so near as to hear it, and all the depositions and witnesses given aloud, that all men may hear from the mouth of the depositors and witnesses what is said.[25]

Shakespeare's theater sought to make judgment as open and accessible (to anyone who could pay the penny it cost to enter the playhouse) as it was imagined by jurists like Smith. The cultivation of popular judgment is a nearly ubiquitous feature of Shakespeare's theatrical art. A good example of how theater cultivates popular judgment is the moment in *Richard II* when Richard and Henry Bolingbroke stand in brief tableau, the hand of each competitor grasping the crown of England. In the fiction they stand before Parliament; in the playhouse the roles of the parliamentarians are taken by the playgoers, the vast majority of them commoners. They are being invited to judge among themselves the justice of the deposition of a legitimate king on account of his gubernatorial incompetence.

*   *   *

The laws of sovereign will, kind, and judgment intermingle and collide in *Measure for Measure*, but the orientation of the comedy, perhaps to a degree greater than in any other Shakespeare play, is toward the cultivation of the law of judgment. The play develops a powerful critique of the laws of both sovereign will and kind. By the end, there is no source of authority or value outside ourselves to which we could surrender the task of judging. There is no refuge for ethical spectators beyond their own abilities to judge the characters, their actions, and the overall meaning and implications of the play.

Even if embodied in the governor, as King James or Carl Schmitt would have it, the law of sovereign will is supposed to be a form of transcendent authority able more or less to guarantee just treatment for everyone. Angelo presents the law forbidding sex outside marriage as a means of fostering a virtuous society (2.2.91–107), but it turns out to be less an instrument of justice and good order than simply a juridical means of getting one's will – getting what one wants. Claudio says that Angelo is enforcing the "fornication law" against him solely in order to establish his, Angelo's, reputation as a law-and-order governor (1.2.154–69). Sovereign will is also a way to get whom you want. "Will" means sexual desire, like the "hot burning will" in *The Rape of Lucrece* (l. 247). In the play, Angelo uses the fornication law as a weapon against Isabella's chastity. "Redeem thy brother," he says to her, "By yielding up thy body to my will, / Or else he must not only die the death, / But thy unkindness shall his death draw out / To lingering sufferance" (2.4.164–8).

The Duke's actions are surprisingly parallel to Angelo's. In response to Friar Thomas's suggestion about a possible romantic tryst, Vincentio explains that his mission is juridical and political and even conversional, something like the moral reform of the city by way of his Deputy's enforcement of the criminal law against venial transgression as well as by his own information-gathering on a number of key citizens. The play provides no disconfirmation of the Duke's professed plan or of his commitment to a chaste life of study and rule, so it is surprising indeed when, as we have seen, he proposes marriage to Isabella and then couples the proposal with a reminder about his power to save her brother from death.

So the law of sovereign will can simply serve the willfulness of the judges. It can also bend to the point of breaking those who fall under its authority. We have seen already Isabella reverse her view of her brother's "crime" of love-making. Claudio himself is harried by the back and forth pressure of the fornication law on one side and the apparent legitimacy of his marriage pre-contract on the other – from likening himself to "rats that raven down their bane, / A thirsty evil" to explaining how "upon a true contract / [He] got possession of Julietta's bed" (1.2.128–9, 143–4).

Worse still, characters can paradoxically instrumentalize the law even as they are being instrumentalized by it. When Angelo rebuffs Isabella early in the play by saying it is the law, not he, that condemns her brother, it is clear that he is exercising his will over her. On her side, does not her espousal of the view that her virginity is an incommensurably higher good than her brother's life suggest that she too might be using the law willfully and for her own purposes? Listen to the unmistakable sound of self-aggrandizement in the soliloquy in which she makes up her mind to sacrifice her brother in order to safeguard her chastity: "Then, Isabel, live chaste, and, brother, die; / More than our brother is our chastity" (2.4.185–6). Angelo's legal formalism and Isabella's absolute privileging of chastity illustrate Shakespeare's keen alertness to how people are able to project their own desires and aspirations onto the law as if they are required by law to do the very thing they in fact want to do.

A law of sovereign will that is at once so unstable, so unjust, and so destructive seems ripe to be supplanted by the law of kind, which would normally be the case in Shakespeare. In this play, however, kind cannot overrule will and cannot emerge as the ground of legitimacy as it does, with various complexities, in plays such as *Richard II*, *King Lear*, *Love's Labor's Lost*, and *The Winter's Tale*. It cannot do this because the core natural attributes in the playworld are not living with bread, feeling want, tasting grief, needing friends. Instead the defining natural attribute is carnal desire. Great creating nature has been assimilated into the tavern, the whorehouse, and the courtroom wrenched to the willful uses of the judges.

The exemplary low point in the fortunes of the law of kind is Pompey's defense of the sex trade. He answers Escalus's charge of pimping by insisting on the naturalness, not of sexual desire, but rather of how desire naturally makes all the young people in the city into prostitutes and johns:

Escalus: Pompey? Is it a lawful trade?
Pompey: If the law would allow it, sir.
Escalus: But the law will not allow it, Pompey, nor it shall not be allowed in Vienna.
Pompey: Does your worship mean to geld and splay all the youth of the city?
Escalus: No, Pompey.

Pompey: Truly, sir, in my poor opinion, they will to't then. If your worship will take order for the drabs and knaves, you need not to fear the bawds. (2.1.214–24)

In light of the fact that in *Measure for Measure* the law of kind can rise not much higher than carnal lust, the trade in flesh, the natural contagion of venereal disease, and the representation of babies *in utero* as the embodied sins their mothers must carry and for which they are enjoined to repent, it can come as no great surprise that the Duke's proposal of marriage at the end, not to mention the weddings of Angelo and Marianna or Lucio and Kate Keepdown, cannot signify the happy victory of natural desire over social and legal obstacles, the triumph of kind over sovereign will, as it would in another comedy. Instead it is bound to arouse suspicion in the spectators and bound to call on us for judgment. Lucio plays an indispensable role here. His slanders of Vincentio, while unsubstantiated, nevertheless encourage us to question the motives and actions of the Duke.

The whole play is bent toward the fostering of public judgment. It begins with the Duke's speech to Angelo about the necessity for someone like him to take on a public juridical role. It is how we fulfill ourselves, he says, serve the community, and honor heaven and nature: "Heaven doth with us as we with torches do, / Not light them for themselves; for if our virtues / Did not go forth of us, 'twere all alike / As if we had them not" (1.1.33–60). The play culminates with the explicitly and relentlessly public scene of judging that fills Act 5, which is in part an image of the playgoers' own interpretive, juridical practices.

The arc of the Duke's story is of a piece with the play's drive toward public judgment. Vincentio begins the play by expressing his distaste for publicity:

I'll privily away. I love the people,
But do not like to stage me to their eyes.
Through it do well, I do not relish well
Their loud applause and Aves vehement (1.1.68–71)

Before his formal return to his position as Duke, however, he instructs Angelo to "proclaim it, in an hour before his entering, that if any crave redress of injustice, they should exhibit their petitions in the street" (4.4.7–9). He even orders up trumpets (used also to announce the start of playhouse performances) to herald his arrival and to summon the citizens to the gates of Vienna.

Of course, the Duke stage-manages what amounts to a drawn-out trial in the open air. Although he has learned the value of public justice, he evidently sees himself as a judge only rather than as one of those being judged. But as I have been suggesting, the play sees things differently. Or, more precisely, the play invites the playgoers to see things differently. The play's invitation is implicit in the strangeness of the Duke's conduct, his apparently secret life as Mariana's confessor (which seems to have been going on before the play's action began – see 4.1.52–3), his surprising proposal of marriage to Isabella, the slanders against him from Lucio, the pardon party he throws at the end of the action, and the title's recollection of Matthew 7.2's message to judges that they too will be judged, and judged by the very measure of their judgments.[26]

* * *

If we imagine ourselves at the Globe in 1604 or thereabouts at a performance of *Measure for Measure*, we might think, as numerous modern critics have argued, that the play has some connections with King James's views of law and governance and that Vincentio is in some degree a figure of the king.[27] But those connections can hardly determine our judgment of the play. The playhouse is uniformly lit and the seating and standing spaces half-encircle the stage so that we can see the players and the other playgoers just as they can see us. We are alert to how others are responding to the play and to what the characters do and say. We are able to judge them as they are judging the play; others in turn might be taking our measure. Duke Vincentio, the judge of others in the playworld, cannot for one moment evade judgment before this heterogeneous assembly in the playhouse. Irony in the theatrical field of vision undoes his design.

To some degree, we are free to roam in the ironizing play-space of theatrical performance. But insofar as there are connections between the world in the play and the world outside the playhouse – after all, the play does seem to touch on hot topics in Jacobean government and law – our engagement with the play will also have a bearing on questions about the state and its rulers.[28] We are having a great time watching a made-up story unfold before our eyes, but we are also doing something socially and juridically creative.

We, most of us mere commoners, move back and forth between make-believe and the possibility of having an effect on the world. That is why it makes sense to say that Isabella is like us. She is the character in Act 5 who most shuttles back and forth between reality and theater. When she accuses Angelo of violating her virginity and cries out for "justice, justice, justice, justice!" she is knowingly play-acting in what the disguised Duke has persuaded her is a theatrical spectacle that will lead to real revelation and justice-making (5.1.42, 26). When she swallows her anger against Angelo and her grief for her brother and kneels to plead for Angelo's life, she is still doing a kind of theater that she hopes will issue in a just outcome, only she no longer knows that it is theater. Since Claudio is not dead, the dilemma she faces is another piece of Vincentio's make-believe. Of course, Isabella has no power either to convict or pardon. Like the playgoers watching her plead for Angelo and judging her words and actions (and judging the words of actions of the other characters) by responding to the play, her capacity to realize justice in the world lies principally in the emotional and intellectual force of her plea for the life of the man she believes killed her brother. By her moving performance of judgment, she leads the members of the audience in the crafting of a practice of popular, public judging of matters of shared concern and in the creation of a system of law in the common playhouses of early modern London.

Notes

1. All quotes from *Measure for Measure* are from the edition by N. W. Bawcutt (Oxford: Oxford University Press, 1991).
2. For early modern legal views of pre-marital sex, see Martin Ingram, "Spousals Litigation in the English Ecclesiastical Court c. 1350–1640," in *Marriage and Society: Studies in the Social History of Marriage*, ed. R. B. Outhwaite (New York: St. Martin's Press, 1981), 35–57.
3. See Constance Jordan, "Interpreting Statute in *Measure for Measure*," in *Shakespeare and the Law: A Conversation among Disciplines and Professions*, ed. Bradin Cormack, Martha C. Nussbaum, and Richard Strier (Chicago: University of Chicago Press, 2013), 101–20: "Ecclesiastical law regarded a contract of the kind Claudio and Juliet had entered – *sponsalia per verba de presenti* – as constituting a legally valid marriage" (110).
4. Indeed, were these questions to go to court, Angelo's situation would be worse than Claudio's since he had broken off the contract to wed his betrothed in advance of having sex with her.
5. Geneva Bible (1599), https://www.biblegateway.com/, accessed November 28, 2015.
6. There are various ways – none of them illegitimate – of alleviating the wackiness of the closing action. One formerly not unusual approach was to allegorize Vincentio as a figure of the divine who at the end extends his mercy and a chance for a new beginning to all the characters.

Another was to characterize the play as a compliment to King James, who had staged a similar pardon party of a group of convicted traitors. A third approach is to focus on Isabella as a solitary figure who closes the play in silent contemplation of the Duke's marriage proposal. For the first approach, see Roy W. Battenhouse, "*Measure for Measure* and Christian Doctrine of the Atonement," *PMLA* 61 (1946): 1029–59; for the second, Wilbur Dunkel, "Law and Equity in *Measure for Measure*," *Shakespeare Quarterly* 13 (1962): 275–85; for the third, Philip C. McGuire, *Speechless Dialect: Shakespeare's Open Silences* (Berkeley: University of California Press, 1985), 63–96.

7. Richard Strier, "Shakespeare and Legal Systems: The Better the Worse (but not vice versa)," in *Shakespeare and the Law: A Conversation among Disciplines and Professions*, ed. Bradin Cormack, Martha C. Nussbaum, and Richard Strier (Chicago: University of Chicago Press, 2013), 174–200 (p. 174).

8. Ibid., 188.

9. Ibid., 189.

10. I am influenced here by thinkers such as Peter Goodrich, Desmond Manderson, and Martha Nussbaum, all of whom have developed a much broader understanding of what law and law-making are, how law relates to other fields of artistic and intellectual work, and how we create a lawful world by way of multiple discourses and practices, not only by those inside the formal world of the law. See Peter Goodrich, *Law in the Courts of Love: Literature and Other Minor Jurisprudences*, (London: Routledge, 1996); Desmond Manderson, *Kangaroo Courts and the Rule of Law: The Legacy of Modernism* (London: Routledge, 2012); Martha Nussbaum, *Poetic Justice: The Literary Imagination and Public Life* (Boston: Beacon Press, 1995).

11. I take 1992 as an approximate starting point for this work; that year saw the publication of two seminal books – Richard Helgerson, *Forms of Nationhood: The Elizabethan Writing of England* (Chicago: University of Chicago Press, 1992); and *Habermas and the Public Sphere*, ed. Craig Calhoun (Cambridge, MA: MIT Press, 1992). The Making Publics (MaPs) project, which Helgerson helped create, has published a number of books and articles on the growth of early modern public life, including, most recently, a collective rethinking of his *Forms of Nationhood* in the book, *Forms of Association: Making Publics in Early Modern Europe*, ed. Paul Yachnin and Marlene Eberhart (Amherst, MA: University of Massachusetts Press, 2015).

12. Peter Lake and Steve Pincus, "Rethinking the Public Sphere in Early Modern England," *Journal of British Studies* 45 (2006): 270–92 (pp. 290–1).

13. King James I, *The Kings Majesties Speach to the Lords and Commons of this Present Parliament at Whitehall* (London, 1609), A4v, B1. EEBO, accessed December 3, 2015. The spelling of this text and other early modern texts has been modernized.

14. For the differences between James and the common lawyers on the sources of legal authority, see Richard Helgerson, "Writing the Law," Chapter 2 in *Forms of Nationhood*, 63–104.

15. Carl Schmitt, *Political Theology: Four Chapters on the Concept of Sovereignty*, trans. Geroge Schwab (Cambridge, MA: MIT Press, 1985), 5.

16. Ibid., 10.

17. All Shakespeare citations except for those from *Measure for Measure* are from *The Riverside Shakespeare*, ed. G. Blakemore Evans, 2nd ed. (Boston: Houghton Mifflin, 1997).

18. Henry de Bracton, *On the Laws and Customs of England*, trans. Samuel E. Thorne, 4 vols. (Cambridge, MA: Harvard University Press), 2:33.

19. For an overview of the play's debate about power, see "Introduction," *Richard II*, ed. Anthony Dawson and Paul Yachnin (Oxford: Oxford University Press, 2011), 16–33.

20. Quoted in Polly J. Price, "Natural Law and Birthright Citizenship in Calvin's Case (1608)," *Yale Journal of Law and the Humanities* 9 (1997): 73–145 (p. 115). http://digitalcommons.law.yale.edu/cgi/viewcontent.cgi?article=1170&context=yjlh. Accessed December 7, 2015.

21. First noted by Eleanor Prosser, "Shakespeare, Montaigne, and the 'Rarer Action,'" *Shakespeare Studies* 1 (1965): 261–4.

22. Michel de Montaigne, "Apologie for Raymond Sebond," in *The Essays*, trans. John Florio, ed. for Kindle, John McArthur, loc 10082.

23. *Kings Majesties Speech*, C3.

24. Ian Ward, *Shakespeare and the Legal Imagination* (London: Butterworths, 1999), 25.

25. Sir Thomas Smith, *The Common-Wealth of England, and Manner of Government Thereof* (London, 1601), 104.

26. For a discussion of the role of the judge in *Measure for Measure*, see Desmond Manderson and Paul Yachnin, "Shakespeare and Judgment: The Renewal of Law and Literature," *The European Legacy* 15 (2010): 195–213, esp. 206–9.

27. See Josephine Waters Bennett, *"Measure for Measure" as Royal Entertainment* (New York: Columbia University Press, 1966).

28. See Jordan, "Interpreting Statute in *Measure for Measure*."

Chapter 7

Prospero's Plea: Judgment, Invention, and Political Form in *The Tempest*

Kevin Curran

Theatrical epilogues – onstage speeches addressed to the audience at the end of a performance – were a common feature of English Renaissance plays. They were typically read rather than memorized, sometimes by a character in the play, sometimes by someone else. An epilogue asserts the merits of the play it punctuates and asks for audience approval in the form of applause. Far more epilogues occurred in performance than survive in print and of those that do survive, most were occasional. That is, they were designed for particular venues, particular audiences, or particular performances, though some epilogues may have been more permanent features of the plays they accompanied. What all epilogues have in common is their capacity to effect what Robert Weimann describes as a "redistribution of authority in the playhouse."[1] When an epilogue speaker requests applause, this changes the relationship between actors and audience and between fiction and life. Playgoers are now expected to do something, to respond based on the kind of emotional and intellectual experience they have had up to that point. The epilogue, in other words, draws attention to the active and participatory nature of theatrical spectatorship and the degree to which audiences were implicated in the imaginative world of the plays they attended.

This chapter concerns Prospero's epilogue in *The Tempest*, a particularly well-known example of the form and one that has become a standard feature of the play in performance. It occurs in the final moments of the play, just after Prospero has released the island castaways and set his servant Ariel free. Addressing the audience directly, Prospero says,

> Now my Charmes are all ore-throwne,
> And what strength I have's mine owne.
> Which is most faint: now 'tis true

> I must be heere confinde by you,
> Or sent to Naples. Let me not
> Since I have my Dukedome got,
> And pardon'd the deceiver, dwell
> In this bare Island by your Spell,
> But release me from my bands
> With the helpe of your good hands:
> Gentle breath of yours, my Sailes
> Must fill, or else my project failes,
> Which was to please: Now I want
> Spirits to enforce: Art to inchant,
> And my ending is despaire,
> Unlesse I be reliev'd by praier
> Which pierces so, that it assaults
> Mercy it selfe, and frees all faults.
>   As you from crimes would pardon'd be,
>   Let your Indulgence set me free. (2322–41)[2]

Prospero presents his case to the playgoers who are expected to consider two related questions: (1) Was the play good? (2) Has Prospero behaved in an ethical manner? In considering these questions, the audience is being asked not simply to pass judgment, but more precisely, to imagine *through* judgment a future for Prospero, an imaginative addendum to the fiction presented on stage. If the audience disapproves and does not clap, Prospero will remain imprisoned on the island. If it approves and does clap, he will return to Milan. My aim in the pages that follow is to both historicize and theorize the connection between these two seemingly distinct requests. First, I will show that Prospero's epilogue participates not only in the theatrical convention of soliciting audience applause, but also in an intellectual tradition that views judgment and invention as closely related concepts. This will involve positioning the epilogue in relation to Renaissance performance practices and Aristotelian rhetorical theory, two contexts which I suggest find a point of intersection in Prospero's closing speech. The final move of the chapter will be to use this historical understanding of Prospero's epilogue to arrive at a new set of insights about the relationship between theatrical and political form. For this I will be turning to the work of Hannah Arendt and Jacques Rancière in order to articulate more precisely how the particulars of Prospero's epilogue instantiate broader philosophical ideas about the place of judgment in political life.

Judgment in the Theater

Printed epilogues in playbooks are an important component of the archive of early modern judgment, but they present certain interpretive challenges as well. In particular, these printed texts can give the misleading impression that epilogues were stable and enduring features of the plays for which they were written when, in fact, they were usually composed with a first performance in mind. Because they carried a higher-than-usual entrance fee, first performances attracted a different kind of audience than one might find at a play later in its run. First-performance audiences were composed of educated playgoers – precisely the sort of people who might think themselves in possession of superior powers of discernment. What is more, as Tiffany Stern notes, many at first performances would have felt that the high price of admission granted them a right to critique. "At publique Stage-Playes," writes Dudley North in 1645, "whoso-ever censures" is "entituled to it . . . for his money."[3] This sense of entitlement was fueled by the promise of a very real form of theatrical authority since audiences at first performances largely determined the fate of the plays they watched. Usually, a new play would only be granted a second performance if the audience responded encouragingly to the epilogue.

Epilogues, then, constituted the ritual core of a broadly adjudicatory set of conditions that were central to the culture of professional theater. Playwrights make frequent reference to this phenomenon. The Prologue to John Marston's play, *The Dutch Courtesan* (1605), for example, admonishes playgoers as follows:

> . . . know that firme art cannot feare
> Vaine rage: onely the highest grace we pray
> Is you'le not taxe, until you judge our Play.
> Think and then speake: tis rashnesse, and not wit
> To speake what is in passion, and not judgment fit.[4]

The audience may acquire a right to judge when they pay their entrance fee, but as far as Marston is concerned, judgment also requires a certain level of responsibility and skill. It is part of a larger rational procedure that originates in thinking and culminates in speaking and leaves no place for rash emotionalism. Marston clearly harbors some latent skepticism about the ability of theater audiences to judge well. Ben Jonson goes further, expressing outright derision at being held in thrall to the tastes of playgoers. In his epistle to the 1612 quarto of *The Alchemist*, he opines,

> How out of purpose, and place, doe I name Art? When the Professors are growne so obstinate contemners of it, and presume on their owne Naturalls, as they are deriders of all diligence that way, and, by simple mocking at the termes, when they understand not the things, thinke to get of wittily with their Ignorance. Nay, they are esteem'd the more learned, and sufficient for this, by the Multitude, through their excellent vice of judgment. For they commend Writers, as they doe Fencers, or Wrastlers; who if they come in robustly, and put for it with a great deale of violence, are receiv'd for the braver fellowes.[5]

This is the sort of contemptuousness that Jonson is famous for, but his attitude here becomes more understandable when we recall that his play *Sejanus* (1603) was rejected by its first Globe audience and never made it past its opening performance.

With its rituals of evaluation, public-theater epilogues bore a striking resemblance to the procedures of law courts. A number of playwrights even described their relationship to their audiences in overtly legal language. In *The Novella* (1653) by Richard Brome, for example, the playwright is imagined as a defendant in a law court: "Hee'll 'bide his triall, and submits his cause / To you the Jury."[6] The prologue to Thomas Dekker's *The Wonder of a Kingdom* (1636) frets about "what Judges sit to Doome each Play."[7] And *The Coxcomb* (1647), by Francis Beaumont, John Fletcher, and Philip Massinger, features the sarcastic declaration, "Now 'tis to be tri'd / Before such Judges, 'twill not be deni'd / A . . . noble hearing."[8] These legal references would have made sense to the community of theatergoers in Shakespeare's time, a sizeable portion of which was affiliated with the Inns of Court, the institution that trained young men for careers in law.[9] A number of playwrights, too, had connections with the Inns. John Marston was a member of the Middle Temple in the 1590s, as was John Webster, and John Ford was admitted in 1602. Ben Jonson, though he did not attend the Inns himself, was close friends with prominent jurists such as John Seldon, with whom he corresponded about transvestism on the stage, and John Hoskyns, who was also a respected poet and wit. There was significant overlap between the culture of theater and the culture of law in Shakespeare's time and epilogues constituted a formally compact instance of this crossing.

This much we know, then: Prospero's invocation of audience judgment is part of a larger theatrical convention, one which has clear legal coordinates. What about his invocation of audience *imagination*? I quote the relevant lines once again:

> I must be heere confinde by you,
> Or sent to Naples. Let me not
> Since I have my Dukedome got,
> And pardon'd the deceiver, dwell
> In this bare Island by your Spell,
> But release me from my bands
> With the helpe of your good hands: (2326–32)

One way of looking at this passage is as a bid for creative input, and to this extent it fits comfortably under the umbrella of epilogue convention. As Stern writes, "From a time in theatrical history hard to date precisely, some plays on their opening performances were offered as mutable texts ready for audience revision."[10] There is evidence of this practice in printed playbooks. For example, the prologue to John Marston's *Antonio and Mellida* (1602) invites the audience to "polish these rude Sceanes."[11] Similarly, in Thomas Heywood's *Mayden-Head Well Lost* (1634), the audience is told, "Our Play is new, but whether shaped well / In Act or Seane, Judge you, you best can tell."[12] These sorts of invitations made playgoers collaborators in the fiction. Most often, this took the form of cutting. Spectators would communicate which parts of the play they didn't like and these sections would be excised for subsequent performances.[13] In Prospero's epilogue, however, there is something slightly different going on. Here, playgoers are not being asked to "polish" or cut; they are being asked to elaborate and expand. This difference is important because it means their charge is not to perfect something that is already there, but rather to make something that is not: namely, a future for Prospero. Judgment, in other words, leads to invention in Prospero's epilogue. Understanding the link between these two concepts requires us to look beyond the walls of the theater to a larger tradition of rhetorical thought and practice.

Judgment and Invention

The idea that judgment and invention are fundamentally connected would have been familiar to many in Shakespeare's time, including a considerable number of playgoers and playwrights. The link finds its source in a long tradition of rhetorical learning. Thomas Blundeville's commentary in *The Arte of Logicke* (1599) is fairly standard. While "invention finds matter," Blundeville explains, judgment "frameth, disposeth, and reduceth the same into due forme of argument."[14] This formulation derives from Roman rhetorical theory, which has deeper roots in Aristotle. Texts like Cicero's *De inventione*, the anonymous *Rhetorica ad Herennium*, and Quintilian's *Institutio oratoria* describe invention (*inventio*) as the skill of deciding which line of reasoning is most likely to strike a particular audience as especially compelling. Judgment's role is to break that line of reasoning down into component parts and then arrange them in a sequence calculated to achieve maximum persuasiveness.[15] Judgment, in other words, turns ideas into arguments by lending them organizational form. Along with invention, it was an essential component of what Aristotle termed the *genus iudiciale*, the kind of speech typically found in the law courts.[16] In Shakespeare's time, anyone with a grammar school education was likely to have encountered rhetorical handbooks like *De inventione*, *Rhetorica ad Herrenium*, and *Institutio oratoria*, or vernacular manuals like Thomas Wilson's *The Art of Rhetorique* (1553), which drew on the Roman handbooks.[17] Accordingly, Blundeville's simple description of judgment would have sounded familiar to many early moderns, including Shakespeare, who would have been exposed to rhetorical texts as a student at the King's New School at Stratford-upon-Avon.[18]

With this in mind, we can begin to see how judgment might be conceived as one crucial point along a continuum of creative endeavor. For those with some training in rhetorical theory, judgment was a form of *making* rather than a form of decision, as we would now tend to view it. This creative component of judgment is even more apparent in the vernacular literary criticism of sixteenth- and seventeenth-century England, which was heavily influenced by, and sometimes indistinguishable from, rhetorical theory. Central to literary critical judgment was the notion of *decorum*, which involved following carefully prescribed rules about how, for example, certain types of characters require the use of certain kinds of language, how certain styles of argument require particular metaphors, or how a given genre necessitates a specific type of plot.[19] These precepts reached Renaissance readers through either direct or mediated exposure to the ideas in Aristotle's *Rhetoric* and Horace's *Ars Poetica*, as well as through grammatical and rhetorical commentaries attached to the comedies of Plautus and Terence, which were among the mainstays of elementary and intermediate education in Latin.[20] For Renaissance critics and theorists writing in this vein, the aesthetic quality and even the moral viability of imaginative writing depended on how well the rules of *decorum* were followed. Thomas Wilson in his pioneering manual, *The Arte of Rhetorique*, uses the word "aptness" for *decorum* and stresses that writers must choose "words most apt for their purpose. In weighty causes grave words are thought most needful, that the greatness of the matter may the rather appear in the vehemency of their talk."[21] Robert Ascham, in *The Schoolmaster* (1570), prefers the word "propriety," and tells his readers that it applies at all levels of a composition, "in choice of words, in framing sentences, in handling of argument, and use of right form, figure and number."[22] George Puttenham goes on to lay out these precepts in impressive detail in *The Art of English Poesy* (1589). Consequently, for many readers in the sixteenth and seventeenth centuries, the process of appraising the aesthetic worth and the moral viability of imaginative writing was guided by simple questions that linked reading to judging: were laws broken or adhered to? What are the implications? Within this general interpretive framework, someone like Sir John Harington could defend Ariosto against charges of obscenity by pointing out that "there is so meet a decorum in the persons that speak lasciviously, as any of judgment must needs allow."[23]

Philip Sidney's *The Defense of Poesy* (c.1580; printed 1595) is the first attempt at sustained literary criticism in English. In it, Sidney expands on the idea that judgment forms the basis of sound reading to argue, in addition, that our ability to judge well can be sharpened by good poetry. All the wisdom that philosophy has to offer, Sidney says, "lies[s] dark before the imaginative and judging power if they be not illuminated or figured forth by the speaking picture of poesy."[24] Sidney goes on to describe how religious scripture "inhabit[s] . . . the judgment" precisely because it functions like poetry, which is neither wholly conceptual (as philosophy is) nor wholly particular (as history is), but something in between, which illustrates universal precepts with specific instances and images:

> Even our Saviour Christ could as well have given the moral commonplaces of uncharitableness and humbleness as the divine narration of Dives and Lazarus, or of disobedience and mercy as that heavenly discourse of the lost child and the gracious father, but that his through-searching wisdom knew the estate of Dives burning in hell and of Lazarus in Abraham's bosom *would more constantly, as it were, inhabit both the memory and judgment* (truly, for myself, me seems I se before my eyes the lost child's disdainful prodigality turned to envy a swine's dinner), which by the learned divines are thought not historical acts but instructing parables.[25]

The charge of English poetry, then, is to help build a community of rational, moral, right-thinking people. Samuel Daniel, for instance, tasks poetry with "setting up the music of our times to a higher note of judgment and discretion" in *A Defense of Rhyme* (1603).[26] It is also true, though, that bad poetry can weaken judgment. The Scottish poet, courtier, and statesman William Alexander has a method for avoiding such problems:

> When I censure any poet, I first dissolve the general contexture of his work in several pieces, to what sinews it hath, and to mark what will remain behind when that external gorgeousness, consisting in the choice or placing of words, as if it would bribe the ear to corrupt the judgment, is at first removed, or at least marshaled in its own degree.[27]

Good poetry builds and fortifies judgment; bad poetry erodes it. And since, as Wilson, Ascham, and Puttenham show us, judgment is the cornerstone of responsible reading – of being able to discern what is good and what is bad – the whole process is circular. The more good poetry one reads, the better equipped one will be to identify other examples of good poetry, and the better disposed one will be to produce good (moral, decorous) poetry oneself. This last point is important. For it is sound judgment, Henry Peacham tells us in *The Garden of Eloquence* (1577), that transforms wisdom, through the application of rules of decorum, into the kinds of eloquent and persuasive verbal packages that affect people:

> Many, not perceiving the nigh and necessary conjunction of these two precious jewels [wisdom and eloquence], do either affect fineness of speech and neglect the knowledge of things, or, contrariwise, covet understanding and contemn the art of eloquence. And therefore it cometh to pass that such take great pains and reap small profits; they ever seek and never find the thing they would fainest have – the one sort of these speak much to small purpose, and the other (though they be wise) are not able aptly to express their meaning. From which calamity they are free, that do use a right judgment in applying their studies so that their knowledge may be joined with apt utterance: that is to say, that their eloquence may be wise, and their wisdom eloquent.[28]

Each of the writers mentioned above has a slightly different way of invoking judgment, a slightly different way of positioning it in relation to the ethical affordances of English poetry and rhetoric. What is clear, though, is that judgment is a practice suspended within a larger web of ideas about literary evaluation and invention: it is part of the reading process, since all art is, or should be, rule-bound; it is a faculty that stands to be strengthened or weakened depending on what one chooses to read; and it is a mediating force between pure ideas and the embodiment of those ideas in a structured expressive form. Prospero's epilogue expresses a similar set of associations. The request for judgment is also an appeal to the audience's capacity for literary invention, specifically its ability to craft an imaginary afterlife for Prospero: "release me from my bands / With the helpe of your good hands," he implores; "As you from crimes would pardon'd be, / Let your Indulgence set me free." According to the terms set by Prospero, then, clapping is an act both evaluative and generative, a verdict on the past and a vision for the future.

Judgment and Responsibility

With these cultural-historical coordinates in place, I want now to pose a larger question. Not just, what are the sources and contexts for the link between judgment and invention, but instead, what are the effects and implications of such a pairing for the audience and for our own understanding of the nature of theatrical experience? One thing is certain: bringing judgment and invention together as Prospero does gives theatergoers a different kind of ethical stake in the play they are watching than would otherwise be the case. As fellow makers, rather than just consumers, the audience's collective sense of the good, of what is right and what is wrong, is implicated in the play's imagined conclusion, and all the more so for the moral freight Prospero so insistently attaches to the epilogue. Viewed from this perspective, judgment develops less out of an evaluative impulse and more out of a sense of responsibility to communal norms (norms which are both moral and aesthetic). Not to judge, accordingly, would be a failure of responsibility. In the final section of this chapter, I will delve deeper into the ethical dimension of theatrical judgment. My guides in this undertaking will be Hannah Arendt, the thinker who more than anyone else sought to understand the conceptual link between judgment and responsibility, and Jacques Rancière, the most influential commentator on the relationship between political and literary form.

Arendt became interested in judgment when she covered the 1961 trial of Nazi leader Adolf Eichmann for *The New Yorker*. Her articles were later expanded into the book, *Eichmann in Jerusalem: A Report on the Banality of Evil* (1963). Arendt was profoundly underwhelmed by Eichmann. She thought he was forgettable, unintelligent, unfrightening. She was also critical of the trial itself. It seemed to her a show trial, one that used Eichmann as a proxy to condemn and punish antisemitism in general. Against this method of retribution, Arendt argued that the Holocaust called for specific and nuanced forms of condemnation, mostly of Nazis, but also of Jewish leaders who cooperated with the Nazis. That this did not happen represented for her a "fundamental problem" common to "all these postwar trials," which had to do with "the nature and function of human judgment." She writes,

> What we have demanded in these trials, where the defendants had committed "legal" crimes, is that human beings be capable of telling right from wrong even when all they have to guide them is their own judgment, which moreover happens to be completely at odds with what they must regard as the unanimous opinion of all those around them. . . . Since the whole of respectable society had in one way or another succumbed to Hitler, the moral maxims which determine social behavior and the religious commandments – "Thou shalt not kill!" – which guide conscience had virtually vanished. Those few who were still able to tell right from wrong went really only by their own judgments, and they did so freely; there were no rules to be abided by, under which the particular cases with which they were confronted could be subsumed. They had to decide each instance as it arose, because no rules existed for the unprecedented.[29]

Judgment for Arendt, in other words, is not an expression of external social or legal norms, but rather an expression of personal responsibility. So long as you are human, there is an expectation that you will be able to tell "right from wrong."

What postwar trials like Eichmann's threw into sharp relief for Arendt was the degree to which so many were willing to shirk this responsibility, either by refusing to judge or by issuing a sort of judgment that was so broad, so resistant to the concrete threshold between right and wrong, that it amounted to non-judgment. Arendt describes the phenomenon as follows:

> Another such escape from the area of ascertainable facts and personal responsibility are the countless theories, based on non-specific, abstract, hypothetical assumptions – from the *Zeitgest* down to the Oedipus complex – which are so general that they explain and justify every event and every deed . . . Among the constructs that "explain" everything by obscuring all details, we find such notions as a "ghetto mentality"

among European Jews; or the collective guilt of the German people, derived from an *ad hoc* interpretation of their history; or an equally absurd assertion of a kind of collective innocence of the Jewish people. All these clichés have in common that they make judgments superfluous and that to utter them is devoid of all risk.[30]

Arendt understood the reluctance of both Germans and Jews to examine closely what took place in Europe between 1933 and 1945, to pinpoint definitively the many groups and individuals – Nazi officers and bureaucrats, "Christian churches," members of "the Jewish leadership" – who had a hand in what she calls "the totality of moral collapse." However, she concludes that "this understandable disinclination is insufficient to explain the reluctance evident everywhere to make judgments in terms of individual moral responsibility."[31]

In the years following her coverage of the Eichmann trial, Arendt finally did arrive at an explanation. In an essay called "Personal Responsibility Under Dictatorship," she recalls, "I was told that judging itself is wrong: no one can judge who had not been there."[32] At the heart of this fiercely neutral stance, Arendt decided, was deep skepticism about the possibility of human freedom:

> There exists in our society a widespread fear of judging that has nothing whatever to do with the biblical "Judge not, that ye be not judged," . . . For behind the unwillingness to judge lurks the suspicion that no one is a free agent, and hence the doubt that anyone is responsible or could be expected to answer for what he has done. . . . we're all alike, equally bad, and those who try, or pretend that they try, to remain halfway decent are either saints or hypocrites, and in either case should leave us alone.[33]

What Arendt does brilliantly in her writings on judgment is to triangulate between three large, difficult concepts – judgment, responsibility, and freedom – in a way that deepens our understanding of all three. Judgment is an expression of responsibility and responsibility, in turn, is a condition of being a free agent capable of moral decision and active worldmaking. Viewed thus, judgment is a way of manifesting our status as free agents in moral terms – in terms, that is, of a collective obligation to the good that only a free agent could enter into. The refusal to judge is troubling to Arendt because it indicates an unwillingness to be accountable for the world we all must share. It rehearses a vision of politics as something that works upon rather than through human actors and in this way advances precisely the sort of detached acquiescence that forms the necessary conditions for totalitarian disasters like the Third Reich. That "judgment itself is wrong was Eichmann's own argument against the district court's judgment," Arendt is careful to remind her readers.[34]

Arendt's work on the Eichmann trial establishes a framework for thinking about judgment that helps us uncover some of the political deep-structure of Prospero's epilogue. Specifically, she equips us with a vocabulary and a set of concepts that allow us to think about the audience's evaluative response in *The Tempest* as an expression of responsibility rather than authority, and therefore as something grounded in, and oriented toward, sociality and recognition. This has the effect of lifting Prospero's epilogue out of the historically specific world of Renaissance drama and rhetorical theory and reframing it in terms of the ethical dynamics of participatory politics. It shows us, in other words, that at the heart of Prospero's judgment–invention linkage is an implicit assumption that the playgoers assembled in the theater are free agents and therefore not just *able* to judge, but also *expected* to judge. For it is through judgment that they shape the moral contours of the future – Prospero's future.

On a pragmatic level, of course, the clap-to-free-me-from-my-island conceit is simply a trick to help ensure that the audience will indeed clap. But even if this passage is not political by design, it is still political in form. This, Jacques Rancière has argued influentially, is the most important way in which literature and theater are always political. He writes,

> The politics of literature is not the same thing as the politics of writers. It does not concern the personal engagements of writers in the social or political struggles of their times. Neither does it concern the way writers represent social structures, political movements or various identities in their books. The expression "politics of literature" implies that literature does politics simply by being literature . . . It assumes that there is an essential connection between politics as a specific form of collective practice and literature as a well-defined practice of the art of writing.[35]

Likewise, we could say that theater does politics simply by being theater, or, more specifically, that theatrical epilogues do politics simply by being theatrical epilogues. "It is not enough that there be power for there to be politics," Rancière reminds us. "It is not even enough that there be laws regulating collective life. What is needed is a configuration of a specific form of community."[36] Prospero's epilogue embodies politics precisely through the "specific form of community" it establishes – a community of judgment founded on shared responsibility and the collective freedom to craft a world.

Prospero's epilogue establishes a point of intersection for a variety of different forces at work in English Renaissance theater. It indexes not only the material and economic conditions of play-writing and performance, but also the cultural sources and ethical implications of collective discernment. For this reason, the epilogue places a particular demand on us as scholars, insisting that we practice a pluralistic and intellectually non-partisan criticism. This involves attending to both theater-historical and intellectual-historical contexts of audience judgment – the way Prospero's final speech is shaped by the conventions of playgoing, but also, in a more general way, by Renaissance legal culture and a long tradition of rhetorical theory. At the same time, while all this tells us where Prospero's epilogue came from, it tells us very little about what it makes possible, conceptually and experientially, in the theater and in the world. To begin to address this question, we have to attend to the way audience judgment generates its own context by mobilizing that unique configuration of agency and accountability that is common to political and theatrical form.

Notes

1. Robert Weimann, *Author's Pen and Actor's Voice: Playing and Writing in Shakespeare's Theatre* (Cambridge: Cambridge University Press, 2000), 241.
2. Quotations from *The Tempest* follow *The Norton Facsimile: The First Folio of Shakespeare*, ed. Charles Hinman, 2nd ed. (New York: W. W. Norton, 1996) and are referenced with the through-line numbers.
3. Dudley North, *A Forest of Varieties* (London, 1645), A2a, quoted in Tiffany Stern, *Documents of Performance in Early Modern England* (Cambridge: Cambridge University Press, 2009), 88. See also Stern's larger discussion, 88–9.
4. John Marston, *The Dutch Courtezan* (London, 1605), A2r.
5. Ben Jonson, *The Alchemist* (London, 1612), A3r.
6. Richard Brome, *The Novella*, in *Five New Playes* (London, 1653), H4b.
7. Thomas Dekker, *The Wonder of a Kingdome* (London, 1636), A2a.
8. Francis Beaumont, John Fletcher, and Philip Massinger, *The Coxcomb*, in Francis Beaumont and John Fletcher, *Comedies and Tragedies* (London, 1647), 2P3b.
9. See Denis Kezar, *Solon and Thespis: Law and Theater in the English Renaissance* (Notre Dame: University of Notre Dame Press, 2007).
10. Stern, *Documents of Performance*, 89.
11. John Marston, *The History of Antonio and Mellida* (London, 1602), B1b.

12. Thomas Heywood, *A Pleasant Comedy, called A Mayden-Head Well Lost* (London, 1634), 13a.
13. Stern, *Documents of Performance*, 92.
14. Thomas Blundeville, *The Arte of Logicke* (London, 1599).
15. Quentin Skinner, *Forensic Shakespeare* (Oxford: Oxford University Press, 2015), 11–25; Henry S. Turner, *The English Renaissance Stage: Geometry, Poetics, and the Practical Spatial Arts* (Oxford: Oxford University Press, 2006), 45–55.
16. Jon Hesk, "Types of Oratory," in *The Cambridge Companion to Ancient Rhetoric*, ed. Erik Gunderson (Cambridge: Cambridge University Press, 2009), 145–61 (pp. 150–6).
17. Peter Mack, *Elizabethan Rhetoric: Theory and Practice* (Cambridge: Cambridge University Press, 2002), 11–47; Skinner, *Forensic Shakespeare*, 25–41.
18. See further, T. W. Baldwin, *William Shakespeare's "Small Latine & Lesse Greeke,"* 2 vols. (Urbana: University of Illinois Press, 1944); Emrys Jones, *The Origins of Shakespeare* (Oxford: Oxford University Press, 1977); Joel B. Altman, *The Tudor Play of Mind: Rhetorical Inquiry and the Development of Elizabethan Drama* (Berkeley: University of California Press, 1978); for studies that show how Shakespeare and other playwrights made use of their training in rhetoric and dialectic when crafting speeches and plots having to do with evidence, proof, or doubt, see Kathy Eden, *Poetic and Legal Fiction in the Aristotelian Tradition* (Princeton: Princeton University Press, 1986), 176–84; Lorna Hutson, *The Invention of Suspicion: Law and Mimesis in Shakespeare and Renaissance Drama* (Oxford: Oxford University Press, 2007) and *Circumstantial Shakespeare* (Oxford: Oxford University Press, 2015); Joel B. Altman, *The Improbability of Othello: Rhetorical Anthropology and Shakespearean Selfhood* (Chicago: University of Chicago Press, 2010); and Skinner, *Forensic Shakespeare*.
19. Discussions of *decorum* can be found in Michael Moriarty, "Principles of Judgement: Probability, Decorum, Taste, and the *je ne sais quoi*," in *The Cambridge History of Literary Criticism, Volume 3: The Renaissance*, ed. Glyn P. Norton (Cambridge: Cambridge University Press, 1999), 522–8, and Brian Vickers, ed., *English Renaissance Literary Criticism* (Oxford: Oxford University Press, 1999), 44–55.
20. Madeleine Doran, *Endeavors of Art: A Study of Form in Elizabethan Drama* (Madison: University of Wisconsin Press, 1954), 16–17, 33–4, 148–71, 174–5, 234–5.
21. Thomas Wilson, *The Arte of Rhetorique* (London, 1553), 123.
22. Robert Ascham, *The Schoolmaster* (London, 1570), 151.
23. Sir John Harington, *Apology for Ariosto* (London, 1591), 318.
24. Philip Sidney, *The Defense of Poesy* (London, 1595), 17.
25. Ibid., 18 (emphasis added).
26. Samuel Daniel, *A Defense of Rhyme* (London, 1603), 213.

27. Sir William Alexander, *Anacrisis. Or a Censure of some Poets Ancient and Modern* (London, 1634), 298.
28. Henry Peacham, *The Garden of Eloquence* (London, 1577), 250.
29. Hannah Arendt, *Eichmann in Jerusalem: A Report on the Banality of Evil* (London: Penguin, 2006), 294–5.
30. Ibid., 297.
31. Ibid., 297.
32. Hannah Arendt, "Personal Responsibility Under Dictatorship," in *Responsibility and Judgment*, ed. Jerome Kohn (New York: Random House, 2003), 17–48 (p. 18).
33. Ibid., 19.
34. Ibid., 18.
35. Jacques Rancière, *The Politics of Literature* (Cambridge: Polity Press, 2011), 1.
36. Ibid., 3.

Part III

The Ethics of Judgment

Antinomian Shakespeare: English Drama and Confession Across the Reformation Divide

John Parker

On St. Stephen's Day in 1604 the King's Men performed at court a play about a duke who retreats from the strain of his own misrule to visit a friary in secret. For years, he confides to his confessor there, he has neglected to enforce the law and quietly tolerated all manner of transgression. Justice of the talionic kind that supplies the play with its title – eye for an eye, measure for measure[1] – had once been able to dissuade malefactors by threatening the most unforgiving retaliation, but now, with *de facto* grants of immunity grown so customary, his empty fulminations no longer curb the least illicit impulse. On the contrary they inspire open mockery, as though tit-for-tat requital were a farcical joke played on true discipline, a comedy in which "Liberty plucks Justice by the nose"[2] to unrestrained laughter. Such uninhibited freedom has led to an upside-down state of anarchy, not unlike the carnivalesque atmosphere on St. Stephen's but otherwise at odds with normative convention: "the baby beats the nurse," complains the duke, "and quite athwart / Goes all decorum" (1.3.30–1).[3] Worse still, according to him, the current chaos is wholly his fault; by giving the people scope to offend, he has actively suborned their moral abandon: "for we bid this be done," he explains, "[w]hen evil deeds have their permissive pass, and not the punishment" (1.3.37–8).

This private exchange between Duke Vincentio and Friar Thomas provides *Measure for Measure* with its backstory in more than one sense: we glimpse here the fictional events that precede the action onstage as well as the actual history from which the play as a whole draws its urgency and aura of relevance. At the most topical level is its holiday performance (the first recorded) before a king who had likewise admitted to an excess of leniency during an earlier phase of his rule: "For I confess," he writes, "where I thought (by being gracious at the beginning) to win all mens heartes to a louing and willing obedience, I by the contrarie founde, the disorder of the countrie."[4]

He learned from that disorder to temper grace with judgment – mercy with amercement, as it were – but nonetheless claims to have retained an element of his former clemency lest strict penalization compound the crimes it tries to correct: "Vse Iustice, but with suche moderation, as it turne not in[to] Tyrannie," he advises, before adding a sentiment he must have been pleased to see diffused throughout this particular entertainment: "otherwaies *summum ius, is summa iniuria.*"[5] The next king, he recommends, should reverse the order of his career – and, as it happens, the duke's: start off merciless and *then* soften your blows. "When ye haue by the seueritie of justice once setled your countries, and made them knowe that ye can strike," he writes, "then may ye thereafter all the dayes of your life mixe justice with mercie, punishing or sparing."[6]

Much of the play's historical density stems from its transposition of current events – the new king's ascent to power, the rise of militant puritans wanting to treat sexual misconduct as a killing offense – to a setting that had ceased to exist by James's reign but whose key religious rite his admission of leniency incidentally names: "I confesse." Auricular confession had once been a mandatory step in the sacrament of penance but had since been abandoned in England, along with the mendicants who commonly administered it, for reasons that Vincentio's confession notably dramatizes: a ruler who seeks spiritual solace from a friar for his overly forgiving reign appeals to the same culture of indulgence he claims to repent. Mendicants in particular had for many centuries been widely considered "hypocrites, entertainers and enterprising merchants,"[7] infamous for using penance to sow duplicity and sensuous freedom wherever they preached. "Ful swetely herde he confessioun," says Chaucer of his amorous friar,

> And plesaunt was his absolucioun:
> He was an esy man to yeve penaunce,
> Ther as he wiste to have a good pitaunce.[8]

The passage echoes a standard complaint of contemporary moralists that, in fraternal hands especially, penance gave people "leue to dwellen in synne fro ʒer to ʒer . . . and comunly al here lif, ʒif þei paien bi ʒere [each year] twenty shillyngis or more or lesse."[9] Such was the pay-for-play culture that the English Reformation had tried to abolish, though we can already see in Chaucer's cheerfully ironic appreciation for religious malfeasance why the pleasantries of absolution continued to haunt English literature, drama especially: from his day to Shakespeare's, representations of penitential wrongdoing seemed to draw from the rite a way of indulging in transgression, under color of moral correction, for the sheer enjoyment of it.

The theater had a special stake in representing confession if for no other reason than that critics consistently argued penance itself was already a form of theater. Of course nearly every aspect of Catholicism at some point came under suspicion for its externalities and the constant need for believers to perform their faith. But from this perspective penance often appeared as the worst of the sacraments because it "depended so much on external show on the part of both penitent and confessor,"[10] and then handed absolution to good performers; which is to say, it dispensed its rewards to those who produced the most convincing effects of sincerity – tears above all – for the benefit of a cleric whose authority could be just as readily impersonated. By the time of *Measure for Measure* nothing could have seemed more generic than a ruler with a confessed lack of morals asking his friar confessor for both a costume and course of instruction, amounting to acting lessons, so that he too might "formally in person bear / Like a true friar" (1.3.47–8). Centuries of antifraternal literature in England had made it wholly expected that dressing up like a mendicant (or, really, at this point, any other member of the Catholic clergy), whether you did it for real or merely pretended, put you in a class of professional role-players where your personal bearing was always at best a persona.[11] The truest of friars stood out for that reason as particularly suspect: truth was the one thing every *falsus frater* knew how to fake. Hence Faustus's request that Mephistopheles adopt the appearance of an old friar, "the holy shape [that] becomes a devil best"[12] and one, not incidentally, whose accouterments actors kept ready to hand. Despite the friars' banishment, the abolition of mandatory confession, and the loss of penance as an official sacrament, the old machinery persisted on stage, as players regularly revived for popular merriment the lost institutions that according to critics had made ethical lapses fundamental to church policy. It was as though the commercial theater itself, emerging in the friaries' absence – sometimes on their same grounds, for example at Blackfriars – had replaced confession and the sacrament of penance with another, equally extravagant sanctuary.

"The crossover of penitential modes into temporal governance that the duke makes happen," writes Deborah Shuger in a major study of *Measure for Measure*, "defines a model of Christian polity that goes back to the patristic era," recapitulating in particular the ancient complaints that Christians "condoned law-breaking; they disregarded public safety; they allowed wickedness to escape due punishment."[13]

Try as she might to mitigate the force of these accusations, by her own admission they are not "easily dispelled" since the Fathers' talk of redemption and the eternal welfare of souls could sometimes trump secular calls for punishment: "S. Augustine by this example of our Maister," comments the Douai-Rheims Bible on the woman taken in adultery (another of *Measure for Measure*'s major intertexts), "proueth that Clergie men specially should be giuen much to mercie: and that they ought often, as the cause and time require, to get pardon of the secular Magistrates for offenders that be penitent" (John 8.11). I mean to put forward on this model a less defensive version of Shuger's insight – namely, that the London theater was irresistibly drawn by its own liminal and mimetic status to the antinomianism inherent to every operation of Christian mercy; that its historicity therefore cannot be confined to the immediacy of Court politics (though the Court was a powerful factor), nor to the aftermath of the Reformation (though the resurrection of otherwise forbidden medieval performances could not help but contribute to a drama's appeal), and least of all to Shakespeare's peculiar gifts, in light of which his plays are sometimes made to stand divinely above and removed from the common sources they openly reformulate. Shakespeare's friar-confessors partake of a rich tradition, long preceding the Reformation, in which artists given by trade to feigning took a deep, if also deeply conflicted, interest in their own proximity to religious hypocrisy.[14] Medieval drama, I will argue, does not always differ from Shakespeare in its exploitation of the lawlessness and metatheatrical potential of confession. At the same time this very continuity underscores what separates post-Reformation England from the Middle Ages: mandatory auricular confession was gone, and so were the friars. Their fraudulent station, together with its benefits, players now had all to themselves. Uniquely suited to market nostalgia, they sold the version of Catholicism that had been most vilified for being freer, more sexually liberated, more comfortable with theater and disguise of all kinds because more devoted to worldly pleasure, above all that of exercising power under a show of humility.[15]

Confession in Roman antiquity largely meant admitting defeat.[16] It was a weakness akin to despair, a degrading welcome to anguish. In court the Romans consequently prized every stratagem, so long as it did not concede guilt. "Nothing can be worse than confession," writes Quintilian.[17] To confess left the accused without remedy or recourse while stripping him of the dignity of expressing defiance. From the Twelve Tablets forward, a confession of guilt legally took the place of judgment, so that execution proceeded as if there had been a trial and conviction when in fact the defendant had obviated the need by convicting himself.[18] "The one who confesses in front of a judge is condemned, in a way, by his own sentence"[19] – so ran the ancient version of Angelo's later dictum: "Let my trial be mine own confession" (5.1.372). Only a broken spirit – or, as we will see, a crafty one – could reach such a point. There was something in confession's nature that made it seem like an act of compulsion, the result of madness, inebriation, or pain.[20] "There is no confession," writes Seneca the elder, "except when the accuser elicits it, the accused denies it, the torturer has extorted it."[21]

A voluntary confession like Angelo's, "when the defendant acknowledges that he has given offense and has done so intentionally and still asks to be forgiven," could only happen "very rarely" according to Cicero, if it happened at all, because it guaranteed that all hope was lost and yet by this very means staged a last-ditch attempt at reprieve.[22] A convict adopted the posture of hopelessness, that is, if it was his only hope of escaping punishment. The effectiveness of his confession rested on its façade of impotence, on the pretext that it could have no effect and deferred without reservation to the *fides* or grace of a superior power whose mercy could not be prompted or in any way coerced. After all, the great and noble man, Seneca the younger explains, does not bother to acknowledge the faults of his inferiors, much less to punish them.[23] Admissions of wrongdoing and pleas for mercy could therefore flatter their target by flaunting his higher status. They were also an accusation: namely, that anyone who would stoop to punish the deserving had given himself over to the thrill of cruelty. Such is the man made happy by harm and insult, provided only he may retaliate, "whose purpose in desiring to beat and to mangle is not vengeance but pleasure."[24]

Then came Christianity and its fusion of guilty confessions with ostentatious professions of faith. The change in outlook was made all the more radical by an idiosyncrasy of the Hebrew Bible, which had used one and the same word for confessing (a crime) and praising (the Lord).[25] The Vulgate followed suit, despite *confiteor* in Latin having never before been any kind of accolade, with the result that the very thing pagan authorities condemned, Christians were now supposed to praise. Not everyone immediately grasped the reversal. Augustine wrote more than one sermon explaining to his congregants that they need not beat their breasts with shame and self-loathing, as though admitting to terrible depravity, whenever a psalm invited them to confess the Lord.[26] Meanwhile pagan judges had had their own kind of trouble understanding why so many Christian prisoners conceded with utmost enthusiasm the accusations against them: that they gathered together, for example, under cover of darkness to worship an executed outlaw or refused all sacrifice, even to the cult of the emperor. Pliny the younger (as governor of Bithynia-Pontus) wrote a letter to Trajan asking how to handle this curious group of dissidents, specifically whether "repentance entitles them to a pardon, or if once a man has been a Christian it avails nothing to recant; whether the mere profession of Christianity, without any criminal acts, is itself punishable or only the crimes inherent in the profession; on all these points I am in great doubt."[27] When the accused persistently embraced their guilt, he felt he had no choice but to follow the course of Roman law to its foregone conclusion: "I interrogated them whether they were Christians; if they confessed it, I repeated the question twice, adding the threat of capital punishment; if they still persevered, I ordered them to be executed" (ibid.).

There was still time, Pliny advises Trajan, to arrest the alarming popularity of this superstition – to halt its "contagion," as he puts it – but a hundred years later adherents were still actively boasting of their invulnerability to criminal accusation. Much to the bishops' dismay, some even invited persecution as the surest sign that God had smiled on their flouting of pagan morals. Tertullian captures the mood in the following juxtaposition:

> Criminals long to hide, avoid appearing, are frightened when caught, deny guilt when accused; even if tortured, they do not easily or always confess; when condemned, they grieve . . . [and] impute their bad impulses to fate or the stars . . . But there is nothing at all like this among Christians. No one is ashamed or feels regret, except at not having been a Christian earlier. If he is pointed out, he glories in it; if he is accused, he offers no defense; interrogated, he freely confesses; condemned, he gives thanks.[28]

Of course, Christians found in their transgression, such as it was, a radical form of innocence: not only because their belief posed no legitimate political threat (or so they thought) but because it was supposed to free them from a deeper, more persistent, more spiritual guilt. Confessing Christ, though to temporal authorities an espousal of vice, exculpated believers for all of eternity. It encouraged them to worship as they liked, with no regard for worldly consequence. Suffering even the most extreme and unjust punishment became a testament to the strength of their faith, an inverse omen of future bliss.

Of all the transvaluations that attended the long process of Christianization, perhaps none was more momentous for the subjective inner life of such interest to Shakespeare studies than what happened with confession. By means of penance medieval Christians seemingly internalized the persecution on which their faith was symbolically and historically based. It took many centuries of uneven, piecemeal development to move away from the spectacular, public confessions in which penitents blazed "their own faults as it were on a stage"[29] to the private, mandatory rite of the High Middle Ages that emphasized motive over effect and considered the full range of individuating circumstance,[30] but through it all the basic model of self-hood arguably gravitated toward a forensic archetype until it became the duty of all believers to accuse themselves of their inevitable misconduct, to act as both prosecution and defendant in their own private court of conscience and, as a defendant, to own through confession every truthful accusation.[31] The key moment of self-consciousness, on this model, was the trial of self by oneself – "bitter, speedy, complete and frequent," to give the classic medieval formulation.[32] The result, according to one interpretation, was that "the personal confession and interrogation of every single layman" had the potential to become "an altogether more comprehensive system of social discipline than the isolated prosecution of relatively notorious offenders."[33] By mimicking confession in the external forum, we are often told, the internal forum created a uniquely austere self-monitoring culture.

It would be easy to read *Measure for Measure* along these lines – to describe, for example, the thorough conflation of state power with pastoral care in the person of the Duke, then to imagine various ways the play explores "both kinds of discipline, the enforced and the internalised."[34] And yet this vaguely Lutheran suspicion that confession served mainly to keep people in a permanent state of terror and guilt was not the only or even the most urgent worry. On the contrary, the confessional's overall objective of exonerating wrong-doers perpetually threatened to contaminate juridical proceedings and replace legal penalties with the anarchy of indiscriminate absolution: for "if we confess our sins," says the first epistle of John, "he who is faithful and just will forgive us our sins and purify us from all unrighteousness" (1 John 1.9; cf. James 5.6). Since canon law held that "divine clemency does not permit sins, once dismissed, to be further punished,"[35] canonists had to deliberate very carefully to explain how crimes forgiven in penance could still be pursued by the courts – especially since the sanctity of the seal forbid a confessor from sharing with other authorities the crimes he discovered by way

of the sacrament. That is one reason confession had to be auricular rather than written: any incriminating words instantly dissipated
and were thereafter unavailable as evidence.[36] The Church was, of
course, able to defend a massive punitive apparatus from neutraliza-
tion by contrite performances, whether by differentiating *culpa* from
poena, mortal sin from venal, the internal forum from the external,
and so forth; but according to much of the reformist tradition, it was
not able to diminish at all the deviant faith in impunity that penance
appeared to facilitate. For we bid this be done, as the Duke says,
when evil deeds have their permissive pass.

His formulation derives straight from polemics against confession
that accused it of inciting the infractions it claimed to regulate. For
someone like Wyclif, this did not even primarily mean that power
requires aberrance to ensure its constant exercise (what we might
think of as the Foucaultian-Pauline position: "for where there is no
law, there is no transgression" [Romans 4.15]). It meant, as Foucault periodically verges on arguing, that the disciplinary process
itself could cross over into "something like the errant fragments of
an erotic art."[37] The fact that everything said in confession was said
in strict privacy (hence "privy shrift") and then *forgiven* made it the
perfect venue, in critics' minds if nowhere else, for every kind of
perversion. As Wyclif described it, the demand for yearly auricular
confession – "þis rotten lawe þat was þus late made of antecrist" –
created a situation in which "a frer & nunne may synne to-gidre; and
close hemsilf in a chaumbre bi lok."[38] Once there, ascetics bound by
oath to a life of abstinence could do whatever they liked with the
blessing of a "feyned assoylynge." Would God (as opposed to Antichrist) really have demanded "þat prestis & wymmen shulde turne
her faces to-gider, & speke of lustful þoutes & dedis, which myʒt do
harme to hem boþe?" Assoiling, for Wyclif, was at bottom a form of
self-soiling, a revolting and unparalleled refuge for the free exercise
of dirty talk.

If these are malicious calumnies, they are calumnies that eerily
resemble the Fathers' arguments in *defense* of confession. According
to them, Christ's odd parable about a fruitless fig tree rejuvenated
by excrement (Luke 13.6–9) was an allegory for penance; confession was a purgative, in their view, with the power to fertilize souls.
"Great indeed is the power of dung!" writes Ambrose – setting in
motion a line of thinking that will extend from Augustine, Jerome,
and Gregory the Great to a host of medieval commentators – "which
is so strong that it makes the barren fertile, the withered green, the
sterile fruitful. Job was sitting on dung when he was tempted and

could not be conquered [Job 2.8], and Paul accounts [everything he has lost] as dung that he may gain Christ [Philippians 3.8] . . . Therefore, good is the dung which is sent!"[39] Confession might have seemed to critics like a "filthy rite"[40] (to lift a phrase from Stephen Greenblatt), but to its defenders that was exactly the point. Only by wallowing in their own indecent smut could sinners be purified. "Therefore let us also dung this field which we possess!" Ambrose writes on the sacrament of penance. "Let us imitate farm workers, whom it does not shame to glut the ground with rich excrement, and to sprinkle the field with filthy ashes that they may cultivate a more copious harvest."[41] A liberal spewing of sewage in confession made one's virtues all the more fecund.

Religious drama in English found in this dual theological legacy – both the attacks on and apologies for confession – an opportunity to recommend penance with the most raucous impiety imaginable. It seems to have been difficult to stage the benefits of confession without staging its scandalous premise, as *Mankind* does in notoriously scatological (if traditional) terms. The play's incredible "Chrystemes songe," containing the refrain "he þat shytyth wyth hys hoyll,"[42] involves a motif common to medieval art but hard for modern audiences to grasp: "instead of the lips opening to read sweet prayers," Michael Camille writes, "the anus, the 'other' mouth, opens to spout faeces or farts."[43] In the case of *Mankind*, this is less a carnivalesque inversion than a literal, if gleefully demonic, embrace of the incarnation – which, early objectors pointed out, implicitly equated the godhead with shit.[44] Mercy, the play's one advocate for virtue, insists that the soul can be saved exclusively "whyll þe body wyth þe sowle hath hys annexion" (863) because only then can the soul participate in Christ's humanity and sacrifice. As a consequence, the body paradoxically conjoins sin with its cancelation in such a way as to loan the vices, their comic bawdiness and endless quibbling, a glorious excess in prefiguration of heaven's cornucopia.

Mankind's moral education, that is, consists of learning to embrace in confession a version of the thing he has been told to disdain everywhere else – namely, gratuitous and obscene speech. Nothing makes it more difficult for him to accept Mercy's advice to repent and confess than Mercy's own talionic admonition at the beginning of the play to "Mesure yowrsylf euer; be ware of excesse" (238) in preparation for the "streyt examynacyon" (42) of final judgment when "for euery ydyll worde we must ȝelde a reson" (173). If that sounds like a recipe for damnation, it should be – except that after Mankind predictably fails to take his advice, Mercy advocates instead for a more genuine form of forgiveness, one that "ys euer habundante" (22), whose "mesure ys tresure" (237) because it literally overwhelms the most inexhaustible sins (verbal and otherwise). By the end of the play the same virtue who had earlier counseled restraint begs the Virgin to show none: "Lett mercy excede justyce," he prays, addressing the chief medieval intercessor for every kind of ethical shortcoming (especially, given her own circumstances, sexual lapses):[45]

> amytt þis supplycacyon,
> Equyte to be leyde onparty [aside] and mercy to prevayll. (758–9)

Tapping into Mercy's reservoir of superabundance does not so much require a lifetime of constraint, it turns out, but a lifetime of confession and supplication – that is, an incessant discourse on sin in a quasi-dramatic dialogue with a friar or priest.

Mankind, like Wyclif – or, for that matter, Marlowe's Faustus or Shakespeare's Claudius – objects to this penitential process on the grounds "þat god were unry3tfyll, 3yf he 3af hym mercy" (as an important source text puts it).[46] Asking for a mercy that exceeds justice, an equity set aside, is for him a dangerous, adolescent fantasy; after all isn't the promise of forgiveness simply iniquity in its most cunning disguise, a ploy to convince him that sin has no meaningful consequence? (The play strengthens this suspicion by allowing the same actor to play Mercy and the chief devil, with each offering kindred temptations.) "What, aske mercy 3et onys agayn?" complains Mankind,

> Alas, yt were a wyle petycyun.
> Ewyr to offend and euer to aske mercy, yt ys a puerilite.
> Yt ys so abhominabyll to rehers my iterat transgrescion,
> I am not worthy to hawe mercy be no possibilite. (819–22)

We can hear in this speech an echo of the ancient Roman disapproval of confession: it is a vile or – given the ambiguities of medieval orthography – wily petition, puerile in the expectation that someone can offend with impunity so long as he admits the offense and says he's sorry. Sin, already obsessively iterative, merely repeats itself in confession, where Mankind is expected to "rehearse" yet again the endless refrain of his profligacy. And yet just before exiting the stage he bends at last to God's will (as does Genus Humanum after a similar lifetime of sin in *The Castle of Perseverance*) and pleads for the forgiveness he does not deserve but, we are given to understand, will now undoubtedly have: "God send ws all plente of hys gret mercy!" (900).

Drama like this went a long way toward justifying certain Protestants' opposition to both penance and play-acting. Sacramental confession, and the fraternal orders' scandalous promotion of it, remained a lucrative and alluring spectacle on the commercial stage, however – nowhere more so, prior to Shakespeare, than in Marlowe, whose capitalization on the sacrament's antinomian implications in *The Jew of Malta* deeply marks the work of his rival. Like Vincentio, Abigail first joins a religious order under false pretenses; she eventually leaves but then, seized with remorse (or something like it), wants to rejoin. It is this oscillation that makes her father confessor, the friar Jacomo, worry that if he readmits her, she will only backslide again the way she already had ("ever to offend, ever to ask mercy," in Mankind's words). She convinces him with a seemingly heartfelt speech that he nonetheless correctly intuits someone else has scripted in advance: "who taught thee this?"[47] Her answer – "the abbess of the house" where she had formerly pretended to convert – has a pious ring to it, as Maria's responsibilities would have included instructing novices in their new spiritual commitments, but the portrait that emerges here is less of successful catechization than belated indoctrination into a system of Christian deceptions running parallel to the "Jewish" misdirections of Barabas: Friar Jacomo readmits Abigail to the convent only after learning that her chief mentor in the mysteries of the faith has been the nun with whom he most likes to fraternize. Maria calls for Jacomo specifically on her deathbed, and he already knows all too well the wrongs she will need to admit: "O, what a sad confession will there be!" (3.6.4). For the rest of the play he and Barnadine (whose name returns in *Measure for Measure* as a resolutely dissolute prisoner) openly display all the hypocrisy and self-indulgence that the penitential system had been said to promote – above all, its unbridled sexual licentiousness, whereby "the nuns [have] fine sport with the friars" (3.3.36), just as reformers since Wyclif had always alleged.

In fact Abigail's penitential speech, evidently learned from a fellow sinner accustomed to performing regret, replaces the full confession that absolution would normally require, and it greatly complicates her ability to confess again later at the moment of her death. Rather than owning the specifics of her misbehavior, she claims the fault is ultimately her father's while vowing never to say exactly how:

> Jacomo: Thy father's how?
> Abigail: Nay, you shall pardon me. [*Aside*] O, Barabas,
> Though thou deservest hardly at my hands,
> Yet never shall these lips bewray thy life. (3.4.75–8)

Presumably she wants to show her father some mercy by withholding a report of his crimes, but even this charitable act collaborates with his subterfuge and deepens her guilt. Her colloquial excuse for not speaking more fully – "pardon me" – demands an absolution that speaking fully alone could earn. The complementary vow never to betray Barabas with her "lips" means any subsequent attempt at a thorough confession will entangle her in yet another sin – that of breaking an oath. Her wrong, like Claudio's in *Measure for Measure*, is now "what but to speak would offend again" (1.2.128).

As a result her final deathbed confession involves a casuistic ruse fully on a par with her father's cunning. Speaking to Barnadine rather than Jacomo, who has left to confess the abbess, Abigail says all she can about her help in engineering the fatal rivalry between Mathias and Lodowick (another name that returns in *Measure for Measure*, as the Duke's alias) until she hits the stumbling block of her earlier oath:

> Barnadine: So, say how was their end?
> Abigail: Both, jealous of my love, envied each other:
> And by my father's practice, which is there
> Set down at large, the gallants were both slain . . .
> To work my peace, this I confess to thee.
> Reveal it not, for then my father dies . . .
>   . . . Ah, gentle friar,
> Convert my father that he may be saved,
> And witness that I die a Christian . . .
> Barnadine: Ay, and a virgin too; that grieves me most. (3.6.26–9)

Rather than an auricular confession, that is, she offers her final, most damning admission in writing. This is no small substitution, as it transfers her private, exculpatory confession into the public domain of documentary evidence where it could be potentially all the more damaging to her father than if she had betrayed him with her "lips." Written confessions, as we have seen, had always posed the greatest risk of eliding the separation between the sacrament and a juridical proceeding – or worse, between the sacrament and blackmail.

Her substitution therefore raises an obvious question: is Abigail sincerely pleading with Barnadine to respect the sanctity of the seal ("reveal it not, for then my father dies") or is she providing him with material to blackmail Barabas into converting so that he "may be saved"? Barabas's entire motive for poisoning her, once he learns (from another piece of her writing) that she has rejoined the convent, was to prevent her from making a disclosure of precisely this sort. Indeed her letter informing him of her reconversion foreshadows, and perhaps directly inspires, Ithamore's plan to write a letter of his own threatening that, without extravagant compensation, he too "will confess" (4.3.4). And, of course, whatever Abigail's intention, blackmail is predictably the use to which Barnadine immediately puts her confession, leading to Barabas's own, comically insincere mimicry of remorse:

> Barnadine: Barabas, thou hast – [waving Abigail's confession?]
> Jacomo: Ay, thou hast –
> Barabas: True, I have money. What though I have? (4.1.29–31)

He readily admits the scale of his wealth so that he can promise to give it to whichever friar will prescribe the least rigorous penance. This admission then occasions a competition between them over whose monastery is more lax, which reprises the cause of his being blackmailed in the first place – his contrivance of a rivalry between Mathias and Lodowick. If there is a moment when Barabas miscalculates prior to his poor construction of the play's final trap, it is here in his oddly principled unwillingness to convert to a religion that is more than happy to accommodate, via penance, his every desire. The friars' attempt to blackmail him actually strengthens the sanctity of the seal for the simple reason that blackmail remains profitable only so long as the blackmailer *declines* to publish his victim's secrets. The confessor's silence, like any other indulgence from the Church, works best when underwritten, in Chaucer's words, by a "good pitaunce."

Shakespeare's borrowings from *The Jew of Malta* make it difficult to sustain Sarah Beckwith's recent proposition that his "own friars, prior to *Measure for Measure*, are emphatically not in this [antifraternal] tradition."[48] It is certainly true that Shakespeare taps into various positive memories of the orders that England had lost – the selfless servants of the community who could be counted on to mediate local disputes, care for the poor, and salve troubled consciences because they themselves had elected to join a collective beyond the narrow claims of family, class, or kingdom. Even here, however, their strength was often at one with their appetite for deviance, for repudiating social norms, and for throwing in their lot with the abject and reprobate. As in Marlowe, I think we can see evidence throughout Shakespeare's corpus for a kind of nostalgia somewhat different from the one usually described by early drama studies – which is to say, we can see a longing for the old penitential system, as overseen by mendicants in particular, not with the hope that the uncountable accusations against it had been unfair, but with the hope they were true.

In *Romeo and Juliet*, for example, Friar Lawrence's opening soliloquy raises the cultural ambivalence surrounding the fraternal orders almost to the level of a credo. His celebration of herbs – which will have a pivotal role when he provides the potion that allows Juliet to feign her death – invokes an ancient paradox appertaining to doctors but in this case also evocative of how the clergy works: as in modern chemotherapy, they used poisons to cure. Doctors cut, bled, and burned in order to heal. The idea here is that Romeo and Juliet are lovesick, that only a member of the clergy can cure them through the sacrament of marriage, but that this virtuous treatment will require the vice or poison of deception. In effect, the friar must act, according to the dictates of his conscience, as a surreptitious bawd. On the one hand, we can see how his moral flexibility might be all to the good: the dogmatic intolerance of the two clans has led to a destructive and unending blood feud. It takes a man of great spiritual depth to step away from the groupthink and antagonism that dominate the culture of Verona, in pursuit of higher, more charitable ends – the ends of "love." On the other hand, we can see in this a familiar version of all the old antifraternal criticisms and a forerunner to the duke of dark corners: the friar as internecine figure of intrigue, fostering shadowy dealings and, in this case, offering through confession to exonerate disobedient children. Friar Lawrence is, in short, both an agent of liberation and an enabler of libertines.

The cover of confession is indispensable to Romeo and Juliet's illicit affair – they will be married, for instance, by devising false "means to come to shrift."[49] When Juliet first arrives in the friar's cell, she playfully extends this hoax by greeting Lawrence as her "ghostly confessor" (2.6.21), thereby stressing how cavalierly they are using his spiritual or "ghostly" calling as camouflage. After the marriage ceremony, Juliet will again pretend to go to confession in order to find a "remedy" for her forced union with Paris (3.5.231ff.), at which point Friar Lawrence will propose that she fake her own death. His advice cues her to perform a penitential change of heart: she returns to her parents "from shrift with a merry look" (4.2.15), claiming to have learned "to repent the sin / Of disobedient opposition" (4.2.17–18), when in reality the confessional has directly abetted her insubordination by offering her a kind of asylum. Lawrence's cell seems to be the only space that allows for the social reconciliation commonly touted as a primary virtue of the sacrament of penance, and yet in this case it makes that possible by providing a sanctuary for romantic trysts, exactly as its critics said. Meaningful social reconciliation, if there were to be any in this play, would come at the cost of breaking the social and moral codes restricting sexual contact to people from the correct families. Confession here provides the perfect warrant for such infractions, as it will again in *Measure for Measure* by rescuing the illicit union between another Juliet and her lover, which they too "thought it meet to hide" from friends and family, "till time had made them for us" (1.2.141–2).

When Duke Vincentio visits Friar Thomas, he explicitly cites this convention of turning to confession in order to find a release for all kinds of libidinal blockage: "No. Holy Father, throw away that thought," he says as the two first enter in mid-conversation:

> Believe not that the dribbling dart of love
> Can pierce a complete bosom. Why I desire thee
> To give me secret harbor hath a purpose
> More grave and wrinkled than the aims and ends
> Of burning youth. (1.3.1–6)

If *Measure for Measure* is a "problem play," the problem stems primarily from this disavowal: Vincentio will use his fake ordination, and the power of the seal that comes with it, to pursue almost exclusively sexual objectives. His wrinkled purpose – supposedly free from the erotic agenda of youth – turns out to require him to listen to the confessions of others and arrange assignations among them while at the same time scheming to satisfy his own sexual needs: hence the other bed-trick in the play, whereby the Duke replaces Angelo as Isabella's coercive suitor. Evidently Friar Thomas suspected all along an outcome of this sort: "Holy father, throw away that thought" protests – too much, we can see in retrospect – what must have been a suggestion that Vincentio discuss his bedroom issues. Thomas's prescience raises the rather extraordinary possibility that the Duke's confession from the very beginning is a *confessio ficti*:[50] it only seems as if he is admitting to an overly lenient rule and then concocting with the friar's help a Machiavellian dodge to restore order. In fact his remorse for having been excessively indulgent is itself *already* a disguise for the randy old lecher who finds in his subsequent disguise as a friar what friars had supposedly always sought out – every variety of sexual chicanery. He was concerned from the start about justice and mercy not for the ethical and political quandaries they raise, but for the kinks that their administration turns out to entail.

We cannot know what would have happened had Isabella remained in the convent rather than intervening (up to a point) for her brother, just as we cannot know whether the play ends in her marriage or a return to the sisterhood. But given that "Angelo's behavior is exactly what one would expect of someone who assumes that all sexual expression is tantamount to moral ruin," I think we have reason to imagine that Isabella's similar rectitude ultimately affords her plenty of "enjoyment by other means," whether in or out of the convent.[51] I am struck by the exchange, immediately after Vincentio's adoption of the habit, that depicts Isabella's parallel introduction to the convent: "have you nuns no farther privileges?" (1.4.1) she asks, ostensibly chafing already from pious constraints that famously inspired all manner of flouting. Then, when her guide lightly reprimands her – "are these not large enough?" (1.4.2) – we see the first hint of Isabella's knack for holier-than-thou poses when confronted with less than holy proposals: far from desiring more privileges, she says, she wishes rather for "a more strict restraint" (1.4.4). This seems like an impromptu lie to cover for her inadvertent confession of a desire for a different kind of freedom, but even if true, it is hard not to think that stricter restraints would merely result in more elaborate pleas for forgiveness. At any rate, from here on out the intimation is never far from the surface that Isabella, like both of her suitors, is at heart a hypocrite – except that when she is given a chance to exercise her duplicitous talents toward the end of saving her brother, she reveals herself to be not quite hypocritical enough. And that is a sin no one can believably admit.

Notes

1. Exodus 21.23–35; Leviticus 24.20; Matthew 7.2.
2. William Shakespeare, *Measure for Measure*, ed. J. W. Lever (London: Bloomsbury, 2012), 1.3.27–9. All further quotations are from this edition.

3. For the atmosphere of St. Stephen's, see Leah Marcus, *Puzzling Shakespeare: Local Reading and its Discontents* (Berkeley: University of California Press, 1988), 154–8.

4. *The Basilicon Doron of James VI*, ed. James Craigie, 2 vols. (Edinburgh: William Blackwood & Sons, 1944), 1:65 (1603 text). For discussion of and further bibliography on the play's topicality, see Julia Reinhard Lupton, *Citizen-Saints: Shakespeare and Political Theology* (Chicago: University of Chicago Press, 2005), 151–2.

5. *Basilicon Doron*, 1:139 (1603 text).

6. Ibid., 1:63 (1603 text).

7. Barbara H. Rosenwein and Lester K. Little, "Social Meaning in the Monastic and Mendicant Spiritualities," *Past & Present* 63 (1974): 24.

8. Geoffrey Chaucer, *The Riverside Chaucer*, ed. Larry D. Benson, 3rd ed. (Boston: Houghton Mifflin, 1987), 27, ll. 221–4.

9. Quoted in Anne Hudson, *The Premature Reformation: Wycliffite Texts and Lollard History* (Oxford: Clarendon Press, 1988), 297.

10. Penn R. Szittya, *The Antifraternal Tradition in Medieval Literature* (Princeton: Princeton University Press, 1986), 159.

11. Cf. John Parker, "Persona," in *Cultural Reformations: Medieval and Renaissance in Literary History*, ed. Brian Cummings and James Simpson (Oxford: Oxford University Press, 2010), 591–608.

12. Christopher Marlowe, *Doctor Faustus: A- and B- Texts (1604, 1616)*, ed. David Bevington and Eric Rasmussen (Manchester: Manchester University Press, 1993), 1.3.27 (A-Text).

13. Deborah Shuger, *Political Theologies in Shakespeare's England: The Sacred and the State in Measure for Measure* (Basingstoke: Palgrave Macmillan, 2001), 137.

14. Cf. John Parker, *The Aesthetics of Antichrist: From Christian Drama to Christopher Marlowe* (Ithaca: Cornell University Press, 2007).

15. I am building here on my earlier arguments in Parker, "Faustus, Confession, and the Sins of Omission," *ELH* 80 (2013): 29–59.

16. The following discussion is particularly indebted to Jean Michel David, "La faute et l'abandon: Théories et pratiques judiciaires à Rome à la fin de la République," in *L'aveu: Antiquité et Moyen Âge: Actes de la table ronde organisée par l'École française de Rome avec le concours du CNRS et de l'Université de Trieste, Rome 28–30 mars 1984* (Rome: École Française de Rome, Palais Farnèse, 1986), 69–87; Yan Thomas, "Confessus pro iudicato: L'aveu civil et l'aveu pénal à Rome," in *L'aveu*, 89–117; Carlin A. Barton, *Roman Honor: The Fire in the Bones* (Berkeley: University of California Press, 2001), 136–95; Joseph Ratzinger, "Originalität und Überlieferung in Augustins Begriff der confessio," *Revue des études Augustiniennes* 3 (1957): 375–92.

17. *The Institutio Oratoria of Quintilian*, trans. H. E. Butler, 4 vols. (London: Heinemann, 1933–39), 2:317 (5.13.8; trans. modified). Cf. *Inst. Orat.* 7.4.17: "In the last resort we may plead for mercy,

although most writers deny that this is ever admissible in the courts" (ibid. 3:115).

18. H. F. Jolowicz and Barry Nicholas, *Historical Introduction to the Study of Roman Law*, 3rd ed. (Cambridge: Cambridge University Press, 1972), 182.

19. Quoted in David, "La faute," 69.

20. Ps.-Quintilian, *The Lesser Declamations*, ed. and trans. D. R. Shackleton Bailey, 2 vols. (Cambridge, MA: Harvard University Press, 2006), 2:18–19 (§314).

21. Seneca the Elder, *Declamations*, trans. Michael Winterbottom, 2 vols. (Cambridge, MA: Harvard University Press, 1974), 2:185 (*Controversiae* 8.1).

22. Cicero, *De Inventione, De Optimo Genere Oratorum, Topica*, trans. H. M. Hubbell (Cambridge, MA: Harvard University Press, 1949), 31 (*De inven.* 1.11.15), speaking of the formal legal strategy of *deprecatio*.

23. Seneca the Younger, *Moral Essays*, trans. John W. Basore, 3 vols. (Cambridge, MA: Harvard University Press, 1928), 1:238–9 (*De ira* 2.32.3).

24. Ibid., 1:174 (*De ira* 2.5.2).

25. See *tôdâ* in Joshua 7.19; Cesare Giraudo, "Confession of Sins in the Old Testament," in *The Fate of Confession*, ed. Mary Collins and David Power (Edinburgh: T. & T. Clark, 1987), 85–9.

26. *Exposition of the Psalms* 117.1, 137.2 in *Works of Saint Augustine: A Translation for the 21st Century*, ed. Boniface Ramsey (Hyde Park, NY: New City Press, 1990–), III/19:333 and III/20:242.

27. Pliny, *Letters*, trans. William Melmoth, rev. by W. M. L. Hutchinson, 2 vols. (London: Heinemann, 1915), 2:401 (*Ep.* 10.96; trans. modified).

28. Tertullian, *Apology, De Spectactulis*, trans. T. R. Glover; *Minucius Felix*, trans. Gerald H. Rendall (Cambridge, MA: Harvard University Press, 1966), 7 (*Apol.* 1; trans. modified).

29. Richard Hooker, *Laws* 6.4.11; quoted in Deborah Shuger, *Censorship and Cultural Sensibility: The Regulation of Language in Tudor-Stuart England* (Philadelphia: University of Pennsylvania Press, 2006), 145.

30. Still the most comprehensive history is Henry Charles Lea, *A History of Auricular Confession and Indulgences in the Latin Church*, 3 vols. (Philadelphia: Lea Brothers, 1896). See also Thomas Tentler, *Sin and Confession on the Eve of the Reformation* (Princeton: Princeton University Press, 1977).

31. See especially Mike Hepworth and Bryan S. Turner, *Confession: Studies in Deviance and Religion* (London: Routledge & Kegan Paul, 1982).

32. Ramon de Peñafort, quoted in Lea, *History of Auricular Confession*, 1:347.

33. Keith Thomas, *Religion and the Decline of Magic* (New York: Scribners, 1971), 155; cf. Thomas Tentler, "The Summa for Confessors as an Instrument of Social Control," in *The Pursuit of Holiness in Late*

Medieval and Renaissance Religion, ed. Charles Trinkaus and Heiko A. Oberman (Leiden: Brill, 1974), esp. 123.

34. Jonathan Dollimore, "Transgression and Surveillance in *Measure for Measure*," in *Political Shakespeare: New Essays in Cultural Materialism* (Ithaca: Cornell University Press, 1985), 75.

35. R. H. Helmholz, *The Spirit of Classical Canon Law* (Athens, GA: University of Georgia Press, 1996), 298–302, esp. 298, quoting *Decretum Gratiani, De pen. Dist.* 4 c. 24.

36. Lea, *History of Auricular Confession*, 1:362–7.

37. Michel Foucault, *The History of Sexuality*, vol. 1: *An Introduction*, trans. Robert Hurley (New York: Vintage, 1990), 71.

38. *The English Works of Wyclif*, ed. F. D. Matthew (London, 1880), 300.

39. Ambrose, *Exposition of the Holy Gospel according to Saint Luke, with Fragments on the Prophesy of Isaias*, trans. Theodosia Tomkinson (Etna, CA: Center for Traditionalist Orthodox Studies, 1998), 299 (*Expositio ev. Lucam* 7.168).

40. Stephen Greenblatt, *Learning to Curse: Essays in Early Modern Culture* (London: Routledge, 1990), 77–104.

41. *De poenitentia* 1.3 in *Patrologiae cursus completus, Series Latina*, ed. J. M. Migne, 221 vols. (Paris, 1844–64), 16:0496D.

42. *The Macro Plays*, ed. Mark Eccles, Early English Text Society 91 (Oxford: Oxford University Press, 1969), 165 (l. 337). All further citations from *Mankind* refer to line numbers of this edition.

43. Michael Camille, "Play, Piety and Perversity in Medieval Marginal Manuscript Illumination," in *Mein Ganzer Körper ist Gesicht: Groteske Darstellungen in der europäischen Kunst und Literatur des Mittelalters* (Freiburg im Breisgau: Rombach, 1994), 175. Cf. Paula Neuss, "Active and Idle Language: Dramatic Images in *Mankind*," in *Medieval Drama*, ed. Neville Denny (London: Edward Arnold, 1973), esp. 63.

44. See, for example, Tertullian, *Adv. Marc.* 3.10 in *Ante-Nicene Fathers*, ed. Philip Schaff, 10 vols. (Grand Rapids, MI: Eerdmans, 1950–53), 3:329.

45. Emma Solberg, "Madonna, Whore: Mary's Sexuality in the N-Town Plays," *Comparative Drama* 48 (2014):191–219.

46. From *Jacob's Well*, quoted by Neuss, "Active and Idle Language," 66.

47. Christopher Marlowe, *The Jew of Malta*, ed. N. W. Bawcutt (Manchester: Manchester University Press, 1978), 3.3.69. All further quotations are from this edition.

48. Sarah Beckwith, *Shakespeare and the Grammar of Forgiveness* (Ithaca: Cornell University Press, 2011), 76.

49. William Shakespeare, *Romeo and Juliet*, ed. René Weis (London: Bloomsbury, 2012), 2.4.173. All further quotations are from this edition.

50. For this term, and a fascinating overview of confession in general, see Lee Patterson, *Chaucer and the Subject of History* (Madison: University of Wisconsin Press, 1991), 400.

51. Katharine Eisaman Maus, *Inwardness and Theater in the English Renaissance* (Chicago: University of Chicago Press, 1995), 163, and Lupton, *Citizen-Saints*, 142, respectively.

Chapter 9

Bracketed Judgment, "Un-humanizing," and Conversion in *The Merchant of Venice*[1]

Sanford Budick

In sooth I know not why I am so sad.
It wearies me, you say it wearies you;
But how I caught it, found it, or came by it,
What stuff 'tis made of, whereof it is born,
I am to learn.[2]

I propose that the famously unexplained mood of emotional help-lessness with which Antonio thus opens *The Merchant of Venice* is the first of many prompts for an efficacious counter-mode of self-reflection that is deeply embedded in the play's language. This is a modality of language in symbolic action that is linked, in reaction, to the morally problematical manifestations of the surface drama. Many commentators have noted the degraded values for which the play's apparent heroes stand, especially the way their claims for Christian mercy are belied by merciless legalism and unabashed greed.[3] I believe that a reactive reflection on the surface drama is an inner necessity generated by the play itself. Yet the widely divergent responses that constitute the history of reception of *The Merchant of Venice* turn precisely on whether one recognizes that inner necessity. A. D. Nuttall puts his finger directly on this question – "the most difficult point," he calls it – and decides against the recognition. His reasoning, and what I believe are its flaws, are telling:

> Half-buried echoes and subauditions in the play really do compose a structure, and an exciting subversive thesis. But they are not the play. After years of pious criticism the views of A. D. Moody and H. C. Goddard are very seductive. Moody says, "Shylock avows the moral sense by which they actually live. We can see that by condemning

Shylock they are condemning their own sins. It would seem that they are making him literally into their scapegoat . . . or, A. C. Goddard puts it, 'They project onto him what they have dismissed from their own consciousness as too disturbing.'" But in agreeing with this we are in danger of forgetting the real generosity, however produced, of the Christians, the real ferocity, however explained, of Shylock. They did forgive Shylock. Shylock would have torn open the breast of Antonio. These are things which no theatrical experience of the play will ever let you forget. . . . The subversive counter-thesis is itself too easy.[4]

A great deal is at stake in describing as "real" both the Christians' "generosity, however produced" – after all, "They did forgive Shylock" – and the "ferocity" of Shylock – after all, he "would have torn open the breast of Antonio." What status of reality do we assign to these "real" things? If we apprehend these things as dubious representations of the human reality they allege, can we then disclose – in Shakespeare and in ourselves – an inner actuality of the human that is for us beyond such dubiety? One litmus test for identifying how, at the end of the day, one apprehends the status of the real in this play is seeing how one grasps the forgiveness, in forced conversion, that the Christians grant Shylock. Stanley Cavell expresses his sense of what that forgiveness amounts to at the final moment, when Portia demands, "Art thou contented, Jew? What dost thou say?" and Shylock echoingly responds, "I am content" (5.1.389), says nothing more (ever), and disappears. Here is Cavell on Shylock at that moment:

> I find I can only assume that he is not convinced by Portia's mock Talmudism but is, at a stroke, spiritually overborne, rendered helpless or hopeless to expect mere tolerance of his existence, let alone whatever is to be called justice. . . . I take it that we are to perceive Shylock's ending, his continued mere repetition of words he once upon a time could mean and could use to effect in confronting others, as showing him now working to cover the vanishing powers, or the increasing consciousness of the emptiness, the suffocation, of his possibility of speech; put otherwise, showing him becoming drained of the effort to continue assuming, to the extent he has ever assumed, participation in the human.[5]

Has "real" forgiveness wrought this? And we must ask as well, is the "ferocity" of Shylock – he "would have torn open the breast of Antonio" – "real" as well? Shakespeare troubles to bestow moving features of the human upon Shylock. Yet on an entirely different level of the real, which breaks violently into the play from outside the play, Shakespeare nevertheless has made himself party to the most vicious form of medieval and early modern antisemitism, namely, the so-called "blood libel" that represents the Jew in a state of continually thirsting for Christian blood. It is untidy for a suspension of disbelief but on some level it is impossible, for us at least, to forget that, after all, that is the "real" reason Shylock "would have torn open the breast of Antonio." Shakespeare seems to affirm Shylock's humanity by having him say, "if you prick us do / We not bleed?" (3.1.50–1). Of course this could be reckoned as mere insidious irony, but might one not at least question whether Shakespeare can here be totally suspending his own disbelief in the blood libel? In the marketplace of this play can he simply be retailing, at face value, the "real" of representing Shylock's fictional desire to tear open Antonio's breast?

In themselves these are undecidable questions. Yet the upshot of these kinds of possible counter-reasonings to Nuttall's reasonings is that we need to reconsider the evidence for deciding, nevertheless, whether the "half-buried echoes and subauditions in the play" – even more of these than Nuttall has noted – provoke a counter-thesis that is not "subversive" but integrally constructive. These amount to subauditions in the precise sense of mentally supplying, upon reflection, something that is not immediately expressed. The play itself, in other words, sets in motion the spectator's sharing in the reflective, onlooking intelligence that revolves around the play's worldly surface. The activity of reflection, worked through in painstakingly generated structures of reflection, is central to the meaning of *The Merchant of Venice*.

Taken as a whole, the surface drama of the play projects the lowest common denominator of an unimproved natural attitude of humanity: this is mirrored in the romance of wealth, power, beauty, brash sexuality, sophistic cleverness, and, most fiercely, destruction of the Other. In this play hatred of the Other is manifest both in Shylock's hatred of Christians, a hatred that the Christians neutralize, and in the Christians' pervasive Jew-hatred that leads to the onstage eradication of even the minimal being-human of a human being. Shakespeare's representation of Shylock eschews the reductionism of the Pantalone of Commedia dell'arte or the comic devil of the morality plays. Yet by bestowing dimensions of humanity upon Shylock, Shakespeare has knowingly plunged his play into a moral dilemma from which there is no obvious worldly exit. His play commits imaginary erasure of a human being, allegedly for the sake of the moral imagination. The irresolvable clash of values thus created, together with other forces of suspending judgment in the play, determine that the so-called judgment scene finally suspends the idea of meaningful judgment altogether. We need to see how the play's structures of reflection indeed compel suspension, even cancelation, of one kind of alleged human judgment while showing how a truly human judgment might be disclosed.

Although the play's outward action sanctions both the romanticization of superficial values and the obliteration of the Jew, Shakespeare creates a protesting counter-life of language. This he achieves in a set of acute divergences from the outward meanings of a set of key terms, namely, *nothing, hazard, three* or the *third*, and *conversion*. These divergences within some meanings do not amount to subversions of all meaning, such as a deconstructionist reading might aim to uncover. Rather, the play's pattern of inner signification is established by its strong web of interconnecting language. Yet the articulation of this inner meaning also does not bring with it an expectation that it can easily displace the allure of worldly values. To hear the inner meaning of the play's inner drama we need to be self-disciplined in a difficult language of self-reflection that is distinctly secondary in the order of the play's unfolding of meanings. Paradoxically, however, it is this secondary activity that can produce a sense of the solid actuality of being, while the outward reality represented in the play remains wrapped in mists of romance.

Shakespeare's language of subauditions in *The Merchant of Venice* follows patterns of a meditational discipline that he need not have derived from a particular source. Rather, at very different times and places, both in antiquity and in modernity, those patterns have been seen as an available, even if difficult, path within human consciousness. In this mental discipline ways are found – or are even thought to be inevitable – to suspend momentarily, to *bracket*, consciousness of the spatio-temporal world. Since the activity of this bracketing of judgment has a pivotal but not obvious place in the history of thought, it is important to be as clear as possible about what it means and does not mean, especially because Shakespeare is decidedly of one mind and not the other.

As if on either side of a great divide, opposing basic intuitions concerning this act of bracketing have long been strongly in evidence both East and West – in the West, particularly in the twentieth and twenty-first centuries. On one side of the divide we find the intuition that in the moment after such bracketing the mind discloses a sense of self that is prior to, and largely (but not completely) independent of, experience of the world outside the mind. Concepts and procedures that are based on this grounding intuition were anciently elaborated, for example, in the Yoga Sutras. In the modern era, closely resembling but not derived from such concepts and procedures, is the self-reflective act of "bracketing" in Edmund Husserl's "phenomenological reduction."[6] In its turn, Husserl's act of bracketing bears strong resemblances to, or even filiations with, Kant's radical suspension of consciousness of the world in the experience of the sublime, as well as Søren Kierkegaard's suspensions of one's accustomed self in the "anxiety of the nothing."[7] The thinking of Emmanuel Levinas adopts Husserl's and Kant's (and Kierkegaard's) intuitions concerning suspension or bracketing of this kind. On the other side of the divide we find (among many others) Heidegger and Derrida. Although their philosophical careers both commence from Husserl's thought, they absorb bracketing into an entirely different grounding intuition, one that finds in bracketing an unstable back-and-forth movement of *Destruktion* (Heidegger) or deconstruction and *différance* (Derrida) in and around the bracketed space of absence or emptiness.[8]

I will not try to adjudicate the contest, in these arenas, between the views of Husserl–Kant and Heidegger–Derrida. Rich as the afterlives and counter-lives of Husserl's concept of bracketing have been, for the purposes of illuminating Shakespeare's meanings Husserl's own method and application of bracketing have an integral unity and cogency that need to be preserved. This unity and cogency have a striking capacity for allowing one to hear consciously what Husserl would approvingly call the "unnatural" inner language of *The Merchant of Venice*. For Husserl's system as well as for Shakespeare's play the most radical implication of the bracketing of judgment is an "un-humanizing" of allegedly human thought (an *Entmenschung* that is not a *dehumanization*) that can enable a "conversion" to truly human thought. The philosophical side of this method of reflection needs to be spelled out as clearly as possible, even if only briefly. For Husserl as well as Shakespeare the reflective concepts and methods involved here strangely move the center of being human to the phase of the secondary that reflection creates. Yet Shakespeare's language in *The Merchant of Venice* elevates the significance and centrality of that secondariness by revealing the actions of reflection and bracketing that can inhere in fateful double meanings.

Husserl in general took care to escape dualistic views of human consciousness, yet, following Kant's dualistic idea of an "actuality" that is perceived "in an *a priori* manner . . . in accordance with . . . the analogies" of experience, Husserl early identified a "dormant actuality [*Inaktualität*]" that is "ever prepared to pass into the wakeful mode" of "focal actuality [*Aktualität*]."[9] In his later thought (as described below) Husserl elaborated the ways in which awareness of this actuality is paradoxically dependent on a struggle to think with negativity, which is to say, to employ bracketing (*epoché*) structures of thought that build in acknowledgment of the unrepresentable dimension of language and of reality. Kant's non-spatio-temporal negativity, achieved, among other ways, in the momentary suspension of consciousness of the world in the experience of the sublime, discloses an a priori self that abides in freedom and in the possibility of choosing action from freedom and moral feeling. In parallel, Husserl's spatio-temporal negativity, achieved in the bracketing or "universal *epoché*" of consciousness of the world discloses the actuality of the transcendental ego/I/self that can enable one to choose an action that freely expresses that self.

Here, gathered from Husserl's explanations (and those that he approved in the work of his close associate, Eugen Fink), are the terms of and concepts of Husserl's method of reflection. It is worth remarking again that though the meditative method described here may sound like Husserl's pure invention, we could produce closely equivalent terms and concepts from ancient texts. So too, without reference to any questions of influence, Shakespeare's method of reflection in *The Merchant of Venice* stands independently somewhere between that antiquity and this modernity. If there is an assertion of anything metaphysical in all three of these reflective methods, it is only that there is a pre-reflective self that exists prior to experience of the world (which is exactly what Kant means by the term transcendental). The inner strength of *The Merchant of Venice* is disclosed when the close equivalences to these terms and concepts of reflection are seen at work within the play's doublings of language. In the following glosses culled from Husserl's and Fink's writings we should not be thrown by the term "phenomenological" which, given the functional directness of their explanations of that which is phenomenological, is here virtually redundant:

1. *The natural attitude and the phenomenological [un-natural] attitude*

> In the natural attitude we simply effect all the acts by virtue of which the world is there for us. We live naively in perceiving and experiencing, in these acts of positing in which unities <and realities of every kind> appear and not only appear but also are given with the characteristic of things [that seem] "on hand," "actual." . . . In the phenomenological attitude . . . we *prevent the effecting* of all such cogitative positings, i.e., we "parenthesize" [bracket] the positings

effected; for our new inquiries we do not "participate in these positings." Instead of living *in* them, instead of effecting *them*, we effect
acts of *reflection* directed to them; and we seize upon them themselves as the *absolute* being they are. We are now living completely
in such acts of the second degree.[10]

2. *Epoché (bracketing) and the reduction*

In contrast to the natural theoretical attitude, the correlate of which
is the world, a new attitude must in fact be possible which, in spite
of the "exclusion" of the psychophysical universe of Nature, leaves
us something: . . . instead of naively *effecting* the acts pertaining
to our Nature – constituting consciousness with their positings of
something transcendent, and letting ourselves be induced, by motives
implicit in them, to effect ever new positings of something transcendent – instead of that, we put all those positings "out of action," we
do not "participate in them."[11]

3. *Two simultaneous "moments"*

Epoché [bracketing] and the reduction proper [carried out in "radical reflection"] are the two internal *basic moments* of the phenomenological reduction, mutually required and mutually conditioned
. . . "in which we *blast open captivation-in-an-acceptedness* and
first recognize the acceptedness *as* an acceptedness in the first
place."[12]

4. *Un-humanizing and the onlooker*

In the universal epoché, in the disconnection of all belief-positings,
the phenomenological onlooker produces himself. The transcendental tendency that awakens in man and drives him to inhibit
all acceptednesses nullifies man himself; man *un-humanizes*
[*entmenscht*] himself in performing the epoché, that is, he lays bare
the transcendental onlooker in himself, he passes into him. This
onlooker, however, does not first come to be by the epoché, but
is only *freed* of the shrouding cover <barrier of anonymity> of
human being [*Menschsein*].[13]

5. *Un-humanizing and the residuum*

Pure consciousness in its absolute being. That, then, is what is
left as the sought-for "*phenomenological residuum*," though we
have "excluded" the whole world with all physical things, living beings, and humans, ourselves included. Strictly speaking, we
have not lost anything but rather have gained the whole of absolute being.[14]

Phenomenologizing . . . signifies precisely *the un-humanizing of
man* [*Entmenschung*], the passing of human existence [*Existenz*] (as

a world-captivated naïve self-apperception) into the transcendental subject.[15]

6. *Conversion and humanity's existential task*

The total phenomenological attitude and the epoché belonging to it are destined to effect, at first, a complete personal transformation, comparable in the beginning to a religious conversion, which then, however, over and above this, bears within itself the significance of the greatest existential transformation which is assigned as a task to mankind as such.[16]

In *The Merchant of Venice* the activity of bracketing accepted judgment of what is human is carried out, first of all, within a sustained language of the "nothing" that takes its rise in reaction to Antonio's words that open the play. It is crucial for absorbing the impact of everything that transpires in this play to take in that Antonio opens the world of the play with an act of self-reflection, even and especially because he does not recognize that his self-reflection is about "nothing." Beginning with Antonio's self-reflection of the nothing, which is matched by kindred reflections of Gratiano, Bassanio, and Portia, the spectator is drawn into an ever more inward act of this kind, although for the spectator, as for Shakespeare, the object and meaning of reflection on the nothing will become something altogether different.

Shakespeare immediately leads us to the double language of the nothing in Solarino's diagnosis of Antonio's mood. Solarino sees that that mood – Husserl would call it part of the "natural attitude" – has somehow to do with a deep anxiety of being "worth nothing" (1.1.36), of being dispossessed of everything worldly that seems to makes one who he or she is. Solarino's response to Antonio's fear of the nothing unknowingly hints at the complexity of reflection that would be required for clarifying and re-thinking the thought of the nothing:

Shall I have the thought
To think on this [i.e., being "worth nothing"], and shall I lack the thought
That such a thing bechanced would make me sad? (1.1.36–8)

Shakespeare will show that the answer to this question is, indeed, that even if we can think *about* this thought and be made chronically *sad* by it, in the natural attitude that characterizes Antonio and Solarino and their company we will miss completely the potentiality of a constructive thinking of the nothing. Although the nothing in itself is invariable (zero), how it is framed determines very different thoughts of the nothing. In *The Merchant of Venice* there are principally two framings of the nothing: one is the monetarized or sexualized thoughtlessness that pretends to fullness but conceals emptiness; the other is a beginning of the human in the thinking created by acceptance of our own potential nothingness and concomitant suspension of accustomed ideas of the human. This latter thinking of the nothing is at the furthest remove from either nihilism or dehumanization since it poises us for finally being able to affirm the human without prejudgments or prejudices. This active thinking of the nothing corresponds to Husserl's bracketing and "radical self-reflection" (both "acts of the second degree") that silently disclose the mind's consciousness of being. In Husserl's theory and Shakespeare's practice this is a consciousness which, instead of possessing the objects of the world, effects "acts of *reflection* directed to them" and grasps the actuality their own being.[17]

Shakespeare's bracketing and residuum certainly leave no doubt about the prevalence of the degraded antithesis to a morally purposive thinking of the nothing. He even seems to invent an entire character, Gratiano, whose main role in life is to trumpet the low form of "nothing." Early on, Bassanio seems to distance himself from that form of nothing by reflecting on Gratiano's mindless task: "Gratiano speaks an infinite deal of nothing, more than any man in all Venice" (1.1.114–15). Shakespeare's acknowledgment of the continuing triumph, in the real world, of the outward spectacle of the nothing is made clear in his placement of Gratiano's nothing as the closing words of the play. These consist of Gratiano's bawdy play with the nothing or "no other thing" of Nerissa's vaginal "ring"-space that his virility must make itself (or her self) "sore" with satisfying: "Well, while I live, I'll fear no other thing / So sore as keeping safe Nerissa's ring" (5.1.306–7). Gratiano's words would leave the natural mind with the impression that Belmont is a *mons veneris*, an ideal playground for sexual friction in the nothing.

Despite Bassanio's supposed insight into Gratiano's nothing, he is himself caught in its emptiness. While Shakespeare shields him from direct condemnation, Bassanio nevertheless stigmatizes himself with something materially akin to the nothing for which he has criticized Gratiano. To Portia, Bassanio laments his worldly nothingness in a way that demonstrates his incapacity to imagine a nothing that is not money-determined:

> dear Lady,
> Rating myself at nothing, you shall see
> How much I was a braggart. When I told you
> My state was nothing, I should have told you
> That I was worse than nothing. (3.2.255–9)

There is, one may believe, an intolerable pain in acknowledging, even subliminally, that one's life is centered in the nothingness of total material dependency. Denying to oneself that that is one's case can have violent consequences, such as the attempt to commit the Other – especially the Other who offers unceasing reproach – to nullification. Gratiano, who lives purely by the material nothing, openly demands Shylock's annihilation: "A halter gratis – nothing else, for God's sake" (4.1.375). Portia, Belmont's super-rich mistress, fulfills Gratiano's desire for that nullification, that particular "nothing":

> The Jew shall have all justice; soft, no haste;
> He shall have nothing but the penalty. . . .
> Thou [Shylock] shalt have nothing but the forfeiture,
> To be so taken at thy peril, Jew. (4.1.317–18; 439–40)

But the peril or hazard of forfeiting the human is ultimately not only or principally Shylock's.

In this play, coordinate with the language of being nothing is the language of being at "hazard" of reduction to the nothing. Shakespeare here employs the hazardous potential of fission within language's double meanings to create, most of all, his structures of reflection. One might say that this is a lesson that has been driven home by Deconstruction. We can certainly learn from this, but we need not therefore conclude our reflection with deconstructionist inconclusiveness. Shakespeare's deepening of the hazard of language overleaps deconstructionist premises and provides means for reflection that are even beyond Husserl.

Antonio and Shylock are not the only ones at hazard in this play. In *The Merchant of Venice* everyone, including Shakespeare, faces hazard of one kind or another. With regard to the *dramatis personae* this is repeatedly made obvious. Bassanio is the first to speak of the "hazard" of dubious fortunes that he is proposing to Antonio and which he knows only dimly will entail Antonio's own "hazard" (1.1.139–51). So, too, Portia's destiny, her very person, are locked into the whims of a silly game. Of course all the hangers-on to Bassanio's and Portia's fortunes are subject to the same or similar hazards, while Jessica throws herself upon the mercies of a Christian lover who, as has been pointed out, by Venetian law cannot confer Christian status upon her.[18]

Shakespeare's own hazard in producing the text and the performance of this play may be less apparent yet it is actually far more dramatic than any suffered by the characters within his play. And it is

Shakespeare's hazard that projects the deeper hazard that we all face in *The Merchant of Venice*. No matter how insistently we suspend disbelief in the fictionality of the *dramatis personae*, we know, on some level, that their hazard is fictive. Shakespeare's hazard is a function of the fictive yet it remains, for him and for his audience – on the level of the real world – alive and glaring after the play is done. Knowingly but beyond his full control, Shakespeare has here put his moral consciousness – his humanity – at overwhelming hazard. The magnificently human speech that he has given Shylock shows that Shakespeare vividly comprehends the abyssal danger (to one's capacity for imagining the human) incurred by imagining the erasure of the Jew. We do not have to be members of Shylock's "tribe" (3.1.61) to hear that in *The Merchant of Venice* the word Jew is consistently charged with obliterative violence. Ranged as a choric team against Shylock, the other characters of the play repeatedly spit out the Jew-word as a fierce execration, just as Antonio "did void" his "rheum" upon Shylock's Jewish "beard" (1.1.109). As even the briefest survey of the word's occurrences in the play shows, the Jew malediction here explodes from an atavistic, affricative *J*, as if prior to formed language, against an object that, most of the time, hardly rates an individual name.[19] Shakespeare's representation of the total muting of Shylock is itself shockingly muted. It vanishes suddenly and totally, without a later trace or vibration to tell us where it once occurred. Yet, as I have suggested from the outset, although Shakespeare cannot directly avoid participation in this pathology, he poises himself for leaping over it in a reflection on the play's own emptinesses and nullifications.

Here we encounter an intensely difficult form of reflection on the nothing and un-humanizing. I suggest that in *The Merchant of Venice* the chief hazard of bracketing the human is incurred in the intrusion, en bloc, of Christian Jew-hatred directly from Shakespeare's (and Marlowe's) own place and time into the space and time of the play. To describe how this intrusion is effected I apply to Carl Schmitt's concept of an "intrusion of the time," an *Einbruch* or "breaking-in" of an extra-fictional reality into the reality represented on stage. In *Hamlet* Schmitt finds an *Einbruch* in an intrusion of the time's (Shakespeare's time's) shared political-theological anxieties concerning monarchical election.[20] I propose that in the case of *The Merchant of Venice* there is also a deep anxiety concerning election that has political-theological roots. Yet here the intrusion – historical and "of the time" as it surely is – is more profoundly elemental and more exhaustively encompassing. Here election means laying claim to the moral grounds that define the human. The anxiety that characterizes this intrusion concerning election is closely connected to the historical and political-theological antagonisms between Christianity and Judaism. The intrusion of this historical, extra-fictional time acts as a wedge that opens an infinite space of nothingness which defies intellectual containment. As a result the intrusion or *Einbruch* in the experience of this play dislocates claims to the human rendered by both Christian Jew-hatred and Jewish Christian-hatred, although it is finally the Jew alone who is obliterated here. In the play's steady movement toward this outcome, the thinking of the nothingness of the human hardly seems to be thinking at all. In the play's counter-life of language, however, the space of the nothing that is thus broken open is paradoxically a prime building block.

The play's hazard of un-humanizing is completed (secondarily, as usual) by a further element of reflective, doubling language, namely, the homonymous language for two different structures of judgment that both hang on the number *three* and its variants, the *third*, *thrice*, and *treble*. This number or numbering, including doubling and trebling of three, is heard throughout the play, where the game of the three is outwardly played with reference to two specific themes: the game of hazard that risks the worldly nothing and the drive to convert the Jew.[21] In the worldly game of hazard the winning hazard number is by Bassanio, Portia, and their cohorts imagined to be three. This is indeed the lowest possible winning number, the "hazard" or sudden death winning score, in the rules of the game of hazard.[22] In *The Merchant of Venice* this game is apparently played out with full success in Bassanio's cast for the "third" casket (2.7.8) and by Antonio's winning gamble at sea with his "three" argosies (5.1.276). These threes will presumably seal the success of the winners as a group, who (taking their cue from Bassanio, as well as giving it to him) actively promote the three. If three and the third are the magic number for the winners in this play, it is not because of Trinitarian associations. This three is only the risking and recuperating of everything financial, legal, and sexual on the table. In addition, these gamesters stake their hazard number on another wager that almost seems spiritual: Shylock's conversion.

Michel Foucault and others have explained that, historically and philosophically considered, *epistrophe* is far more than a figure of rhetoric. *Epistrophe* is the crowning third stage of *conversion* in the triple pattern of the original (*mone*), emergence (*prodos*), and conversion (*epistrophe*) that was taken up from Plato's term for the object of education – "*epistrophe*," the "turning around of the soul"

(*Republic*, 7.521c) – and given new life in Neoplatonism and early Christianity.[23] In *The Merchant of Venice* the conversion of Shylock that is demanded by the Christians would be the legitimation and confirmation of their winning, worldly hazard, three. In Shylock's hypnotic echoing of the terms of "three" in the drawing up of the bond we may hear the doom of an unwitting prophecy of the moment when he, not Antonio, will be "bound" – bound, that is, to a total loss of will, to disintegration into what the Christians will call conversion: "Three thousand ducats, well. . . . for three months . . . for three months, well . . . Three thousand ducats for three months, and Antonio bound" (1.3.1–9). The fulfillment of the three in Shylock's conversion seems inevitable, just as Antonio will require. Yet in this play the whole package of the Christians' hazard of three begins to unravel in the grotesque claim that Shylock is converted. Instead of a totally unbelievable conversion to Christian belief, Shylock has now merely been reduced to a nothingness of the human. In experiencing this bracketing of the human, Shakespeare and the spectator, as onlookers, reflect on this accepted, natural un-humanizing in order to reveal a very different conversion, this one to a purified acceptance of being itself, including human being.

Looking back at this trajectory of the play's inner language we may come to see or hear another flight of thought, this one, too, converting thought to a non-exclusionary sense of being. This is a trajectory in a double language of arrows. To raise this possibility I return to Bassanio's initial deployment of the term hazard:

> In my school-days, when I had lost one shaft,
> I shot his fellow of the selfsame flight
> The selfsame way, with more advised watch,
> To find the other forth; and by adventuring both
> I oft found both. I urge this childhood proof
> Because what follows is pure innocence.
> I owe you much, and like a wilful youth
> That which I owe is lost; but if you please
> To shoot another arrow that self way
> Which you did shoot the first, I do not doubt,
> As I will watch the aim, or to find both
> Or bring your latter hazard back again
> And thankfully rest debtor for the first. (1.1.139–51)

At this point Bassanio cannot be blamed for not foreseeing that Antonio's own hazard will be lethally hazardous, yet his words astonishingly miss even the immediate danger in the hazard that he is proposing. What if his second arrow, his second venturing of Antonio's capital, should also be lost? What possible grounds does he have to be certain that in the worst case he will be able to "bring your latter hazard back again / And thankfully rest debtor for the first"? At this point he and Portia are virtual strangers. Bassanio's blindness even to obvious danger, or elementary realism, is an omen of intensely bad things to come. But there is perhaps a good deal more to what Bassanio fails to see or hear here.

It has been noticed by many before that Bassanio's and Antonio's relationship has an obvious parallel in David's and Jonathan's relationship described in the Book of Samuel. Not only does the unusual ardor of Bassanio's and Antonio's love for each other recall the extraordinary intensity of the love of Jonathan and David, but a death-threat hovers over both pairs (in David's case it comes from Saul). S. J. Schönfeld and Zvi Jagendorf have drawn attention to the fact that the two pairs of friends make vivid use of the motif of shooting arrows to chart their destinies.[24] Given the unfolding of an alternative, inner language in *The Merchant of Venice*, this possible biblical allusion to the arrows episode in Samuel, counterpointed against the fortune-hunting and shallowness of Bassanio's appeal to Antonio, may be seen as possessing a particularly appropriate inner or partly hidden depth. In addition, lest we think that the Book of Samuel and David's hiding from danger is alien to the mindset of this play, we should recall that they are in fact directly alluded to in Morocco's figure of the bravery that would "Pluck the young sucking cubs from the she-bear" (2.1.29). This is an allusion (calculated, it would seem, to impress the Christians with Morocco's biblical knowledge) to 2 Samuel 17.8–9 where Hushai tells Absalom,

> You know your father and his men; they are fighters, and as fierce as a wild bear robbed of her cubs. Besides, your father is an experienced fighter; he will not spend the night with the troops. Even now, he is hidden in a cave or some other place.

Here, from the Authorized Version, are verses 36 and 37 of 1 Samuel 20, recording the moment when the signals agreed upon by Jonathan and David are set in motion to try to ward off the extreme danger to David, who must go into hiding:

> And [Jonathan] said unto his lad, Run, find out now the arrows which I shoot. *And* as the lad ran, he shot an arrow beyond him. [37] And

when the lad was come to the place of the arrow which Jonathan had shot, Jonathan cried out after the lad, and said, *Is* not the arrow beyond thee?

Contrasted, that is, with Bassanio's projection of a beyond that is the hoped-for success at fortune-hunting, the beyond of Jonathan and David is a leap into an unknown future that is fortified only by personal courage and by faith in God's ultimate blessing for all of humanity. (David will be the progenitor of the Messianic line.) In the playing out of Bassanio's game of arrows, after the two arrows will come, indeed, the winning "third" of his casket choice, the arrow of love, almost, that Portia anticipates from Bassanio, "quick Cupid's post" (2.9.99). In Bassanio's imagination of "adventuring" his two arrows, the fulfillment of the threefold epistrophic pattern will thus come from what Portia calls his "hazard" at Belmont (3.2.2). Portia has her own merely material formula of trebling and conversion. To Bassanio she says, "for you / I would be trebled twenty times myself; . . . what is mine, to you and yours / Is now converted" (3.2.152–67). By contrast, the arrow pact of Jonathan and David requires translation to an unrepresentable sphere. Here the completing third is imagined (as in the triple-braided cord of Ecclesiastes 4:12) to be God the onlooker and guarantor:

> [41] And when the lad was gone, David arose and . . . fell on his face and bowed three times: and they kissed one another, and wept one with another. . . . [42] And Jonathan said to David, Go in peace, forasmuch as we have sworn both of us in the name of the Lord, saying The Lord be between me and thee.

The presence, the necessary involvement, of the onlooker is the determinative difference between the arrow pacts of Jonathan–David and Bassanio–Antonio. If one sees and hears the parallelisms of these exceptionally intense friendships (each unique, whether in the Bible or in the world of Venice) and the uses they both just happen to make of an arrow pact, the effect itself is of a silent onlooking, that is, by the metaphysically charged biblical text and episode. The presence of unseen onlookers in this play may thus be thought to be significantly highlighted by means of this buried allusion, if we hear it.

Be that as it may, it is time to return to the principal emergence of the onlooker, both in Husserl and in Shakespeare. To recapitulate for Husserl: in his meditative method the bracketing of the spatio-temporal world, reducing it to nothingness most especially in the act of un-humanizing, makes possible the emergence, in the residuum, of an onlooker consciousness. This is the disclosure of a purified consciousness of being that includes a renewed commitment to the human. This onlooker consciousness is the consummation of radical self-reflection, the bringing of a hidden part of the self to full converted awareness, the breaking of the barrier of anonymity so that the onlooker now achieves self-conscious actuality. As Husserl and Fink say, however, all of this must somehow take place in a mutual conditioning of simultaneous "moments." Despite the great impetus of Husserl's thought, however, it is not obvious where or how his discursive language can produce such a simultaneity. Shakespeare's art in *The Merchant of Venice* is a working through of just such a simultaneity of the acts of self-reflection that disclose the actuality of the onlooker – Shakespeare and/or the spectator. This kind of onlooker is physically detached from, yet mentally deeply involved with, the worldly things of the play. As Husserl puts it: "Instead of living *in* them, instead of effecting *them*, we effect acts of *reflection* directed to them; and we seize upon them themselves as the *absolute* being they are. We are now living completely in such acts of the second degree."[25] In his play Shakespeare or the spectator, having experienced the un-humanization of a prejudgmental humanness, lays bare the onlooker within, passes into that onlooker. It may be that this strategy for creating meaning is even signaled by the famous ambiguity of the title of the play. Antonio and Shylock, who seem to vie for that title, are not the only, or the chief, merchants in this play. In the play's inner drama, in the transaction that converts one kind of nothing to another, the presiding merchants are finally the onlookers. They are the ones who convert the play's currency from apparent reality to real actuality. These onlookers stand at a dire threshold: on one side the nothing of merely obliterating the human; on the other, an un-humanizing of the human that can lead to a conversion that is otherwise unimaginable – the disclosure of a form of human judgment that is all inconclusive.

Notes

1. For stimulating discussion of *The Merchant of Venice* I am grateful to Michael Kaufman and Henry Weinfield. One of the starting points for this chapter was Julia Reinhard Lupton's essay, "Exegesis, Mimesis,

and the Future of Humanism in *The Merchant of Venice,*" *Religion and Literature* 32 (2000): 123–39, which applies the thinking of Emmanuel Levinas to difficult aspects of the play (135–6).

2. Citations from the play are to *The Merchant of Venice,* ed. M. M. Mahood (Cambridge: Cambridge University Press, 2003), which with few exceptions follows the First Quarto.

3. Among many others who discuss this exchange, see Janet Adelman, *Blood Relations: Christian and Jew in The Merchant of Venice* (Chicago: University of Chicago Press, 2008).

4. A. D. Nuttall, *A New Mimesis: Shakespeare and the Representation of Reality* (New Haven: Yale University Press, 2007 [1983]), 130–1. Nuttall quotes from A. D. Moody, *Shakespeare: The Merchant of Venice* (London: Edward Arnold, 1964), 32. Nuttall's comments on the play in *Shakespeare the Thinker* (New Haven: Yale University Press, 2007), especially 255–62, enrich and somewhat qualify his earlier reading, though he still largely accepts the mercifulness of the Christians' forgiveness of Shylock and he still cannot see the possibility of the play's non-subversive counter-thesis.

5. Stanley Cavell, "Saying in *The Merchant of Venice,*" in *Shakespeare and the Law: A Conversation among the Disciplines,* ed. Bradin Cormack, Martha C. Nussbaum, and Richard Strier (Chicago: University of Chicago Press, 2013), 223, 229.

6. Fred J. Hanna, "Husserl on the Teachings of the Buddha," *The Humanist Psychologist* 23 (1995): 365–72, includes an English translation of Husserl's brief but enthusiastic late essay "On the Teachings of Gotama Buddha" (367–8). Hanna quotes the assertion of Husserl's close associate Eugen Fink that "the various phases of Buddhistic self-discipline were essentially phases of phenomenological reduction" (366). Beginning especially with Ramakant Sinari, "The Method of Phenomenological Reduction and Yoga," *Philosophy East and West* 15 (1965): 217–28, there have been detailed explorations of the parallels between Husserl's phenomenological reduction and the Yoga Sutras. I regard these parallels as attestations to the wide accessibility of such meditational practices and results.

7. Toward the end of his life (as with his late exposure to the Yoga Sutras) Husserl became intensely interested in Kierkegaard's writings, as Lev Shestov recounts, "In Memory of a Great Philosopher: Edmund Husserl," trans. George L. Kline, www.angelfire.com/nb/shestov/sar/husserl1.html, section 1. For Kierkegaard's concept of the anxiety of the nothing, see *The Concept of Anxiety: A Simple Psychologically Orienting Deliberation on the Dogmatic Issue of Hereditary Sin,* trans. and ed. Reidar Thomte and Albert B. Anderson (Princeton: Princeton University Press, 1980), 65, 96; cf. 41–6, 81–91.

8. The relation of Husserlian bracketing to modern existentialism, especially to the thought of Maurice Merleau-Ponty and Jean-Paul

Sartre, is of course also of salient interest for tracing this divergence of grounding intuitions. On the development of existential philosophies in relation to Husserl, see Herbert Spiegelberg, "Husserl's Phenomenology and Existentialism," *Journal of Philosophy* 57 (1960): 62–74. Elements and potentialities of Husserl's phenomenology are currently enjoying new life in phenomenologically oriented approaches to literary criticism. In their Introduction to a special issue of *Criticism* 54.3 (2012): 353–64, devoted to "Shakespeare and Phenomenology," Kevin Curran and James Kearney indicate how a large variety of such approaches can be used to illuminate Shakespeare's plays.

9. The relevant discussion of Kant occurs in the *Critique of Pure Reason*, trans. Norman Kemp Smith (London: Macmillan, 1993), A 224–6, B 271–4; of Husserl, in *Ideas: General Introduction to Pure Phenomenology*, trans. W. R. Boyce Gibson (New York: Collier, 1972), 107. Husserl's concept of the necessary directedness of consciousness is at least analogous to Kant's placement of the a priori categories of "relation" (i.e. the categories of "relation" in the Analogies of Experience: "permanence," "succession," and "community of reciprocity"). In this instance I have cited Gibson's translation of *Ideas* rather than Kersten's (cited below) because the latter departs from Husserl's term "actuality" (*Aktualität*), which (as has been frequently noted) recalls Kant's discussion of actuality (*Wirklichkeit*).

10. Edmund Husserl, *Ideas Pertaining to a Pure Phenomenology and to a Phenomenological Philosophy: First Book: General Introduction to a Pure Phenomenology*, trans. F. Kersten (Dordrecht: Kluwer, 1998), # 50, 114. Here and in citations from Eugen Fink's *Sixth Cartesian Meditation: The Idea of a Transcendental Theory of Method*, trans. Ronald Bruzina (Bloomington: Indiana University Press, 1988), below, angle brackets indicate Husserl's handwritten insertions.

11. Husserl, *Ideas Pertaining to a Pure Phenomenology*, 113.

12. Fink, *Sixth Cartesian Meditation*, 41. On pages 32–3, the idea of "radical self-reflection" is elaborated together with Husserl's on-the-page notations.

13. Ibid., 39–40.

14. Husserl, *Ideas Pertaining to a Pure Phenomenology*, # 50, 113.

15. Fink, *Sixth Cartesian Meditation*, 120.

16. Edmund Husserl, *Crisis of European Science and Transcendental Philosophy*, trans. David Carr (Evanston: Northwestern University Press, 1970), 137.

17. In this context we might mention that another aspect of Shakespeare's dramaturgy of un-humanizing (*Entmenschung*) and alienation is in the actor's act of acting itself, that is, in the actor's implicit emptying of his own humanness in the interests of enabling the emergence of a more universal kind of humanness. This can be seen programmatically in the

chiastic give and take (and take and give) of theatricalism in *Hamlet*, but that is a story for another occasion.

18. See Adelman, *Blood Relations*, 163 n. 10.

19. For example, those at 2.8.4, 3.1.17–18, 3.2.296, 3.2.315–16, 4.1.112, 4.1.283–8, 4.1.343–4.

20. Carl Schmitt, *Hamlet or Hecuba: The Intrusion of the Time into the Play*, trans. David Pan and Jennifer R. Rust, introd. Jennifer R. Rust and Julia Reinhard Lupton (Candor, NY: Telos Press, 2009).

21. This kind of numbers game is certainly not unique to *The Merchant of Venice*. Shakespeare extensively plays such games with the number three, for example in *Julius Caesar* where the number is a deeply ominous portent. Shakespeare's interest in the game of hazard – the most popular dicing game in Europe throughout the late middle ages and the Renaissance – was already evidenced in *Richard III* where the number three is suggestively linked to a fateful cast of the dice, indeed, in just such a sudden-death roll of the number three as medieval and Renaissance rules of the game of hazard describe. While repeating an epistrophic triplication – "A horse! A horse! My kingdom for a horse!" – Richard declares, "I have set my life upon a cast, / And I will stand the hazard of the die" (5.7.7–13). Even a partial list of the occurrences of three and its variants (including explicit multiples) in *The Merchant of Venice* would include those at the following lines: 1.3.1, 2, 3, 8 (twice), 16, 21, 48, 66 (twice), 95, 96, 114, 152 ("thrice three times"); 2.7.8, 48; 3.1.61; 3.2.146, 153, 297, 298, 299; 4.1.42, 84, 85, 223, 230, 407; 5.1.276.

22. For the rules of hazard, which remained more or less stable well into the nineteenth century, see *Medieval Futures: Attitudes to the Future in the Middle Ages*, ed. John Anthony Burrow and Ian P. Wei (Woodbridge: Boydell Press, 2000), 170–1.

23. For the importance of epistrophe in Foucault's thinking, see Edward F. McGushin, *Foucault's Askesis: An Introduction to the Philosophical Life* (Evanston: Northwestern University Press, 2007), 110–14. Foucault was especially influenced here by Paul Aubin, *Le problème de la 'conversion'* (Paris: Beauchesne, 1963), and Pierre Hadot, *Exercises spirituels et philosophie antique*, 2nd ed. (Paris: Albin, 2000). Epistrophe was already treated extensively by Arthur Darby Nock, *Conversion: The Old and the New in Religion from Alexander the Great to Augustine of Hippo* (Baltimore: Johns Hopkins University Press, 1998 [1933]).

24. S. J. Schönfeld, "A Hebrew Source for *The Merchant of Venice*," *Shakespeare Survey* 32 (1980): 126, and Zvi Jagendorf, "Innocent Arrows and Sexy Sticks: The Rival Economies of Male Friendship and Heterosexual Love in *The Merchant of Venice*," in *Strands Afar Remote: Israeli Perspectives on Shakespeare*, ed. Avraham Oz (London: Associated University Presses, 1998), 27–8. It is worth adding that the

arrows "contract between *Jonathan* and *David*" was familiar enough for Donne to preach about it in 1618 at Lincoln's Inn: see *The Sermons of John Donne*, ed. George R. Potter and Evelyn M. Simpson (Berkeley and Los Angeles: University of California Press, 1955), 2:60.

25. Husserl, *Ideas Pertaining to a Pure Phenomenology*, 114.

Chapter 10

The Judgment of the Critics that Makes us Tremble: "Distributing Complicities" in Recent Criticism of *King Lear*

Richard Strier

Something odd has happened in recent criticism of *King Lear*. Two of the strongest and most influential critics of our time, Stanley Cavell and Harry Berger Jr., have devoted a great deal of their effort in relation to this play to showing that there is virtually no difference, when the play is looked at closely, between the characters normally characterized as "good" (Berger almost always uses scare quotes for this word) or (if I may coin an intuitively obvious ethical category) mixed, and those who are wicked (or "wicked").[1] This critical practice has produced, as I will try to show, some astonishingly bizarre claims along with many less spectacular dubious or false ones. So, to my mind, the interesting question – aside from the analysis of the mechanisms that produce these readings (which will constitute the bulk of this chapter) – is why these readings, if they are as flawed as I suggest, have had the power and influence that they have had. Subsequent critics often take it that "Cavell has established" this or that, or "Berger has established" this or that.[2] I wish I could give a good account of the success of these readings and of these ways of reading. But I will make a preliminary attempt.

Part of the success, I would say, derives from the special standing of Cavell in the world of literary, and especially Shakespeare, criticism. He brings with him the authority that comes from his constantly enacted membership in a more intellectually elite group within the academy than English professors: he is a philosopher. But other philosophers have written on Shakespeare without having made a dent or even a ripple on our field.[3] The reason why Cavell has been so singularly influential may have to do with the fact that he does his philosophical work with literary texts more or less within the protocols of our field, so he speaks as an insider and an outsider simultaneously – a very powerful position. His conception of philosophy does not generally involve any technical work (though he has done this in some of his "straight" philosophical writing),[4] but revolves around terms that are resonant in the worlds of ethics, psychology, and religion: recognition and acknowledgment.[5] His conception of skepticism does not involve us in the quest for certainty or truth but rather in the motives that he sees as underlying these quests, so we are put in the (for us) more comfortable world of existentialized psychology rather than in the (for us) foreign world of sustained epistemological inquiry.[6] So he speaks to us in a language that is almost our language in a voice that is not exactly our normal voice. He speaks, to use the biblical phrase, as one with authority (which is what surprised the rabbis about Jesus).[7]

Berger too – but in his case because of his standing as an established and prolific critic – speaks as one with authority.[8] Both of them make pronouncements that are only thinly backed up by textual analysis or, often, guide the analysis that supposedly supports them. And Berger is a fine writer (Cavell is a very powerful writer, but not a distinguished prose stylist in any normal sense). Both of them are very intelligent, obviously so – which has to be part of their power. But certainly not all of it. I have tried to suggest where some of Cavell's special power for our field comes from. Berger's derives not only from his prolific body of critical work but also partly from consciously appropriating some of the Cavellian *mana* and partly, I think, from our attraction to something like "tough-mindedness." We are suspicious of categories like goodness and more comfortable with low (self-interested) than high (altruistic) motives. So the motives of the "good" (or not obviously wicked) are to be interrogated, where the motives of the wicked are taken to be obvious.[9] Some generalized more or less Freudian psychology easily comes into play here. And what also enters the picture – more so for Berger than for Cavell – is the pleasure of moralizing and of virtual omniscience, of knowing better than the characters what drives them, what their "true" motives are. This is a highly satisfying and implicitly self-congratulatory position, as "tough-mindedness" is in general. So its appeal is reasonably clear.

But let me now turn to specifics. Cavell's essay on *Lear* begins – to my mind promisingly – with a meditation on the odd split in the history of literary, especially Shakespearean, scholarship between "character criticism" and, though he does not call it this, "close reading."[10] He (again to my mind rightly) sees this split as odd and means to oppose it. He seems to oppose in particular a kind of criticism that purports to trace, as he somewhat mockingly puts it, "something called the symbolic structure or the pattern of something or other in the piece" (40). Instead he proposes a kind of reading that attends to the specificity – a repeated word here – of the particular words that particular characters say, a way of reading that sees words as meaning deeply "not because they mean many things [taken to be the New Critical approach] but because they mean one thing completely." This is analogized to the task of "ordinary language philosophy," which, according to Cavell, consists in the task of "placing those words with which philosophers have always begun in alignment with human beings in particular circumstances who can be imagined to be having those experiences and saying and meaning those words" (42). So it looks as if the task will be to try to come to terms with the exact things that characters mean in saying what they say. The "depth" of the meaning will not lie "under" but within the "surface" of them.[11] It looks as if the literal will not have to be transcended in favor of some sort of hidden "symbolic structure."

The main body of the essay then turns, quite logically, to an essay by Paul Alpers that argues for and tries to practice, it would seem, exactly the sort of reading that Cavell seems to advocate.[12] Alpers's essay is a prolonged and eloquent critique of the readings of "symbolic structures" in *Lear* that were put forth by many critics (Robert Heilman perhaps being the most notable). In particular, Alpers rejects the idea of a "sight vs. blindness" pattern in the play, where sight is equated with some sort of "insight" and blindness with some sort of materiality or obtuseness. He wants the blinding of Gloucester to be taken literally – as an act of supreme human cruelty (140) – and not as symbolic of something else. One would think that Cavell would applaud this, and go on to try to be even more consistently literal, and non-moralizing, than Alpers.[13] But Cavell positions his essay not as an extension but as a corrective of Alpers. And that is where the trouble begins.[14]

Cavell finds Alpers's reading of the blinding of Gloucester "over-casual" (46). The action must have some "meaning" – as if, somehow, the literal reading lacked this – and must (here we are getting to the heart of the matter) have some relation "to the necessities of Gloucester's character" (47), and it must have (of all things) "symbolic value" (47). Cavell seems to be falling here into some (unacknowledged) conception of tragedy – presumably versus victimization – and of aesthetic value (presumably relying on perceived patterns). But the explicit motivation for this odd and critically decisive move has to do with Cavell's commitment to making acknowledgment the key concept for understanding the play – which brings the play deeply in line with Cavell's own position with regard to philosophical skepticism, to which he sees acknowledgment as the antidote, if not the answer.[15] Failures (or supposed failures) of acknowledgment are equated with blindness – a refusal to see – and with blinding – a refusal to be seen – and these are taken to be conceptually interconnected, so that blindness requires blinding.[16] *Et voila*! – we have another "sight pattern."[17] And with it come the critical bizarreries and, more disturbingly, the moral obtuseness of the original "sight pattern" in Heilman and company. If there is nothing in Cavell's essay quite like Heilman's delight at the blinding of Gloucester ("[t]he vile jelly, the material seeing, had but caught reflections from the surfaces of life . . . His physical and material loss is his spiritual gain"),[18] Cavell's version of the sight pattern generates almost equally bizarre results.

The first casualty is the reality of the blinding of Gloucester; the second the horror specifically directed at the perpetrators thereof. Very shortly into Cavell's essay we are told that Lear, Goneril, and, most importantly, Gloucester himself have said things that "implicate all of them spiritually in Cornwall's deed" (47). I have to confess that I do not understand what this "spiritual" implication is supposed to mean, and I do not understand how Cavell uses that word.[19] Lear is somehow implicated in Cornwall's "deed" – referred to in this general way (Cornwall grinds the heel of his boot into the bound Gloucester's eyes one by one) – because Lear has mentioned the idea of eyes being plucked out. But Lear did so in an expression of his shame at letting Goneril's actions toward him – dare I say cruelty? – make him weep (Q 1.4.289–91; F 1.4.271–3).[20] It has nothing to do with actual cruelty to anyone, even to himself. "Gloucester himself" is "spiritually" implicated in his own blinding because he is the one who has most recently mentioned blinding in characterizing what he imagines Regan's cruelty might do to Lear (3.7.53–4). He is speaking hyperbolically of almost unimaginable cruelty (his next lines imagine Regan "rash[ing] boarish fangs" into Lear's flesh). The context is one of literally preventing cruelty; Gloucester is explaining why he has sent Lear away, to Dover, where he knows Lear will have "Both welcome and protection" (Q 3.6.85; F 3.6.48). The mere mention of the word or concept of blindness seems, for Cavell, enough to "implicate" anyone using it in an actual act of purposely blinding someone.

And apparently (I have not forgotten) Goneril is also "spiritually implicated" in the blinding of Gloucester. However, she is not "spiritually implicated" in it. She is literally implicated in it. When Cornwall, Regan, and Goneril are contemplating how to treat "the traitor Gloucester" (F 3.7.3),[21] Regan's idea is to "Hang him instantly." Goneril is the one who suggests "Pluck out his eyes" (3.7.4–5). Committed as I am to the literal, I do not want to suggest that Goneril's relation to the blinding of Gloucester is the same as that of Cornwall and Regan. After all, she is on her way out when she makes this (lovely) suggestion, and she leaves before Gloucester is brought in. But it seems possible that once Cornwall has made it clear that he feels that he cannot hang Gloucester (3.7.23–4), he recalls Goneril's alternate suggestion. Whether or not one accepts this, her relation to "Cornwall's deed" seems rather different than that of Lear or of Gloucester himself.

But Cavell thinks that in stressing the human cruelty of Cornwall's deed, Alpers does not "follow the words" (46). Putting aside the fact that cruelty is explicitly mentioned in the scene (by Gloucester), let me examine what Cavell means here. He is right that each time that Cornwall stamps on one of Gloucester's eyes, something is said about punishment catching up to Cornwall. In each case, Cornwall states that he is going to prevent Gloucester from ever seeing such (3.7.64, 80). Cavell is right that Alpers does not mention this. But is what Cornwall is doing really a matter of guarding the self against recognition by another? Is it "to prevent him [Gloucester] from seeing *him* [Cornwall]" (47)? Cornwall has already said that he is going to take "revenges" on Gloucester, and that they will be especially horrible – "not fit for your beholding," he says to Edmund. So there is no doubt that something awful but non-mortal is going to be done to Gloucester. What seems to lead Cornwall to set his foot into Gloucester's eyes is not the idea that *he* (Cornwall) will be seen but the idea that Gloucester will witness or possibly be the agent of some sort of providential punishment of Cornwall.[22] The seeing that is being foreclosed is in the imagined future, not the present. Cornwall – contra Cavell – does not seem to have any shame in the present. He thinks, quite accurately and with good evidence, that he is properly, and with some restraint, punishing a traitor, someone who is in collusion with an invading army, "an intelligent party to the advantages of France" (3.5.9–10). I am afraid that I think that it is Stanley Cavell who does not "follow the words" – or, of course, the plot. Why everyone is focused on Dover is hardly a mystery. Cavell is intent, instead, on the thematic pattern – failures or refusals of acknowledgment – that he sees at work in the "sight pattern."

But I have not yet addressed the claim that the blinding is not only related to "Cornwall's needs," but also, and primarily, to "necessities of Gloucester's character." This is where Cavell joins the moralizers.

Almost every critic of the play thinks Edgar goes too far in making a direct connection between Gloucester's begetting of Edmund out of wedlock and Gloucester's loss of his eyes (Q 5.3.166–7; F 5.3.164–5: "The dark and vicious place where thee he got / Cost him his eyes"), but almost every critic moralizes about Gloucester's supposed bad treatment of Edmund. Cavell, in his own way, comes close to Edgar's view. Gloucester's problem is that he fails to acknowledge Edmund. This is odd, since one of the first things that Gloucester says is that he has repeatedly done so: "I have so often blushed to acknowledge him" (1.1.9). But according to Cavell, he has not done so in the proper way. The (past) blushing is a problem. It connotes shame, which means the desire to hide (not the act but, for Cavell, the self), which means the refusal to recognize an other and a refusal to let oneself be recognized by an other (49). Cavell does acknowledge that Gloucester uses the word – but (I repeat) not in the proper interpersonal way. Of Gloucester's acknowledgment of Edmund, Cavell writes, "He [Gloucester] does not acknowledge *him* [again the pronoun italicized], as a son or a person" (48). But what does this mean? Gloucester does acknowledge Edmund as a son (which he did not have to do), and he has paid for Edmund's education ("his breeding . . . has been at my charge" [8]), which he also did not have to do. Much heavy weather has been made – by Cavell (49) and many others – of the fact that Edmund "has been out nine years, and away he shall again" (1.1.31), but in the Tudor-Stuart period aristocratic children were often sent "out" for a considerable period of time for "breeding."[23]

Cavell says that Gloucester does not acknowledge Edmund's "feelings of illegitimacy and being cast out" (48). But Gloucester states that his legitimate son is "no dearer in his account" than Edmund is – Berger takes this to mean that he likes them both equally little (57) but he knows that that is not the intended (or contextual) meaning. Edmund never expresses any resentment at being "cast out," and – in a line that critics rarely quote – states that he is quite certain that he is indeed as dear to his father as Edgar is. "Our father's love," Edmund asserts quite confidently, "is to the bastard Edmund / As to the legitimate" (1.2.17–18). Edmund is apparently perfectly well acknowledged as a son and as a person. What he is not acknowledged as is as a primary heir, which is a matter of law, not of interpersonal feelings, and is treated by Edmund as such. He resents his legal, not his personal status. The little introductory scene between Gloucester, Kent, and Edmund ends with Gloucester making a gesture of trying to integrate Edmund into the courtly world, and with both Kent and Edmund recognizing and enacting this.[24]

But Cavell is unrelenting. Like almost all other critics, he deplores Gloucester's ribald and casual description of Edmund's begetting. I will not go to the wall for this, but I think it possible to see even these remarks as an attempt on Gloucester's part at acknowledgment, at doing something like acknowledging Edmund's mother: she (unlike him) did not commit adultery – "ere she had a husband"; she was beautiful ("yet was his mother fair"); and the sex seems to have been enjoyable, perhaps all the way around ("there was good sport at his making"). In any case, Cavell sees Gloucester as full of shame here, and once he can establish that, the whole failure to recognize and be recognized dialectic can come into play. Gloucester is not willing to "see'" Edmund, and therefore to be seen by him. This produces a truly astonishing sentence. Like Heilman, Cavell sees a logic in the blinding of Gloucester. Cavell's tone is not as triumphant as Heilman's ("His physical loss is his spiritual gain"), but the moralism is equally strong. And the claim is even more startling (we are accustomed, after all, to the pat kind of paradoxes Heilman postulates). Cavell states, unequivocally: "Gloucester suffers the same punishment he inflicts" (49). This is quite insane. Whatever wrong Gloucester (supposedly) did Edmund, it surely is not "the same" as having one's eyes gouged out. And Cavell's explanation of this claim smacks of bad faith. Cavell says: "In his respectability, he [Gloucester] avoided eyes; when respectability falls away and the disreputable come into power, his eyes are avoided." One hardly knows what to say about such a sentence. "Respectability" is a very odd axis on which to place the events in question, and insofar as one wants to speak in that way, "respectability fall[ing] away" has nothing to do with Gloucester's recent behavior, which has been heroic. There is something really odd in speaking of the outright villains of the play – all of whom, including Edmund in prospect, are highly "reputable" – as "the disreputable." But most of all, the weirdness and moral insanity come in speaking of Gloucester's eyes being "avoided." This is either a bad pun or an intolerable euphemism (or both). His eyes are not "avoided." They are smashed by the heel of a boot.

According to Cavell, practically everyone in the play blinds Gloucester. He sees Lear's mad harping on Gloucester's blindness in the scene between the two old men at Dover as Lear "picking at Gloucester's eyes" (51). He sees it as "active cruelty . . . deliberate cruelty" (50–1). Cavell will not see it as Lear trying, in a mad way, to come to terms with what has happened to Gloucester (which he first discovers here). When Lear says to Gloucester "If thou wilt weep my fortunes, take my eyes" (Q 4.6.164; F 4.6.169), he is not offering Gloucester "a crazy consolation." He is offering him sympathy. To take a gesture, a metaphor, as if it were literal is not to read it but to misread it; it is to read the words but miss the point. Lear is sorrowing for Gloucester. One might well say that he is acknowledging Gloucester's situation, saying (meaning) that Gloucester's situation is such that he (Gloucester) can save his lamenting for himself, since his situation is at least as bad as Lear's own. It is a moment of lucidity, not of madness; the next line is "I know thee well enough; thy name is Gloucester." Cavell sees Lear as asserting the uniqueness of his own suffering, saying "Your eyes wouldn't have done you any good anyway in this case; you would need to see what I have seen to weep my fortunes" (51–2). But Lear is not, at this moment, focused on himself. He is actually focusing on another, on Gloucester. But for Cavell, Lear here joins the crowd of Gloucester's tormenters. We are back to being "spiritually implicated," and the word, in this same odd usage, recurs here. Lear's supposed "picking" at Gloucester's eyes "spiritually relates Lear to Cornwall's and Regan's act in first blinding Gloucester" (52). Again, to use a word that was supposed to indicate Cavell's own commitment, the specificity of Cornwall's and Regan's "act" – again spoken of in the most general way – is lost. They are not the ones who "first" blind Gloucester; they are the ones who *actually* do so.

But the character who is most powerfully tarred by the brush of Cavell's version of the sight pattern is Edgar. Condemning Edgar for not revealing his existence as "Tom" to Gloucester until Edgar is armed and about to duel Edmund is something of a cottage industry in Shakespeare studies.[25] Cavell contributes mightily to it (as does Berger, as we shall see). He sees Edgar as, like almost everyone else in the play, "avoiding recognition," which Cavell immediately – and, again, I would say, bizarrely – equates with "mutilating cruelty" (54). The moment in question is indeed a puzzling one, and something like "avoiding recognition" does seem to be involved. But again Cavell's reading of the passage is oddly tone-deaf and, as in "If you would weep my fortunes, take my eyes" and the analysis of what Cornwall does not wish Gloucester to see, oddly (for someone so powerfully affected by J. L. Austin) unconcerned with identifying the actual speech act being performed.[26] The passage in question is the moment when Gloucester, possibly within the hearing of Edgar (though this is not at all certain),[27] exclaims:

> Ah dear son Edgar,
> The food of thy abused father's wrath,
> Might I but live to see thee in my touch,
> I'd say I had eyes again. (Q 4.1.19–22)

Cavell (like most critics) is certain that Edgar hears this, so that Edgar here "deprives Gloucester of his eyes again" – which "links him, as Lear was and will be linked, to Cornwall and the sphere of open evil"; it shows Edgar's "capacity for cruelty," and, Cavell insists, "the *same* cruelty as that of the evil characters" (55; emphasis Cavell's). But whatever it is that Edgar is doing or not doing here – even assuming that he does hear the relevant words – it is certainly not "the *same* cruelty" as that inflicted by Cornwall on Gloucester ("deprives" is another of those words, like "avoids," which obscures obvious difference, and functions, with regard to Cornwall, as another unbearable euphemism).

But there is more to be said. Again I am not convinced that Cavell is following the words. He treats the "might I" lines as if Gloucester were saying that being able to embrace Edgar would cure his blindness. But Gloucester is not saying this. He is saying that if he could embrace Edgar, he would *say* that he had eyes again. Gloucester is imagining a counterfactual hyperbolic exclamation that he would make in the imagined situation. By not revealing himself, Edgar is depriving Gloucester of the experience of "seeing" Edgar "in [his] touch" and of the chance to make the imagined joyously hyperbolical rhetorical assertion. If we are going to "follow the words," we must take the whole form of the utterance, including the "I'd say," into account. But this is still to avoid the matter of avoidance. Whether or not Edgar hears these exact words, the fact is that he does not reveal himself to his father in this scene, and this is what he is constantly critically rebuked for (and, in the Folio, rebukes himself for – "Never, O fault" is a Folio-only moment; the quarto has "O father" [F 5.3.184; Q 5.3.186]). But the play itself makes it clear that it is not easy for a father who has radically abused a child to deal with what he has done. Gloucester knows that he has (wrongly) disinherited and proscribed Edgar, but he does not know that Edgar was Tom, who "made [him] think a man a worm," though he does have some intuition of a connection to Edgar (4.1.32–3). Lear we are told later (in the Quarto) is avoiding Cordelia out of, as Kent rather wittily puts it, "A sovereign shame" (Q 4.3.42). Cavell seems to think that shame is itself shameful (involving horrid avoidance). But it does not seem "cruel" to want to spare one's parent that, if possible. Edgar's revelation of his identity as Poor Tom to his father at a moment when Edgar is armed (Q 5.3.187; F 5.3.185) can be seen as protective of his father and not – as Cavell takes it – of himself (and it also might be his last chance to reveal himself, since he does not know, as he says, whether he is going to prevail in the single combat with Edmund).

Space does not permit me to deal with Cavell's reading of the "love-test" in the first scene, since I want to move on to Harry Berger's critiques of Edgar and company, but suffice it to say that it does not seem at all obvious to me that Lear is avoiding love in this stretch of text rather than clumsily seeking it, or that what he actually wants is mere flattery and that is why Cordelia responds as she does (Cavell creates a witty paradox in saying that in speaking the truth to Lear Cordelia would not be giving him what he wants but would be giving "*dissembled flattery*" [65; italicized in the original]). This seems to me too clever by half, as the British would say, and wonderfully dismissive of less tricky, more "ordinary" accounts of Cordelia's behavior and Lear's desires.[28]

One of the striking features of both Cavell's and Berger's criticism is that they are both aware of objections to their procedures. In relation to his reading of the opening of *Lear*, Cavell notes that "It may be felt that I have forced this scene too far in order to fit it to my reading" (66), and elsewhere he disdains "moralizing" (78) as he initially did "something called the symbolic structure."[29] Berger is aware that his readings are open to the objection (attributed to a real or fictional C. L. Barber) that they are cynical and lack the "minimal level of sympathy for and generosity toward the fictional objects of his criticism" (the characters in the plays) that is necessary for anything like an adequate response to "the human claims the characters in the play make" on the critic (50).[30] Berger's answer to this is that in his demonstrations of the complicity of the not obviously wicked with the obviously wicked ("spiritual implication" Cavell would say), he (Berger, the "ironic critic") is only assigning "responsibility," not guilt (53); he insists that he is not using "the language of praise or blame" in arguing for such complicity (68). But this – like his even more outrageous claim that his readings of the motives of characters "have nothing to do with the unconscious" (53) – is disingenuous. Complicity is certainly a term of ethical judgment, as its presence in legal contexts confirms. Berger clearly feels the strength of the charge of cynicism.[31] An objection to his readings that he thinks "less securely grounded" is that they can be anachronistic (52). I am not sure that this objection is entirely toothless or groundless. The early moderns certainly did not feel that there was no such thing as goodness, but only "goodness." Even Machiavelli did not think this (he did not deny that goodness was possible; he only held that it was unlikely to succeed).

Berger's position with regard to Cavell's readings of *Lear* is exactly that of Regan in relation to Goneril's protestation of love – it's right as far as it goes but "comes too short" (F 1.1.71). Edgar's complicity (not, of course, guilt) begins before Cavell thinks it does. The key to much of Berger's reading is his commitment to what he calls "the value of the victim's role" (42), where this "value" is seen in its implied (and enjoyed by the agent) accusatory power and implied desire for retaliation. On this view, all suffering can be turned into a version (or enactment) of aggression. With regard to Edgar, the "sight pattern" again rears its distorting head. Edgar as Poor Tom is filled with (unconscious) retaliatory rage. In mentioning that one of the supposed fiends who supposedly torments him "gives the web and the pin, squinies the eye" (Q 3.4.104), Edgar is referring to "the father who has obscured vision"; and in babbling "Look how he stands and glares! Want'st thou eyes at trial madam?" during the quarto's "mock-trial" (Q 3.6.20-1), Edgar is referring to blindness and "conducting his own trial, probably of his father" (62).[32] So what this means is that "Edgar had entertained the idea that blindness would be a just symbol, if not a just punishment" for – and here we see Berger's reliance on Cavell – "Gloucester's inability truly to see him" (63). Edgar is shocked to see Gloucester's condition after the blinding, but for Berger what is affecting Edgar is not the sight of his father being led but "the shock of complicity" in the situation: "Presumably what he cannot bear about his father's maimed appearance is his having entertained this idea" (of maiming and blinding him). Aside from the forced nature of these readings, and the unlikeliness of this reaction within the dramatic situation, this reading does seem to manifest less than a "minimal level of sympathy for and generosity toward the fictional objects of his criticism."

"Presumably what he cannot bear" – this is a deeply characteristic move in Berger's criticism. He always knows better than the characters do what their true motives are, and he is happy, as in this case, to assign their true motives to them. He has no commitment to capturing what the characters ostensibly mean or what is plausible in a dramatic context. His conception of "text" allows this, since it always involves more than its mere surface – which he thinks is all that performance can capture – allows.[33] And what is under the "surface" must always be darker. Even when he attempts acknowledgment of virtuous intent – "There is no doubt in my mind that Edgar's 'Why I do trifle thus with his despair / Is done to cure it' is to be taken at face value" (63) – he cannot take it as such. The next sentence begins "It is nevertheless the case that this is an act of symbolic parricide," and the next paragraph, treating Edgar's revelation of his existence as Tom to Gloucester, begins "The execution of Gloucester." Berger usefully cites a parallel sentence from Sidney's *Arcadia* that is the source for this moment. There a blinded father notes that his good son has been a "poor historian" in not blaming his father. Berger writes – and here it is again – "Edgar was presumably a better historian" – meaning that he did punitively blame his father for his sufferings. But what justifies this "presumably" is never made clear. In a parallel moment, Cordelia says "no cause."[34]

Naturally, she also does not escape the search for darker purposes (here Berger diverges from Cavell, who is sympathetic to Cordelia, in however strained a fashion). Again, a feeling is attributed to a character by sheer postulation – here by way of "must surely" rather than "presumably." With regard to Lear's original plan in the opening scene, we are told that "The thought of Lear's setting his rest on her kind nursery (a heavy phrase! A heavy rest) must surely be oppressive to her, though she is not likely to admit it to herself" (42). The critic knows much better than the character what she is (must be) feeling. Why this "must surely" be so is never explained, but obviously rests on an assumed but never fully articulated psychological theory (one that sees resentment as a fundamental response).[35]

No good deed goes uncriticized. Where Cavell, not afflicted with generalized cynicism, speaks lyrically of the "gratitude and relief" properly evoked by the words and behavior of France in the opening scene (and sees "the validity of such feelings as touchstones of the accuracy of a reading of the play" [65]), for Berger the King of France is too self-satisfied, and "diminishes her [Cordelia] by dwelling on his largesse" (43). The King is chided for "indulging nice antitheses at her [Cordelia's] expense" ("Most choice forsaken, most loved, despised"). Berger makes a fine historical-legal point in stating that France is "invoking the law of salvage" in "I take up what's cast away," but this is somehow held against him, as if he means only the negative sides of the "nice antitheses." That France is doing something unimaginably grand – a king taking a wife without a dowry (truly only possible in a fairy tale) – is irrelevant. One can read the antitheses differently. Shakespeare seems to be showing the character trying to find words to conceptualize the situation and his feelings – "'Tis strange . . . My love should kindle" [Q 1.1.243–4; F 1.1.253–4]). Denigrating Cordelia hardly seems the point. However, Berger is certain (and here we get the word again) – "*surely* France's condescension must rankle" (44; italics mine). Here the issue of anachronism might well be relevant. "Condescension" is a relevant notion, but some historical work could easily be done to recover the very positive sense that the term (and concept) normally had in the

period (a society in which hierarchy was accepted as normal appreci-
ated moments when it was ignored).[36] Cordelia is blamed – I see no
other word for it here – for committing (as she says) her father to her
sisters (Q 1.1.261; F 1.1.271) – as if at this point she had a choice in
the matter. But that is mere plot. Her words committing her father
to the "professed bosoms" of her sisters are seen as intending his
punishment by them – rather than urging them to live up to their
words. But "whatever she consciously intends" does not matter (44).

Berger is committed to reading the play only in personal and psychological terms – the two chapters on *Lear* are "The Lear Family
Romance" and "The Gloucester Family Romance." Cavell's ideo-
logical commitments are less obvious and more original, but he too
shares what might be called the personalist focus. This orientation
leads both critics to occlude entirely one of the most striking and
distinctive features of the play: its concern for the material conditions of human life – that is, of *human* life.[37] Cavell simply doesn't
mention any of this; it doesn't vector into his thematic focus. Berger
is aware of this aspect of the play but finds it ludicrous and/or irrelevant. After quoting the extraordinary speech (prayer in the Folio)
about "Poor naked wretches" (Q 3.4.23–32; F 3.4.28–36) that
Lear makes just before he actually encounters one, Berger states
that, "on the face of it," this speech might seem to be "converting
wretchedness to fellow feeling" and might be "imagining a sce-
nario in which suffering will lead to wisdom and improvement"
(38). But we can never accept anything "on the face of it." Lear
is – and here is one of those words again – "presumably" (38)
imagining himself regaining power (as if, after Lear says, "I have
ta'en / Too little care of this," he were continuing to address himself when he exhorts "Pomp" to "take physic"). Lear is making,
Berger says with a kind of sneer, "what sounds like a suggestion for
better housing and other economic reforms." But that is only what
the speech "sounds like." The main point for Berger is that "these
reflections are conspicuously irrelevant" to Lear's experience and
to the play as a whole (38). The only real function they can have
is psychological. When this speech is brought into alignment with
Lear's rageful fantasy of Cordelia not being "Neighbored, pitied,
and relieved" (Q 1.1.109; F 1.1.117) "the conspicuous irrelevance
of Lear's prayer comes to seem more like conspicuous evasion"
(38) – so we can blame Lear for this speech too. Berger does have a
sharp and practiced eye for verbal connections, and he is right that
this speech connects to the earlier one. But that the earlier speech
already shows (though in a weird context) an awareness in Lear of

the need for human fellowship – that cannot be asserted. The whole meaning of the first two Acts of the play after the opening scenes – the refusal of housing and "accommodation" to Lear by Goneril and Regan and company; the specific "shape" and social position that Edgar adopts; Lear's culminating speech about the special status of human need (Q 2.4.234; F 2.4.253) – is glossed over. The only piece of this aspect of the play considered, the prayer for the poor, is finally judged "facile" and "misdirected" (39).[38]

I hope that it has now become clear that something has gone very wrong in these critical accounts. Obviously they are right about some things: there is language of blindness in the play as well is the enactment of it; the timing of Edgar's revelation to his father as something to be thought about, as is the dynamic that leads Cordelia to so outrage Lear in the opening scene. Stanley Cavell and Harry Berger are intelligent people, as are the critics who have followed them. And so was Robert Heilman. But there is something in the world of literary criticism that allows the odd results that we have examined to emerge – and not only to emerge but to be taken as definitive or at least highly persuasive. It looks as if what is needed in literary criticism is something like ordinary awareness and common sense. In the actual world, the difference between avoidance or delayed revelation and physical mutilation is obvious, does not need to be argued for. Motives – whether an action is done out of love or hatred – matter; conscious intentions matter. The "face value" of an utterance is generally not to be discarded; a special argument is needed for doing so.[39] And the nature of actions matter – sending one's father to be tortured is different from creating a fiction to preserve his psychic equilibrium. Mixed motives are different from wicked ones. And, in the actual world, "better housing and other economic reforms" really do matter.

What is odd is having to say these things. Dr. Johnson rejoiced when he was able, as he said, "to concur with the common reader."[40] As literary critics, and as readers of literary criticism, we need to maintain our common sense, and not (to use one of Wittgenstein's favorite formulations) allow ourselves to be "bewitched" by "shrewd" or "deep" remarks or schemes that cannot survive the light of common day. Literary criticism as well as philosophy sometimes needs to be brought "home."[41] It seems strange to have to say this to an "ordinary language" philosopher, but I think that Stanley Cavell does not in fact do "ordinary language" literary criticism, and that ordinary language and ordinary ethical sense criticism are what is needed.[42] And this need can be reasoned.

Notes

1. For Cavell on *Lear*, see "The Avoidance of Love: A Reading of *King Lear*," which first appeared *Must We Mean What We Say? A Book of Essays* (New York: Scribner's, 1969), 269–353, and then in *Disowning Knowledge in Six Plays of Shakespeare* (Cambridge: Cambridge University Press, 1987), 39–124, and then in *Disowning Knowledge in Seven Plays of Shakespeare* (Cambridge: Cambridge University Press, 2003), 39–124. I cite this essay parenthetically in the text by page number from *Disowning Knowledge* (identical in both versions). For Berger on *Lear*, see *Making Trifles of Terrors: Redistributing Complicities in Shakespeare*, ed. and introd. Peter Erickson (Stanford: Stanford University Press, 1997), chs. 3, 4, 13. I cite this work parenthetically in the text by page number.

2. See, for instance, Richard C. McCoy, "'Look upon me, Sir': Relationships in *King Lear*," *Representations* 81 (2003): 46–60. On one page, "Stanley Cavell points out" and "Harry Berger points out" (49).

3. See, for instance, Colin McGinn, *Shakespeare's Philosophy: Discovering the Meaning Behind the Plays* (New York: HarperCollins, 2006).

4. For Cavell doing "straight" philosophy – philosophical writing that recognizably conforms to the mode of American analytic philosophy (or at least "ordinary language" philosophy) – see the first three Parts of *The Claim of Reason: Wittgenstein, Skepticism, Morality, and Tragedy* (Oxford: Clarendon Press, 1979).

5. See "Knowing and Acknowledging," in *Must We Mean What We Say?*, 238–66.

6. Attempts like that of Reed Dasenbrock and some others to interest literary scholars in what our colleagues in philosophy would consider disciplinarily normal or exemplary have been notably unsuccessful. Despite *Literary Theory after Davidson*, ed. Reed Way Dasenbrock (Philadelphia: University of Pennsylvania Press, 1993), Donald Davidson remains unknown to most literary scholars, as does the work of philosophers who are close in some ways to Cavell like Bernard Williams, Thomas Nagel, or Harry Frankfurt (except possibly for his surprisingly successful – and very minor – essay on bullshit).

7. For Cavell and literary study, see, *inter alia*, Michael Fischer, *Stanley Cavell and Literary Skepticism* (Chicago: University of Chicago Press, 1989), and *Stanley Cavell and Literary Studies: Consequences of Skepticism*, ed. Richard Eldridge and Bernard Rhie (London: Continuum, 2011).

8. For Berger's status (in the humanities as a whole), see *A Touch More Rare: Harry Berger, Jr., and the Arts of Interpretation*, ed. Nina Levine and David Lee Miller (New York: Fordham University Press, 2009).

9. In a remarkable essay on "Harry Berger and Self-Hatred" (in *A Touch More Rare*, 23–30), Kenneth Gross speaks of Berger's "skepticism of the self and its intentions" (25).

10. In his essay on "Reading Harry Berger" (*Shakespeare Studies* 27 [1999]: 65–73), Cavell sees the "conjunction of interests" (65) between Berger's Shakespeare criticism and his own as consisting in their shared return to "a modified character-and-action" (Bradleyan) approach (Cavell, 67, quoting Berger, *Making Trifles*, 25). Where they differ, for Cavell – aside from a dispute about shame vs. guilt (with Berger on the guilt side) – has to do with their attitudes toward the actual words said by characters (73). I should note that Cavell's essay is actually more about Henry James's conception of criticism than about Harry Berger's. I am grateful to Sara Saylor for calling my attention to this essay.

11. This points to where Cavell sees his own way of reading as different from that of Berger (see the previous note).

12. Paul J. Alpers, "*King Lear* and the Theory of the 'Sight Pattern,'" in *In Defense of Reading: A Reader's Approach to Literary Criticism*, ed. Reuben A. Brower and Richard Poirier (New York: Dutton, 1963), 133–52.

13. Alpers himself falls into symbolizing (the storm, "*King Lear*," 140), into moralizing (re Lear, 149), into condescension (re Gloucester, 145), and into an occasional neat paradox (150). I have discussed the general problem of the difficulty of hewing to the literal (and "surface") in criticism in *Resistant Structures: Particularity, Radicalism, and Renaissance Texts* (Berkeley: University of California Press, 1995), chs. 2 and 3.

14. McCoy, "'Look upon me, Sir'," tries to bring Alpers and Cavell together, as if there were no tensions between their essays.

15. See Cavell, "Knowing and Acknowledging," esp. 262–6.

16. The philosophical premise is that "failure to recognize others is a failure to let others recognize you" (49); put positively, the premise is "that recognizing a person depends upon allowing oneself to be recognized by him" (50). As far as I can see, Cavell takes this premise to be, if not intuitively obvious, then obvious upon reflection. I cannot see that an argument is given for it. That there is an ethical relationship between recognizing and being recognized does seem intuitively obvious; that there is a mutually constitutive relationship between them does not seem to me to be so. And I am not sure that Shakespeare believed this. To recognize others without allowing them to recognize you is a characteristic of at least one of Shakespeare's morally complex characters (Prince Hal) and is a fundamental mode of his most developed villain, Iago. It is this that leads Stephen Greenblatt to give Iago's mode the chilling designation of "empathy" (see *Renaissance Self-Fashioning from More to Shakespeare* [Chicago: University of Chicago Press, 1981], 224–9). On the significance of Prince Hal's "I know you all" at the beginning of his soliloquy at the end of scene 2 of *1 Henry IV*, see Richard Strier, "Shakespeare and Legal Systems: The Better the Worse (but not vice versa)," in *Shakespeare and the Law: A Conversation Among Disciplines and*

Professions, ed. Bradin Cormack, Martha Nussbaum, and Richard Strier (Chicago: University of Chicago Press, 2013), 178–83.

17. The problem seems to lie in the "pattern" idea. A series of mentions or actions involving something (here eyesight) must have something in common other than their (ordinary) shared referent. What they have in common is taken to define the pattern, which in turn, is taken to affect the meaning of each instance.

18. Robert B. Heilman, *This Great Stage: Image and Structure in King Lear* (Baton Rouge: Louisiana State University Press, 1948), 50.

19. For a "spiritual instant," see Cavell, "The Avoidance of Love," 40.

20. All citations of *King Lear* are to *King Lear: A Parallel Text Edition*, ed. René Weiss (London: Longman, 1993). When the line or lines in question appear in both versions but are numbered differently, I first give the quarto (Q) and then the Folio (F) reading from this edition. When the line numbers in a scene are identical in both versions, I simply give the Act, scene, and line numbers from this edition. When a formulation is unique to one of the versions, I cite only that version as it appears in this edition.

21. Q has "villain" instead of "traitor," but Gloucester is called "traitorous" in Cornwall's next speech in both texts.

22. That Gloucester might become, and to an extent does become, such an agent is made clear in Q 4.5 (F 4.4), where Regan notes that "It was great ignorance, Gloucester's eyes being out / To let him live" because "where he arrives he moves / All hearts against us" (9–11). Nahum Tate, in his shrewd political adaptation of the play, picks up on this and has Gloucester, though blind, actively lead a popular rebellion. See *The History of King Lear. Reviv'd with Alterations, By N. Tate* in *Five Restoration Adaptations of Shakespeare*, ed. Christopher Spencer (Urbana: University of Illinois Press, 1955), 4.1.36–43. For a reading of Tate's play as primarily motivated by political concerns, see Strier, *Resistant Structures*, ch. 8.

23. See, *inter alia*, Lawrence Stone, *The Family, Sex and Marriage in England 1500–1800* (Oxford: Oxford University Press 1977), 107–13, and Ilana Krausman Ben-Amos, *Adolescence and Youth in Early Modern England* (New Haven: Yale University Press, 1994).

24. Berger (56–7) denigrates Kent's saying to Edmund "I must love you, and sue to know you better" (29). But this statement is clearly meant to be one that acknowledges Edmund's status as Gloucester's son (and therefore to be loved by Gloucester's good friend) and also acknowledges the fact that they have just met. Kent's behavior in this brief prose opening is a model of ideal courtliness (meaning courtesy in the highest sense) and should make it clear that his normal mode was not the "unmannerly" one that he takes on when Lear acts crazily ("be Kent unmannerly / When Lear is mad" [Q 1.1.135–6; F 1.1.143–4]) and that

he continues in his disguise as Caius. One knows what Berger means when he states that "I must love you" is "virtually oxymoronic," but for a clear demonstration that the idea of a duty to love was not conceived as such in the period, see Victoria Kahn, "'The Duty to Love': Passion and Obligation in Early Modern Political Theory," *Representations* 68 (1999): 84–107.

25. Berger, *Making Trifles*, 437 n. 16, gives a good list of the players.

26. For Cavell's account of Austin's impact on him, see "Notes after Austin," *The Yale Review* 76 (1997): 313–22, and the many comments on Austin in *Little Did I Know: Excerpts from Memory* (Stanford: Stanford University Press, 2010).

27. It seems possible to me that this moment could and perhaps should be staged with Edgar-as-Tom hiding off to one side, so that he sees Gloucester and the old man (which he comments on), but cannot hear this dialogue. In support of this staging, I note that if "Tom" were in plain sight, the Old Man would not say "How now, who's there?" right after Gloucester's speech (23), as if the Old Man were just then noticing the presence of another person, whom he cannot see.

28. Cavell's treatment of Cordelia includes an (as far as I know) unre-marked on and very odd moment of misogyny (or something) together with a refusal to credit the (Folio) text. He is unhappy with the fact that (in F) Lear calls Cordelia "least" as well as last (F 1.1.82). Cavell states, very emphatically, that "The idea of a defiant *small* girl seems grotesque" (63; emphasis in the original). I have no idea why he thinks this. There is no reason to believe that Shakespeare did.

29. Elsewhere in *Disowning Knowledge*, Cavell speaks of and defends the "over-excitement" of one of his readings (158). This is in relation to his treatment of *Coriolanus*, which is again oriented against a reading that would insist on the literal – in that case Brecht's rather than Alpers's (146). For a critique of that reading, see Strier, *Resistant Structures*, 52–4.

30. For a discussion of Berger and C. L. Barber (though more sympathetic to the former), see Peter Erickson's Introduction to *Making Trifles*, xxvii–xxx.

31. In the little italicized prelude to his essay on "Bodies and Texts" (*Representations* 17 [1987]: 144–66), Berger speaks of having to "protect" himself against his "own tendencies toward cynical read-ing" of, for instance, Cordelia in *King Lear* (145). I understand this need for "protection" against such, but think that the context of the remark (going to a performance of the play for such "protection") undermines it, and that Berger's deeper commitment is to the "more assertive negations" and "darker sayings" that his encounter with the "textual matrix" allows him – or, he would probably say, forces on him. Gross takes the problem of cynicism in Berger's work seriously, but tries to mute it by speaking of the work as "deeply skeptical but

never cynical" ("Harry Berger and Self-Hatred," 23), and its mode as "loving suspicion" (26). I think that the double way of reading this latter phrase is not intended by Gross, but is apt. In a long footnote (283 n. 4) and in some final remarks (30), Gross asserts the genuine need for the sort of "protection" that Berger only (I think) pretends to need – that is, for limits to ethical and psychological suspicion.

32. There is a possible textual problem here, in "trial madam" (see *The Division of the Kingdoms: Shakespeare's Two Versions of King Lear*, ed. Gary Taylor and Michael Warren [Oxford: Clarendon Press, 1983], 486–8). It is odd that for all Berger's commitment to "text," he is largely uninterested in textual problems. As far as I am aware, there is only one moment when he shows any awareness of the variant texts of the play (301), despite a note characterizing Michael Warren's *The Complete King Lear, 1608–1623* (Berkeley: University of California Press, 1989) as "indispensable" (457 n. 23). Berger's first essay on the play ("*King Lear*: The Lear Family Romance") came out in 1979, before the "textual revolution" was fully visible, but after *The Division of the Kingdoms* the matter of the two versions was conspicuous.

33. Two of the essays in *Making Trifles* are entitled "Text against Performance": the essay on the Gloucester family (ch. 3) and that on *Macbeth* (ch. 5).

34. Naturally this phrase annoys Berger. For his critique of it, see xii and 46–7.

35. One should also note the heavy-handedness of Berger's parenthetical interjections in the key sentence here: "(a heavy phrase! A heavy rest)." This is sheer rhetorical manipulation.

36. When, for instance, George Herbert writes of "The Parson's Condescending" in *The Country Parson*, he is recommending the behavior (and seeing it motivated by love – "his [the Parson's] business, and aime"). *The Works of George Herbert*, ed. F. E. Hutchinson (Oxford: Clarendon Press, 1945), 283–4. A search in EEBO quickly reveals that the normal use of the word in the period is to describe either the "unexpressible condiscention of the Almighty" in the Incarnation ("Oh what condescention is here!") or good behavior reported or urged on the king or other powers. Joshua Scodel has reminded me that Adam is deeply grateful for Raphael's "friendly condescension" at the beginning and the end of Book 8 of *Paradise Lost* (lines 8 and 649). See John Milton, *Complete Poems and Major Prose*, ed. Merritt Y. Hughes (New York: The Odyssey Press, 1957).

37. On this aspect of the play, see Michael Ignatieff, *The Needs of Strangers* (New York: Viking Penguin, 1984), ch. 1 ("The Natural and the Social: *King Lear*"), and Margreta de Grazia, "The Ideology of Superfluous Things: *King Lear* as Period Piece," in *Subject and Object in Renaissance Culture*, ed. Margreta de Grazia, Maureen Quilligan, and Peter Stallybrass (Cambridge: Cambridge University Press, 1996), 17–42.

38. In contradistinction, one might note the use made of this speech as one of the epigraphs to James Agee and Walker Evans's *Let Us Now Praise Famous Men*: [*Three Tenant Families*] (Boston: Houghton Mifflin, 1941).

39. Gross notes that there have to be times when such utterances as "Take this gift" or "I honor you" are not "inevitably subject to suspicion." As Gross beautifully puts it (in a way, I think, that Berger never does): "We need some kind of 'natural piety' toward such ways of speaking and the commitments they imply" ("Harry Berger and Self-Hatred," 30). My own test would be to see whether we could learn to take an utterance like "I am a man / More sinned against than sinning" (*King Lear* 3.2.59–60) "straight." I am not sure that I can do so, but I think that the effort toward this would be a valuable "spiritual exercise" (so to speak). I also think that it would be a valuable piece of historical recovery – avoidance of anachronism – since I think that early modern people would have been able to do this.

40. Samuel Johnson, "The Life of Gray," in *Lives of the English Poets*, ed. George Birkbeck Hill (Oxford: Clarendon Press, 1905), 3:441.

41. Ludwig Wittgenstein, *Philosophical Investigations*, trans. G. E. M. Anscombe (New York: Macmillan, 1953), section 109 ("bewitchment"); section 116 ("home").

42. I believe, in other words, that Cavell's literary criticism – or at least much of his Shakespeare criticism – is at odds with the deepest commitments of his philosophy. I will pursue this claim in a separate essay. As my colleague Lisa Ruddick has pointed out to me, some of the commitments of this chapter are consonant with some of those advocated (or at least explored) in Stephen Best and Sharon Marcus, "Surface Reading: An Introduction," *Representations* 108 (2009): 1–21. In the "Afterword" to that same issue, Emily Apter and Elaine Freedgood suggest that "now might be the moment to give a certain kind of irony a rest" (140). Rita Felski has noted that "the general idea of 'reading for the surface' has been around for a number of decades" ("Digging Down and Standing Back," *English Language Notes* 51 [2013]: 8). Alpers's essay can stand as proof of this (though he is not the sort of figure Felski has in mind). Elsewhere, Felski has noted that a number of contemporary modes "conceive of everyday thinking as an indispensable resource rather than a zone of compulsion and self-deception," and she, with some cautions, endorses this view (*The Uses of Literature* [Malden, MA: Blackwell, 2008], 13).

Index

Act of Supremacy, 72
Act of Uniformity, 72
agency, 45, 61–2, 148, 169
 moral agency, 84
Alpers, Paul, 217, 219
Altman, Joel, 2, 97, 170n18
Ambrose, 182–3
Arendt, Hannah, 2, 11–12, 99,
 103, 111, 129, 158, 165–9
Ariosto, Ludovico, 75, 163
Aristotle, 3–4, 5, 11, 48, 71, 85,
 99, 101, 162
Ascham, Robert, 163, 164
Ashworth, Andrew, 31
Assize courts, 8, 41, 74, 117
Augustine, 178, 179, 182
Austin, J. L., 222

Bacon, Francis, 8
Baker, J. H., 6, 74, 77, 82
Barber, C. L., 224
Bawcutt, N. W., 23
Beaumont, Francis, 160
Beckwith, Sarah, 64n8, 69n55,
 187
benefit of clergy, 27
Benjamin, Walter, 45, 59, 68n34
Berger Jr., Harry, 215–16, 220,
 222–34
Bernard, Richard, 10
Bevington, David, 22, 43n53

Blackstone, William, 30, 35, 37
Blundeville, Thomas, 161, 162
Bracton, Henri de, 136n10, 146
Bradshaw, Henry, 78–9
Brome, Richard, 160
Brook, Robert, 79
Brown, Wendy, 133

Camille, Michael, 183
canon law, 27, 181
Carroll, Noël, 96–7
Castle of Perseverance, The, 184–5
Cavell, Stanley, 65n13, 196,
 215–34
Cervantes, Miguel de, 55
Chancery, 23, 74
Chaucer, Geoffrey, 176, 187
Cicero, 4, 69n40, 101, 162, 179,
 192n22
Coke, Edward, 7–8, 74, 116–17,
 145, 147
Condren, Conal, 26, 27
confession, 6–7, 175–94
Cook, Ann Jennalie, 98
Coriolanus, 100, 232n29

Dalton, Michael, 9, 30, 33, 37
Daniel, Samuel, 5, 7, 164
Davies, John, 8, 116–18
de Grazia, Margreta, 45, 67n33,
 68n35

de la Primaudaye, Pierre, 3
de Mornay, Philippe, 3, 4
Dekker, Thomas, 160
Derrida, Jacques, 49, 199
Descartes, René, 55
Diehl, Huston, 23
Dworkin, Ronald, 32

Eden, Kathy, 2, 5, 170n18
Eichmann, Adolf, 165–8
Elizabeth I, Queen, 72
epilogues, 110, 157–61, 165,
    168–9
epistrophe, 206–7
equity, 22–3, 71, 77–8, 80, 84–6,
    127, 184
Eysten vs. Studd, 71, 82–6

Fidge, George, 24
Fink, Eugen, 200, 210
Fletcher, John, 160
Ford, John, 160
Foucault, Michel, 182, 206
Fraunce, Abraham, 3–4, 101

Garter, Thomas, 7
Gascoigne, George, 71, 75–6
Gosson, Stephen, 100–1, 104
Greenblatt, Stephen, 25, 26,
    49, 183
Gregory the Great, 182
Guazzo, Stephen, 10
Gurr, Andrew, 101

Habermas, Jürgen, 128–31, 134
Hamlet, 4, 16n14, 45–70, 97, 100,
    103, 205, 213n17
Harington, John, 163
Heidegger, Martin, 103, 199
Heilman, Robert, 217, 218,
    221, 228
1 Henry IV, 93, 94, 98, 104–6

2 Henry IV, 94, 106, 109–10,
    143
Henry V, 93–114, 146
2 Henry VI, 100, 119
Herrup, Cynthia, 24, 33, 42n30
Heywood, Thomas, 161
Hindle, Steve, 31
Holinshed, Raphael, 104
Holocaust, 166–8
Horace, 162
Hoskyns, John, 160
Husserl, Edmund, 199–200,
    202–4, 209–10
Hutson, Lorna, 2, 7, 10, 23,
    42n30, 87n13, 117, 118, 119,
    120, 129, 130, 170n18

Inns of Court, 9, 42, 71–6, 78, 82,
    85, 160, 214n14
invention (*inventio*), 4–5, 104,
    128, 162, 164–5, 168

Jacob's Well, 6–7, 184
James VI and I, King, 22, 116–18,
    122, 123, 125, 127, 128,
    131, 132, 145, 149, 150,
    153, 176
Jerome, 182
Jesus, 143, 163, 180, 182, 183,
    216
Job, 182–3
Johnson, Samuel, 228
Jonson, Ben, 2, 159, 160
Judaism, 206
judges, 5, 7–8, 23, 25, 32–3,
    43n47, 77, 82, 87n21, 116,
    139, 140, 141, 142, 149, 150,
    151, 153, 179
jury, 5, 7, 9, 33, 41n26, 42n29,
    117–19, 130
Justice of the Peace, 5, 8–10, 21,
    29–33, 72

Kahn, Paul, 32
Kant, Immanuel, 11, 111, 131, 199–200
Kantorowicz, Ernst, 131
Kierkegaard, Søren, 199
King Lear, 148, 151, 215–34

Lake, Peter, 144
Lambarde, William, 9, 29, 30, 31, 33
Levinas, Emmanuel, 199
lex aeterna, 147
lex talionis, 142
Littleton, Thomas, 6, 74
Lopez, Jeremy, 95–6
Love's Labor's Lost, 148, 151
Lupton, Julia Reinhard, 1–2, 68n34, 191n4, 194n51, 210n1, 213n20
Luther, Martin, 181

Majeske, Andrew, 22, 26
Mankind, 6, 183–5
Marlowe, Christopher, 177, 184, 185, 188, 205
Marston, John, 159, 160, 161
Massinger, Philip, 160
Measure for Measure, 21–44, 115–38, 139–56, 177–8, 181, 186–7, 189–90
mens rea, 78, 142
Merchant of Venice, The, 100, 195–214
Montaigne, Michel de, 148
More, Thomas, 36
Moses, 145

Neoplatonism, 207
North, Dudley, 159

Paul, Saint, 182, 183
Peacham, Henry, 5, 164

Pfau, Thomas, 2, 64n4
Pincus, Steve, 144
Plato, 111, 206–7
Plautus, 162
Pliny the younger, 180
Plowden, Edmund, 6, 71–89
Plucknett, Theodore F. T., 77
Postema, Gerald, 115, 132
Puttenham, George, 5, 102–3, 163, 164

Quintilian, 4, 162, 178, 191n17, 192n20

Rabkin, Norman, 94–5
Rainolde, Richard, 101
Rancière, Jacques, 127, 133, 158, 165, 168–9
Rape of Lucrece, The, 99, 150
Reformation, 176, 178
Reniger vs. Fogossa, 71, 78–82
responsibility, 50, 59, 63, 159, 165–9, 224
Rhetorica ad Herennium, 4, 162
Richard II, 105, 108, 145, 146, 148, 149, 151
Romeo and Juliet, 188
Rousseau, Jean-Jacques, 11

Samuel, Book of, 208–10
Schmitt, Carl, 67–8n34, 145–7, 150, 205
Seldon, John, 160
Seneca, 179
sensus communis, 55, 56, 111, 116
Shaftesbury, Anthony Ashley Cooper, 3rd Earl of, 11, 68
Shakespeare, William *see individual works*
Shepherd, William, 9

Shuger, Deborah, 177–8
Sidney, Philip, 5, 101, 163, 226
Skinner, Quentin, 2, 16n15, 170n15, 170n17
Smith, Thomas, 149
Soni, Vivasvan, 2, 65n14
Star Chamber, 74
Staunford, William, 6
Steiker, Carol S., 30
Stern, Tiffany, 159, 161
Stoicism, 11, 68
Strier, Richard, 1, 25, 28, 43n53, 114n41, 136n10, 137n25, 143–4, 154n3, 211n5, 231n16, 231n22
subjectivity, 13, 32, 45–7, 59–63
Sullivan, Garrett, 3, 16n8
Summers, David, 3

Taming of the Shrew, The, 71, 76–7
Terence, 162

Venus and Adonis, 99

Webster, John, 160
Weimann, Robert, 157
Wilson, Thomas, 162–3, 164
Winter's Tale, The, 2, 148, 151
Wittgenstein, Ludwig, 228
Wright, Thomas, 3, 4
Wyclif, John, 182, 184, 185

Yachnin, Paul, 2, 98, 155n11, 156n19, 156n26
Young, G. M., 74

Zedner, Lucia, 31